Also by Larry B. Silver, M.D.

*The Misunderstood Child*

# Dr. Larry Silver's Advice to Parents on Attention Deficit Hyperactivity Disorder

# Dr. Larry Silver's Advice to Parents on Attention Deficit Hyperactivity Disorder

## SECOND EDITION

*Larry B. Silver, M.D.*

TIMES T BOOKS

RANDOM HOUSE

The first edition of this work was published in 1993 by the
American Psychiatric Press, Inc., Washington, D.C.

Library of Congress Cataloging-in-Publication Data

Silver, Larry B.
   Dr. Larry Silver's advice to parents on attention deficit hyperactivity disorder / Larry B. Silver. — 2nd ed.
      p.      cm.
   Includes index.
   ISBN 0-8129-3052-5 (alk. paper)
   1. Attention deficit hyperactivity disorder—Popular works.
2. Hyperactive children—Family relationships.   I. Title.
II. Title: Doctor Larry Silver's advice to parents on attention deficit hyperactivity disorder.
RJ506.H9S55   1999
618.92'8589—dc21        98-48855

Random House website address: www.atrandom.com
Printed in the United States of America
2   4   6   8   9   7   5   3
Second Edition

# PREFACE
## TO THE SECOND EDITION

School is the lifework of children and adolescents. Thus, anything that interferes with mastery and success in school will cause stress for the student and for his or her family. Attention deficit hyperactivity disorder (ADHD) can be one of the reasons for academic and school difficulties.

ADHD can also lead to emotional or behavioral problems, difficulty with peer relationships, and problems within the family. Unrecognized and untreated, this disorder will interfere greatly with all aspects of the child's or adolescent's life.

Often, by the time a family brings a son or daughter to a health or mental health professional because of academic or school difficulties, there are multiple problems. Each must be identified and addressed. The emotional, social, and family problems may be the most apparent. Parents and teachers may report that the child or adolescent cannot sit still or is easily distracted and unable to stay on task. They may note that the student has trouble learning academic or study skills. These problems may be an indirect or a direct result of the ADHD or may be secondary to another disorder frequently associated with ADHD, a learning disability.

Let me illustrate:

John was seven years old and in the first grade when his parents asked me to see him. He was constantly in trouble at school and at home, and he had no friends. John's parents told me that he had spent an extra year in preschool and two years in kindergarten because of his "immaturity." When I reviewed the teachers' reports for these four years, I found many references to John's inability to sit still or pay attention. These behaviors were the examples teachers used to say he was immature. I also spoke with John's first grade teacher. She described him as restless, saying he was often out of his seat. He never paid attention to her, and he never completed his work. John's mother said that when she did homework with him, she had to remind him to pay attention. He was up and down. She said, "The way I learn is not the way he learns."

When specifically asked, John's parents said that he had always been a hyperactive, distractible, and impulsive child. It was his impulsivity that caused problems at home. He constantly interrupted; he fought with his sister, and he did "wild" things. For example, he would climb out on the roof or climb up on chairs to get things or he would see something he wanted and dash for it, often bumping into things. From helping him with his homework, his parents realized that he could not decode, let alone understand, what he read. He held his pencil in an awkward way and still could not form all of his letters. He could not count to 20.

In my sessions with John, he was fidgety and easily distracted by any sound, as well as by the pictures in my office. It was difficult for him to stay on task when talking or when playing. His choice of play activities and style of interacting with me were appropriate for his age. When I spoke of school, though, he became sad. He felt he was dumb and not as good as the other children in his class. He had had difficulty with early first grade reading, writing, and math tasks.

I called John's teacher again. She agreed that his skills were poor, especially for someone already a year older than the other first graders. She insisted that his difficulties were due to his immaturity. "If his parents made him act his age, he would do so much better."

I diagnosed John as having ADHD and prescribed Ritalin. (Medications will be discussed in Chapter 16.) At a dose of 5 mg, three times a day, there was a dramatic improvement. John became less active, he was better able to stay on task, and he became more reflective rather than impulsive. His teacher said the change was remarkable. "He is such a different child." She insisted that the change was due to my psychotherapy and had difficulty accepting the diagnosis. But she admitted that she had never heard of ADHD. John's parents also reported a major change. He was now calm and pleasant at home. He stopped fighting with his sister. He was able to sit and play by himself. He was able to do his homework, and he played much better with the children in the neighborhood.

A full psychological and educational evaluation revealed major areas of learning disabilities that clearly affected John's academic ability. His parents learned to be assertive with his school system. They had John identified as having a learning disability so that he would receive the necessary services.

John's parent started counseling. As they better understood their son's problems, they were able to modify their parenting behaviors. John started brief therapy. As he better understood his problems and why he was taking medicine and getting special tutoring, he became happier and more pleasant. His behavioral problems at school and at home stopped. He related better to the children his age and began to make friends.

If John's behaviors had been seen only as those of an oppositional child and treated as such, he would have made no progress. Further, such a diagnosis would have added support to the school staff's consistent misunderstanding of his behaviors. With the correct diagnoses and interventions, including recognizing that John's emotional, social, and family problems were a *result* of his ADHD and his learning disabilities and not the *cause* of his problems in school and at home, progress was made.

John's case illustrates the major problems facing parents of a child or adolescent with ADHD. The diagnosis is often missed. The emotional, social, and family problems are seen as the cause rather than the consequence of the behavioral and academic difficulties. Often the focus of treatment in school as well as with mental health professionals is to treat the behaviors without focusing on the underlying causes.

I will discuss each of these problems in this book. The primary focus is on ADHD; however, the problems related to possible learning disabilities and the probable secondary emotional, social, and family problems are also stressed. In addition, I'll review the other neurologically based problems that are often seen with children and adolescents who have ADHD. These, too, must be looked for during the evaluation process.

The diagnosis and treatment of ADHD is getting closer to being a science rather than an art. It is essential that you as parents be as knowledgeable about ADHD and how it is diagnosed and treated as are educational, health, and mental health professionals. This knowledge will help you work with these professionals and help you best understand your son or daughter. In fact, reading this book may make you more knowledgeable about ADHD than the professional you see. If this happens to you, help educate him or her. If you are not successful, seek another professional.

This book is not meant to be a substitute for the more detailed professional guidance and information provided by your family physician or by other health and mental health professionals.

If your child or adolescent also has a learning disability, you might want to read my book for parents on this problem, *The Misunderstood Child: Understanding and Coping with Your Child's Learning Disabilities,* which I wrote as a companion and complement to this guide.

Children and adolescents with ADHD need all the help they can get. Parents of such children are equally in need of information and help. I hope this book helps you become the supportive and helping parent for your son or daughter that you want to be.

# CONTENTS

# Part Three
## The Associated Neurologically Based Disorders

# Part Four
## Social and Emotional Disorders Associated with Attention Deficit Hyperactivity Disorder

# Part Five
## Treatment of Attention Deficit Hyperactivity Disorder

# Part Six
## Special Topics

# INTRODUCTION

Many children get up each school morning and promise their parents that they will try to be good in class that day. They do try. But because these children may be hyperactive, distractible, and/or impulsive, their behaviors disrupt class activities, annoy the teacher, and push their classmates away. Such children cannot help their behaviors. Yet, the message they hear is always the same: "Why can't you be good?" A correct diagnosis and treatment are the only way to erase this painful and inaccurate message. *Attention deficit hyperactivity disorder, or ADHD,* is the current term for such children's problems. Many people believe ADHD is the "disease of the nineties" because they hear so much about the disorder. In reality, it is not a new clinical problem. The only new thing is that a major effort began in the 1980s to educate parents and teachers about ADHD. Thus, more children and adolescents have been recognized.

Physicians and other professionals have observed and managed this problem for many years. I treated my first child with ADHD in 1966. The name for this disorder has changed over the years. Our knowledge of ADHD has expanded significantly in the past twenty years.

In 1863, Heinrich Hoffman wrote a nursery rhyme about a boy who was restless, fidgety, hyperactive, and a behavioral problem to his family. By today's classification system, this boy would be diagnosed as having ADHD.

"Phil, stop acting like a worm,
The table is no place to squirm."
Thus speaks the father to his son,
severely says it, not in fun.
Mother frowns and looks around
although she doesn't make a sound.
But, Phillip will not take advice
he'll have his way at any price.

He turns,
and churns,
he wiggles
and jiggles
Here and there on the chair;
"Phil, these twists I cannot bear."

In Chapter 2, I will review the history of the different labels used in the United States to describe these children and adults. Although the name for the problem has changed over time, the descriptions have remained consistent. These individuals show one or more of three sets of behaviors: hyperactivity, distractibility, and/or impulsivity. Each of these terms will be explained in detail later in the book.

There are several neurologically based disorders that are frequently found with individuals who have ADHD. The most frequently found is a learning disability. If a child or adolescent has ADHD, there is a 30- to 40-percent probability that he or she will also have a learning disability. Other related difficulties include anxiety disorders, depression, anger regulation problems, obsessive compulsive disorder, and tic disorders. These disorders will be covered in later chapters.

## Prevalence of ADHD

Because of the changing criteria for establishing the diagnosis of ADHD and the absence of a reliable or valid diagnostic method, no firm data are available on its prevalence. At least 10 percent of behavior problems seen by general pediatricians are due to ADHD. Up to 50 percent of the children with behavioral problems seen by child and adolescent psychiatrists have ADHD. Studies done in the United States and other countries, especially in New Zealand and Germany, suggest that about 3 to 6 percent of the school-age population has ADHD.

Surveys show that ADHD is more common among boys. In clinic-referred samples of patients, the ratio of boys to girls with ADHD has been reported to be from 2:1 to 10:1. However, among nonreferred children (that is, community surveys rather than clinician surveys), the ratio is closer to 3:1 The higher rate of boys among clinic samples as compared with community surveys probably reflects referral bias. Boys are more likely than girls to express their frustration by being aggressive and/or antisocial. These are the more obvious behaviors that get boys referred for clinical services in the first place.

Previous data suggest that girls are underidentified. The clinical characteristics of girls with ADHD show that although they have attentional problems similar to those of boys with ADHD, they are less intrusive, exhibit fewer aggressive symptoms, and, thus, are less likely to come to the attention of their teachers or other professionals. It is possible that girls who are distractible but not impulsive or hyperactive are often not recognized, referred, or diagnosed.

## Life History of ADHD

Forty to 50 percent of children with ADHD seem to have fewer problems or see their ADHD behaviors disappear after puberty. The remainder will continue to have problems into adolescence and adulthood. The reality that adults can have ADHD has been stressed in the past twenty years, resulting in a major increase in the number of adults being diagnosed. More information on this developmental history of ADHD will be discussed later in this book.

## Why All of the Controversy About ADHD?

Within the scientific community, various aspects of ADHD have generated controversy over the past thirty years. One area of controversy relates to establishing the diagnosis. Unfortunately, there are no hard, biological measures to make the diagnosis. We have no laboratory or radiologic ability to confirm a diagnosis. The diagnosis is made by obtaining the child's history and assessing his or her behavior. There is now general agreement on what criteria lead to the diagnosis of ADHD. (These diagnostic criteria will be discussed in a later chapter.)

Debate over ADHD within the research and medical communities has been minimal and mostly concerned with the subtle details in the diagnostic process and the treatment program. By contrast, highly inflammatory public relations campaigns and pitched legal battles have been waged that seek to label the whole idea of ADHD as an illness a "myth" and to brand the use of stimulants in children as a form of "mind control." The news media have sensationalized the debate, creating anxiety and confusion among the general public.

It is important to separate legitimate concerns raised by scientific studies from abstract, distorted, or incorrect information from other sources. I'll help you do so with this book, but you must also be a discerning critic of information you'll learn elsewhere. When you learn of a controversial issue relating to ADHD, think about the source. Did you read it in a scientific article, or was it a newspaper report of a scientific study? Did you learn it from a radio or television show, possibly stated by someone who does not provide his or her credentials or source of information? Or did you learn it from the Internet? Remember that anyone can have a Web page and can put anything he or she wants on this page without editing or review from anyone.

## Are We Overdiagnosing ADHD?

Studies done by the American Medical Association and by the Centers for Disease Control and Prevention show that we are not overdiagnosing ADHD. You may know someone with a "war story" about a doctor who diagnoses everyone with ADHD. But national surveys do not support this view.

It is true that more individuals are diagnosed as having ADHD today than in the past. There are several reasons for this increase.

First, a major effort was started about fifteen years ago to educate parents and teachers about ADHD. Thus, more children and adolescents were referred for evaluation. Second, more professionals have learned how to accurately diagnose ADHD, using established criteria. Third, we now know that ADHD can continue into adulthood and more adults are now being diagnosed with ADHD.

## Are We Overprescribing Ritalin to Children?

Despite the information sometimes reported by the news media, formal studies show that we are not overprescribing Ritalin, the medication most commonly prescribed to treat ADHD. (I'll describe this medication and its use in Chapter 16.) As noted above, more individuals of all ages are being diagnosed with ADHD. Also, it is more likely now that children placed on Ritalin will continue to use this medication for longer than used to be true. A whole new population is now using Ritalin: adults with ADHD.

A related question might be, is there an increase in the misuse or abuse of Ritalin among adolescents? The Drug Enforcement Administration has had reports of thefts of Ritalin, street sales, drug rings, illegal importation from outside the United States, and illegal sales by health professionals. However, reports of Ritalin abuse by patients with ADHD or their family members are rare. A recent review by the American Medical Association concluded that there is little evidence to suggest that stimulant abuse or diversion is currently a major problem, particularly among those with ADHD.

## Important Concepts to Consider About ADHD

The possibility that a child or adolescent with ADHD might have a learning disability is so high that this disability must be considered whenever the diagnosis of ADHD is made. Often, it is after the ADHD is treated that the underlying learning problems are noticed.

ADHD and learning disabilities are related disorders, *but they are not the same disorder.* A learning disability affects the ability to process and use information, thus interfering with the *ability to learn.* ADHD results in behaviors that make it difficult to sit, attend, or reflect, thus interfering with the *availability to learn.*

ADHD is a *life disability.* Hyperactivity, distractibility, and/or impulsivity are not just a school problem. They are life problems. These behaviors interfere with the student's availability for class-room learning. They also interfere with family life, peer interactions, and successful participation in sports and other activities. This concept is important when we consider treatment. If the clinician treats the child's ADHD during school hours and months only, the child might do well in school but continue to have a behavioral problem at home and with friends.

For the half of children for whom ADHD is a lifetime disability, interventions must be considered for each phase of life. As will be discussed later, for about 50 percent of children and adolescents with ADHD, it is a familial trait. Siblings and/or parents might have the same problem. If so, family members will need help as well.

ADHD is a complex problem. It is critical that any professional working with your son or daughter be aware of your child or adolescent in his or her total world when treatment is planned and carried out. It is equally critical that any related neurologically based disorder be treated as well as any secondary emotional, social, or family problems. Each of these aspects of treatment will be discussed in the book.

It is of equal importance that you, as parents, understand your son or daughter in the context of his or her total world. If the professional is only focusing on one part of your child's or adolescent's life, you must be informed enough to stress that the other problem areas must also be understood and helped.

# Understanding Attention Deficit Hyperactivity Disorder and the Related Disorders

# 1

# A Road Map for Understanding Attention Deficit Hyperactivity Disorder

Attention deficit hyperactivity disorder (ADHD) is a neurologically based disorder. As I will explain in Chapter 3, it is a result of a neurochemical deficiency in specific areas of the brain. There are other problems relating to brain function that might exist along with ADHD. We call problems that exist along with another problem comorbid problems.

I find it helpful to have an overview or road map for making sense of the possible comorbid problems. I occasionally have parents say to me that no one seems to know what is wrong with their child, since every professional they see has a different label or diagnosis. Often, the problem is that the child does have several areas of difficulty and each professional focuses on just one of them.

## The Clinical Road Map

Let me share my road map. For many children, something affects the brain early in development, often during the first part of pregnancy. When this happens, it is unlikely that only one area of the brain is involved. To make it easier to study these individuals, professionals separate each possible problem area and put a label on it. So, depending on which areas of the brain are involved, the person will have different disorders.

For at least 50 percent of individuals, this developmental impact is the result of the genetic code. The problems run in the family because the genetic code tells the brain to wire itself differently. We do not have a full explanation for how the other 50 percent develops these disorders. I will discuss some of these possibilities in a later chapter.

The brain is immature at birth. It constantly grows by having new wires—the connections between neurons, or nerve cells—activated and fired. We call these maturational spurts. This growth takes place throughout childhood, adolescence, and early adulthood. Consider each maturational spurt the equivalent of a new software package. You install it in your computer and suddenly the computer can do things it couldn't do before. So, too, with each firing of new wires in the brain, the brain can do things it couldn't do before. As each new area activates, there are two possibilities. It may be that the wires in this area were not affected initially and are wired "normally." Thus, when this area of the brain begins to work, the individual suddenly can do things that were difficult before. It is also possible that when this area of the brain begins to work, it will be apparent that this area is wired differently. Until the latest maturational spurt, we had no way of knowing that this area of the brain would begin to work—or not to work. For individuals with different wiring, the maturational spurt creates new problems.

This is the reason that some children struggle and struggle, then suddenly master things that were difficult before. It is often rewarding to be the professional working with the child at that time. He or she gets the credit for it. You've heard the story: Mary struggled with reading for several years. Finally, she got Mrs. Jones as a teacher, and within a month she was reading. Often it's hard to say what's responsible for the child's mastery. This activation of new areas is also the reason why some children improve in one area only to have another area of difficulty. For them, the new area of the brain is wired differently as well.

## Faulty Wiring: The Cortex

The cortex, or thinking part of the brain, has many functions. For our discussion, I will say that it has four basic functions: language skills, muscle (motor) skills, thinking (cognitive) skills, and organization (executive function) skills. Any or all of these areas might be wired differently.

If the area of the brain that is wired differently relates to language functioning, the person will have a problem with language, called a *language disability*. The first clue is often a delay in language development. The child is not speaking by age two, or by two and a half or three is using only a few words. Some may be no better by age four. If a speech and language therapist works with this child, it might be possible to speed up the development of language. There is a sigh of relief. Then, by age four or five, another problem becomes clear. This child may have difficulty processing and understanding what is being said (a *receptive language disability*) or might have difficulty organizing thoughts, finding the right words, and speaking in a fluid and clear way (an *expressive language disability*). More help is needed. As this child enters the early elementary grades, another problem might become apparent. The first task in reading is language-based. The child must recognize units of sound (phonemes) and connect these sounds to the correct symbol (graphemes). There are forty-four phonemes in the English language. Each letter has a sound, vowels have two sounds (a short and a long sound), certain combinations (*sh*, *th*, *ch*, etc.) have their own sounds. There are thirty-six graphemes in the English language (*A* through *Z* and *0* through *9*). To learn to read, a child must learn to "break this code" by learning what sounds go with what symbols and sounding out words. Many children with a delay in language development and later receptive and/or expressive language problems have problems learning to read in first grade. Spelling is the reverse process. Children must start with the language in their brain and connect it with the right symbols by writing on the page. Thus, many children with reading problems also have problems with spelling.

Some children might have a delay in language, receive help, improve, and never have another problem. Others might improve but show up later with receptive and expressive language problems. With help, these children resolve these problems, and it's smooth sailing from then on. Other children might progress into reading problems. It just depends on whether the next area of brain activation is also wired differently.

If the area of the brain that is wired differently relates to the use of the muscles, we see what is called a *motor disability*. For some, the primary problems relate to the ability to coordinate and use teams of large muscles (gross motor skills); these kids have difficulty with running, jumping, or climbing. Others might have difficulty coordinating and using teams of small muscles (fine motor skills). They have difficulty learning to button, zip, tie, color within the line, use scissors, and use eating utensils, and, later, using a pencil or pen to form letters and write. Still others might have a broader pattern of motor problems called *sensory integration disorder*. Now, in addition to gross and fine motor planning functions, they might have difficulty making sense out of information coming from nerve endings in the skin. They might be very sensitive to touch or misread temperature or pain. They also might have difficulty processing information from their inner ear (vestibular system), information needed to know where the body is in relation to gravity. They have difficulty with movement in space or position in space. Which of these many possible motor problems are present will depend on the areas of the brain involved.

If the area of the brain that is wired differently relates to the processing of information for learning, we call this a *learning disability*. In some ways, this division of the cortex is artificial. If an individual has a learning disability, more than one area of the brain is involved.

The last area of activation within the cortex is the sophisticated area of the brain that acts like the chief executive officer in a company. This area carries out what is called *executive functions*. It orchestrates behaviors. It assesses a task or problem, decides how to tackle or solve it, orchestrates the necessary activities or functions, continually makes mid-course changes or corrections, and eventually reaches a successful conclusion. If this area of the brain is wired differently, we see people who have difficulty with organizational planning and with carrying out tasks successfully.

## Faulty Wiring: The Area of Vigilance

This problem with wiring might extend beyond the cortex. There is an area of the brain that is often called the area of vigilance. This is the area of the brain found in animals and primitive humans as well as with modern humans. It is the area that allows us to be a hunter. It controls the ability to sit very still so that you do not scare away your prey, the ability to track your prey and not to be distracted by any background activity, and the ability to strike at just the right time. Picture, for example, a frog sitting on a lily pad (so you won't think this is only a human trait). Not a muscle moves lest the fly go away. The eyes track the fly closely. And, at just the right moment, the tongue comes out and catches the fly. Some children have problems with the wiring of this area of vigilance. As a result, they might be hyperactive, distractible, or impulsive. We call this disorder *attention deficit hyperactivity disorder,* or *ADHD.*

This is why some children have a learning disability, while others might have a language disability or sensory integration disorder, and still others might have ADHD. Many kids might have one, two, three, or all four of these problems. Such a child doesn't have multiple disorders. She or he has multiple examples of the initial underlying problem that resulted in areas of the brain being wired differently.

## Faulty Wiring: The Area for Modulation

We have another area of the brain that might be called the modulation area. This is the area that maintains balance or equilibrium, avoiding psychological or emotional extremes. This area modulates many functions. Since this area of the brain has been wired since birth, any specific modulating problem has also been there since birth. Some people have problems modulating anxiety. They have a history since early life of being high-strung or anxious. Over the years, the focus of the anxiety may change, but the central theme is a high anxiety level. They might have a fear of sleeping alone at night. Later it might be a fear of being in part of the house alone or a fear of bees or a fear of something else. As these children move into adolescence or adulthood, they might develop a full-blown *anxiety disorder*. Some may have so much difficulty regulating anxiety that the level gets too high and triggers off a physical (fight-or-flight) response called a *panic disorder*. They break out into a sweat; their heart pounds; they feel weak.

Another regulating problem relates to the ability to modulate anger. These children have been more irritable and angry since early childhood. They have always had tantrums. As they get older, they show a specific form of difficulty regulating anger called *intermittent explosive disorder*. They have a very short fuse. Sometimes they explode so fast you don't know for sure what caused it. Once they passed over their threshold, they lose it. When they get angry, they don't just have a tantrum or pout or slam doors. They yell, scream, curse, hit, throw, threaten. They act in an irrational way and cannot be reasoned with. Sometimes they seem paranoid, saying people are trying to hurt them. The episode lasts up to fifteen or more minutes. Then, it ends almost as abruptly as it began. Once it is over, they may be tired and want to rest or sleep. They usually do not want to discuss what happened and seem confused about their behavior. Later, they might feel remorse about what they did. These are the Dr. Jekyll–Mr. Hyde children.

Some may have difficulty modulating moods. They seem to have been unhappy or sad most of their lives. They are moody or depressed some of the time or all of the time. Some will go on to develop a *depressive disorder*. A very few, in adolescence, may show difficulty modulating not just the down side (depression) but the up side (excitement, manic behavior). This might evolve into a *bipolar disorder* (formerly called manic-depressive disorder).

Another pattern of behavior that seems to relate to these modulating disorders involves the ability to regulate thoughts and behaviors. Some kids will have difficulty controlling their thoughts and feel a powerful need to rethink a thought or thought pattern over and over (obsessive behavior). Others might have difficulty regulating behaviors. They feel they must do certain things (compulsive behavior) or they will get too anxious. They know "it's silly" but cannot stop. They might need to touch things a certain way or number of times. They might need to check and recheck things (like that the front door is locked or the stove is off). They might need to perform certain patterns or rituals. This disorder is called *obsessive-compulsive disorder.*

There is one last area of difficulty with modulation that may or may not turn out to be part of this pattern. However, this problem is a comorbid condition and relates to difficulty regulating certain motor functions. Affected kids experience the contraction of clusters of muscles, causing what are called motor tics. Others may experience the need to say certain sounds or words, called oral tics. These individuals have a *tic disorder* or a specific form of this problem, *Tourette's disorder.*

Our brain is a beautifully functioning, fascinating part of our body. It has many functions. If something affects this brain early in development, this impact will cause areas of the brain to develop differently. Depending on which areas of the brain are involved, one will find different problem areas. We have a name for each.

As I said in the beginning, this road map will help you understand your son or daughter. It may even help you understand yourself. As you read this road map, you will see many familiar trails or sites. It is not unusual for children, adolescents, or adults to have one or more of these disorders. The more one has, the more likely that he or she has even more. So, it is not uncommon to find a child with learning disabilities and ADHD who also has a tic disorder or obsessive-compulsive disorder, or is overly anxious, or is having trouble regulating anger, or . . .

The primary focus of this book is on ADHD. However, each of these related disorders will be discussed as well. I hope this road map helps you orient yourself as you travel from chapter to chapter.

## In Summary

Of all youth with ADHD, between 30 and 40 percent will also have a learning disability. For this reason, this disability will be covered in greater detail in this book than the other disorders.

The likelihood that a child or adolescent with ADHD might have a language, motor, or learning problem is so great you as a parent must know how to clarify whether your child with ADHD might also have one of these problem areas.

Of all youths with tic disorders or obsessive-compulsive disorder, 50 percent will also have ADHD. We do not yet have the data on the reverse—how many children or adolescents with ADHD have a tic disorder or obsessive-compulsive disorder. The suspicion is that the figures, once known, will be greater than expected in the regular population.

# 2

## Attention Deficit Hyperactivity Disorder — What Is It? What Is It Not?

To help your child with ADHD most effectively, you must first have a fair understanding of his or her problems. It may help you to realize that 10 to 20 percent of average school-age children have trouble with academic work. There are many possible reasons. Most fall into several broad categories: (1) Some have mental retardation—that is, they have below-normal intellectual capacities and will therefore always function below normal academic levels. (2) Some have emotional problems that interfere with either the ability to learn or the availability to learn (disruptive behaviors leading to removal from class) (3) Some have average or above-average intelligence, but still have academic difficulties because of the way their brains function. Although such children may have problems with vision, hearing, or both, their learning problems are not caused by these impairments. Kids with learning disabilities fall into this group. They represent about 10 percent of most of the school-age population. (4) Some have difficulty sitting still, maintaining their attention on the task, and thinking through the answer before they respond. These individuals have ADHD.

As discussed in the previous chapter, children and adolescents with ADHD may have one or more of a group of associated neurological disorders. About 30 to 40 percent will have learning disabilities. In addition, some may have a motor tic disorder or Tourette's disorder. Others may have an anxiety disorder, obsessive-compulsive disorder, anger control problems, or depression. Some may have two, three, or more of these difficulties.

Most students with ADHD develop emotional, social, and family problems because of the difficulties they get into and the frustrations and failures they experience. These emotional, social, and family problems are referred to as secondary to emphasize that they are the *consequence* of the academic disability and not its *cause*.

## What Do All of the Terms Used to Explain My Child Mean?

Everyone seems to have a different name for someone with this group of behaviors and problems. With new knowledge, the names or labels have changed. Some professionals still use the old terms or the terms they learned when they were in training. I'm often asked, for example, "Is ADD the same as ADHD?"

Let me give you a quick history of our understanding of these problems, reviewing some of the different labels that have evolved throughout the years. Prior to the 1940s in the United States, if a child had difficulty learning, he or she was considered to have mental retardation, exhibit emotional disturbances, or to be socially and culturally disadvantaged. In the early 1940s, a fourth group of problem children was identified: children who had difficulty learning because of a presumed problem with their nervous system. The initial researchers noted that these students had the same learning problems as individuals who were known to have brain damage (for example, after trauma or surgery to the brain). Yet, these students looked normal; thus, they concluded that they also had brain damage, but that the damage was minimal. The term *minimal brain damage* was introduced. Gradually, however, observations and testing revealed that no evidence of damage to the brain could be found in most of these children. In fact, research began to point to the idea that the cause of the problem lay in how the brain functions—that is, the problem was physiologic and not structural. All of the brain mechanisms are present and operable, but some of the "wiring" is hooked up differently and, thus, does not work in the normal way. Scientists created a term to suggest this concept of faulty functioning. The prefix *dys,* which means "difficulty with," was incorporated, and the term *minimal brain dysfunction,* or *MBD,* came into use. The literature on MBD described such children as having (1) learning difficulties, presumed to be due to a dysfunctional nervous system; (2) problems with hyperactivity and distractibility; and (3) emotional and family problems that were considered to be a consequence of the first two sets of problems.

From the 1950s through the present, professionals from a number of different disciplines intensively studied the problem of MBD. Because each discipline trains its specialists and subspecialists differently and uses a different vocabulary, each investigator described what he or she found somewhat differently, much as the blind men did when they studied the elephant. Only now have we been able to see what the whole elephant looks like.

## Learning Disability

Educators specializing in children with academic problems— the "special education" professionals—studied children's learning problems. Initially, they used labels that had been long established in schools of education to describe the primary presenting problems. Thus, children who had trouble with reading because of language-based problems had *dyslexia* and were called dyslexic. Children with writing problems had *dysgraphia* and were called dysgraphic. Trouble with arithmetic was called *dyscalculia.* Other special educators found these terms too general and not helpful. They decided that they had to look for the specific reasons for the trouble with reading, writing, and arithmetic. These professionals began to look for the underlying learning difficulties that explained the academic skill difficulties. The term *learning disability* was finally selected and is the primary term used today.

If the student has difficulty receiving, processing, and expressing language, the term *language disability* is used. Speech and language therapists use such terms as *receptive language disability, central language disability,* or *expressive language disability.* Special education professionals might call the same problems auditory processing, pragmatic language, or demand language disabilities.

A special education professional might refer to a child's difficulty with motor planning activities as a fine motor or gross motor problem. Occupational therapists might refer to these problems as *motor dyspraxia*. They might identify other problems and refer to the total clinical picture as *sensory integration disorder*.

## Attention Deficit Hyperactivity Disorder

Other professionals studied those children who were described as hyperactive and distractible. The first official term established in 1968 in the medical classification system for these children was *hyperkinetic reaction of childhood*, and with it came the concept of the "hyperactive child." In 1980, the term was officially changed to *attention deficit disorder*, or *ADD*, to emphasize that distractibility with a short attention span was the primary clinical issue and that hyperactivity or impulsivity also might be present. Two subtypes were used: ADD with hyperactivity and ADD without hyperactivity. A child needed only one of the three behaviors (hyperactivity, distractibility, or impulsivity) to have the diagnosis.

In 1987, the official classification for these children changed to *attention deficit hyperactivity disorder*, or *ADHD*, to reflect that although distractibility is the primary issue, hyperactivity is also an important factor of the disorder. Again, children could have any of the three problems and be classified with ADHD. They did not have to be hyperactive.

In 1994, the official classification changed again. The same term was used, *attention deficit hyperactivity disorder*. However, the term *inattention* was substituted for *distractibility*. Three subtypes were established: (1) individuals who are hyperactive, inattentive, and impulsive—mixed type; (2) individuals who are primarily inattentive—inattentive type; and (3) individuals who are primarily hyperactive and impulsive—hyperactive-impulsive type. Despite these changes, many professionals and parents like to use the term *ADD* for children who are only inattentive (distractible) and the term *ADHD* for children who are also hyper-active. It is important to remember that the only official term that can be used on reports or other records is *attention deficit hyperactivity disorder.*

These changes in names over the years do not reflect ambiva-lence on the part of the professionals who develop these classifi-cations and guidelines. They reflect the rapidly expanding knowledge of this disorder.

### Emotional, Social, and Family Problems

Mental health professionals studied the emotional, social, and family problems often seen with children and adolescents with learning disabilities. In addition to describing these problems, these professionals clarified a very important issue. As I've em-phasized, for the individual with a learning disability, the emo-tional, social, and family problems are not the *cause* of the academic difficulties, but the *consequence.*

### Where Are We Today?

At this time, the term *minimal brain dysfunction* is no longer used. In its place, the different components are identified and la-beled individually using current terms. The treatment plan would address each of the individual problems. Thus, today a child whose problem used to be called MBD would be identified as having learning disabilities, ADHD, and secondary emotional, social, and family problems.

Don't let different professionals who use different terms con-fuse you. Nor should you be confused by books you read that use different terms. Often, these terms suggest that the profes-sional using them had trained at an earlier time and has not kept up with the field. If you hear a term at a meeting or see a term in a report and you don't know what it means, don't be embar-rassed to ask for clarification. It is your son or daughter. You need to know what these professionals mean.

# Is an Attentional Disorder the Same as ADHD?

There are many reasons why a child or adolescent might have difficulty maintaining attention. ADHD is but one of the causes. Thus, understanding attentional disorders is important. In Chapter 5 I will discuss in more detail how ADHD is diagnosed. For now, I want to put ADHD in perspective as one type of attentional disorder.

Attentional problems might relate to any of the three general aspects of attending to a task. Specifically:

## TASKS INVOLVED IN ATTENDING

1. The ability to seek out what one wants to attend to and focus on it.
2. Once focused, the ability to maintain this attention.
3. Once the task is complete, the ability to stop attending and move on to something else.

The most common cause of difficulties with the first task, *seeking out and attending,* is avoidance. The child or adolescent knows there is homework to do but keeps putting off the task (procrastinating). "I just want to watch one more TV show," or "I'll do it soon. I promise." Or he or she might start to do the homework, then get up to get a drink, later to get a snack, later to call a friend, later to take a break. Remember what it's like when you have several tasks to do. Somehow, the one you least want to do keeps being bumped to the bottom of the list. Avoidance is best understood by looking at what is being avoided. Perhaps the student does not know how to do the homework or believes it will be too hard. Perhaps he or she has a learning disability. Avoidance is not ADHD.

The second task is the ability to *sustain one's attention* once the task is initiated. Children and adolescents who are anxious or worried or depressed might have difficulty maintaining attention. If the environment is too noisy or stimulating (doing homework at the kitchen table as dinner is being prepared or trying to work in a too-noisy classroom), it will be difficult to concentrate. If the work is too hard or not understood, the child's attention might wander. If the individual has difficulty screening out unimportant stimuli from what is being focused on, sustaining attention will be hard. Only the last of these examples might be ADHD.

The third task, *breaking away from the task* and moving one's attention to another task, might be difficult if the current task is more fun than the expected next task. The child is watching TV and is told it is time to go to bed so the TV has to be turned off. The child will not want to do so. Or the child is playing a computer game and is told to turn it off and start homework. None of these examples is ADHD. Some children have neurologically based disorders that result in difficulty stopping one task to start another. This difficulty is called perseveration. It is not common.

Thus, looking at the full picture of attentional problems, it is clear that ADHD is but one possible cause. With ADHD, the individual has difficulty maintaining attention once he or she attempts to focus. This difficulty is due to difficulty blocking out unimportant stimuli that then compete for attention. In Chapter 5, I will describe the different forms of distractibility found with ADHD.

## Basic Concepts to Remember

As you go about seeking treatment for your child or adolescent, keep these four ideas firmly in mind. You will need them to understand everything that happens to you from now on.

1. Your child or adolescent does not have mental retardation, nor is he or she primarily displaying emotional disturbances.
2. Your child or adolescent probably has a group of difficulties often found together. The most common are learning disabilities and ADHD and the secondary emotional, social, and family problems. There are others that you will learn about in Chapter 7. Know which of these problems your son or daughter has. Each must be addressed to make progress.

3. About 40 to 50 percent of children with ADHD will improve or no longer have ADHD after puberty. However, the other 50 to 60 percent will continue to have ADHD through adolescence and adulthood.

Your child's or adolescent's problems may seem overwhelming. But you must keep in mind that although this condition is unfortunate, it is not the worst thing in the world. Many people can help you understand more, but only you are motivated enough to push for appropriate testing and constructive remedies. Only you know your child well enough to see that he or she gets the best help you can find. When you are ready to give up, remember that you do not have this luxury. Your son or daughter can not afford that luxury on your part. Ready or not, the job is yours. This book will help you accomplish your goals.

# PART TWO

# The Causes and Diagnosis of Attention Deficit Hyperactivity Disorder

# 3

## What Causes Attention Deficit Hyperactivity Disorder?

Once parents become aware that they have a child or adolescent with ADHD and have accepted this reality, they inevitably ask, "How could this have happened? Why did it happen? Why me?" They believe that if they knew what causes ADHD, they would know how to cure it. Or they might be looking for something to blame for the problem or something to avoid so that it won't happen to someone else in the family.

Unfortunately, no one has yet determined the cause for ADHD or any of the other neurologically based disorders discussed in Chapter 2. Most research suggests that for most individuals something influenced the brain during pregnancy, probably early in pregnancy. In about 50 percent of affected children, research shows it is the genetic code that "tells" the brain to wire itself differently. That is, these problems run in the family. For the other 50 percent, we have a lot of information and leads, but no firm answers.

When there is a family history with another sibling, mother or father, or extended family member having ADHD and/or learning disabilities, it is easier to make an assumption on the cause. For the other 50 percent, we will have to wait for more research.

What we do know is that the brain is wired differently. The research on ADHD has shown that it is related to a specific neuro-chemical deficit and a specific neurotransmitter in specific areas of the brain. The details of this neurotransmitter deficit will be discussed in Chapter 3.


## The 50 Percent with a Familial Pattern

As discussed, about 50 percent of individuals with ADHD appear to inherit the problem; that is, there is a familial trait. Let me review what we know about this 50 percent.


### Genetic Patterns

Family studies, twin studies, and adoptee-foster home studies provide the evidence that ADHD has a genetic factor. For example, there is an increased risk for these disabilities in parents or children who have relatives with these disabilities. If one of a pair of identical twins has ADHD or a learning disability, the other twin is much more likely to have these problems; whereas a fraternal twin would be less likely to have these similar disabilities. The familial pattern appears to be clear. Although researchers are getting closer, the specific genetic markers or pathways or processes are not yet known.

The current thinking is that where there is a familial pattern, the genetic code instructs the brain to wire itself differently. If the faulty wiring is in the areas of the cortex, the individual will have a learning disability. With ADHD, the genetic code instructs specific cells to develop without the ability to produce the normal amount of a specific neurotransmitter.

There is a related area of genetic study that might someday help us understand another possible cause of ADHD. Our genetic process takes place through specific units of function called chromosomes. Each chromosome is made up of specific units called genomes. Each genome has a specific task in instructing the body to develop. Studies on these units have identified specific genomes that are related to specific functions and specific genome defects that result in specific diseases.

Each genome is made up of a specific number of basic proteins called amino acids. These amino acids are laid out in a very specific way. One concept is that "something" might influence a genome, causing one or two amino acids to shift position on the chain and changing the specific pattern of the genome. This shift might result in faulty development for the area controlled by that genome. It might someday be clarified that some forms of nonfamilial ADHD are the result of such an accidental shift.

## Adoption

Another interesting observation that has been documented on several occasions is that the incidence of adoption with children and adolescents who have ADHD is five times higher than would be expected from the national norms for adoption. The same incidence has been found with learning disabilities.

One could speculate about the parents of children placed for adoption or about the possible risk factors that were experienced by these youths during pregnancy and delivery. The incidence may be higher with children who were adopted from developing countries, especially from poverty areas within these countries. Often mothers in these places receive minimal or no prenatal care and may have been malnourished. The baby is often malnourished during the weeks or months before adoption. Adequate intake of the appropriate foods, especially protein, is critical during fetal life and during the early months of life if the brain is to develop properly.

At this time, the reasons for such a high incidence of adopted children with these disabilities remain unknown. It must be remembered that the statistics cited refer to the number of children with ADHD who have been adopted. These figures are very different than looking at how many children who have been adopted have ADHD. The number of adopted children with ADHD found in the general population is 1 to 3 percent, the same as with nonadopted children. Parents should not be discouraged from adopting children. However, they might try to learn as much as possible about the birth parents, the pregnancy, and the life of the baby between delivery and placement.

# The Other 50 percent of Children

What might cause ADHD with the 50 percent of individuals who do not have a familial pattern is less clear. We do have some information.

## The Chemical Systems of the Brain

The brain is made up of trillions of nerve cells, each of which communicates with other specific cells. This communication has to take place in such a way that each cell stimulates only one other cell, the right cell. Each cell produces minute amounts of a specific chemical that passes across a microscopic space (called a *synapse*) and stimulates the next, correct cell. These chemicals that transmit messages from one nerve cell to another are called *neurotransmitters*. Once this neurotransmitter crosses the synapse and stimulates the other cell, another chemical process occurs that neutralizes or breaks down the neurotransmitter. How does this work? Each nerve cell releases a specific neurotransmitter with a specific structure. It passes over thousands of cells. The cell that is supposed to be stimulated has a specific site, called a receptor site, on its surface. When this specific neurotransmitter passes over this specific cell, it connects with this specific receptor site and the new cell is stimulated.

The brain produces many different types of neurotransmitters. We know of about fifty. It is estimated that there are as many as two hundred. This new knowledge of the neurochemistry of the brain has resulted in a rapid expansion of knowledge of brain function and dysfunction. As will be discussed later, ADHD is the result of a deficiency of a specific neurotransmitter in a specific area of the brain. Certain types of depression are the result of a deficiency of another specific neurotransmitter in another area of the brain. No data suggest that a neurotransmitter dysfunction might be the cause of learning disabilities.

There are other chemical activities related to the developing brain and an expanding body of knowledge on these activities. These chemicals control brain and behavioral interactions. New research at the molecular level on the genetic process of transmitting messages from the heredity-carrying gene to the developing brain offers much promise for clarification. Specific chemical messengers called neuroendocrines, travel to the brain throughout fetal development. Each binds with a particular cell or cell group that has the correct receptor site for this chemical. This binding results in growth of these cells. Each day, different sites are stimulated to grow in a very exact and orchestrated complex process, slowly weaving together the networks of nerves that make up the human brain.

Could these genetic messengers be affected or influenced, resulting in a differently functioning brain? Could this explain learning disabilities? Might certain drugs or other chemicals interfere with the biochemical messenger process, resulting in the absence of brain growth for that particular time when that messenger should have been active? Would such a block during a brief time affect other brain growth that should link later with this area of nongrowth? Research in molecular genetics and cellular biology offers promise of such answers. With these answers lies hope not just for understanding but for prevention or possibly for treatment.

One set of studies was of enough concern that the information resulted in prevention efforts even before all of the facts were known. Researchers found that 80 percent of pregnant women in the United States took over-the-counter or prescription medications during pregnancy or at the time of delivery. It was not known which of these medications crossed through the placenta into the fetus nor what effect these chemicals might have had on the chemically driven genetic process described above. Further, some of the medications used at the time of delivery could, after delivery, no longer pass back to the mother to be metabolized by her liver. Thus, they remained in the infant's blood for a longer period until his or her immature liver could metabolize them. Could these medications explain the more subtle changes found in the brain or in other organ systems of the children? The answer is not available. However, as a preventive effort, pregnant women are advised to take no medications during pregnancy unless under close medical supervision, and there is an increasing effort to use no medications at delivery, encouraging women to use more natural childbirth methods.

## Fetal Development

Socioenvironmental factors also can have a negative impact on the developing brain. Examples include poor nutrition, absence of prenatal care, metabolic or toxic factors, infections, or stress. Each can result in difficulties during pregnancy, premature delivery, and low birth weight. Studies, for example, show a relationship between low birth weight and prematurity and the later development of academic difficulties or hyperactivity and distractibility. However, there is no consistent pattern. Many children who are premature or of low birth weight do not develop ADHD or learning disabilities.

Two major national collaborative projects are in process, one in the United States and one in England. These studies have followed children since the mothers first learned of their pregnancy and volunteered for the study. Extensive observational information on these children at certain ages has been accumulated. These children are now approaching adulthood.

Studies done at age seven (second grade) and at age ten (fifth grade) identified those who were having academic difficulties (for any reason) or who showed evidence of hyperactivity, distractibility, and/or impulsivity. Efforts were made to find statistical patterns or correlations with specific factors.

It must be noted that such data are suggestive at best and that socioeconomic status was not factored into the results. The information at both age periods found a suggestive correlation between the development of ADHD and learning disabilities and the following factors: maternal cigarette smoking during pregnancy, convulsions during pregnancy, low fetal heart rate during the second stage of labor, lower placental weight, breech presentations, and a specific type of inflammation called chorionitis. There was also a correlation in mothers who consumed two or three alcoholic drinks a day during their pregnancy, far less than that consumed with a more serious disorder called fetal alcohol syndrome.

Although there is not a firm association between these factors and problems found with the children, preventive efforts are in effect. Pregnant women are told not to smoke or drink during the pregnancy. Proper nutrition throughout the pregnancy is stressed. For reasons discussed earlier, mothers are told not to use over-the-counter or prescription medication during pregnancy or at the time of delivery unless it is essential and directed by the physician. Although the final results are not in, these preventive efforts seem more than appropriate to do.

## Metabolites and Toxins

Metabolites are chemicals naturally seen within the body. Toxins are chemicals present in the body that are not naturally there. Metabolites would include glucose, specific hormones, electrolytes, and other chemicals. For each, there is a normal range of expected levels. If the level is too high or too low, there can be difficulties. There are no specific studies relating ADHD or learning disabilities to either high or low levels of these metabolites. However, all of the facts are not yet in.

Toxins in the blood and brain during pregnancy, during the early months of life, and, for some, throughout childhood, can result in brain dysfunction or brain damage. The toxin most studied is lead. Depending on the amount present during fetal development, the result could be mental retardation, learning disabilities, or milder forms of academic difficulty. Many other toxins are being studied.

## Substance Abuse

Studies of substance abuse during pregnancy are distressing. As many as 50 percent of the babies of mothers who used crack cocaine during pregnancy show evidence as they grow of learning disabilities, ADHD, and impulse problems. The data on other drug use during pregnancy is not as complete but the pattern appears to be the same.

Recent studies show that the problem is not just with a mother who uses drugs or alcohol during pregnancy. Evidence now shows that if the father is using drugs or alcohol at the time of conception, the genetic patterns of the sperm might be affected, resulting in difficulties in the child.

## Problems at Delivery

Many studies have been done to ascertain the impact, if any, later in life of complications during delivery. The long-term impact of such factors as a long labor, the use of forceps, the position of the baby, and fetal distress is unclear. There is no direct correlation. However, fetal distress noted at delivery (for example, low APGAR scores) that persists over minutes and a bilirubin level that persists above the accepted safe level seem to suggest a higher likelihood of learning disabilities later in life.

## Factors in Childhood

Infections such as encephalitis can cause changes in the brain, resulting in ADHD or learning disabilities. Trauma can also result in structural changes and academic difficulties.

Fascinating findings from brain research offer another view both of brain development and the potential for brain dysfunction. Key to much of this developmental research is that the electrical and chemical activity of the brain cells change the physical structure of the brain.

At birth a baby's brain contains 100 billion nerve cells (neurons), roughly as many neurons as there are stars in the Milky Way. Also in place are a trillion cells that protect and nourish the neurons, called glial cells. But while the brain contains virtually all of the nerve cells it will ever have, the pattern of wiring between them has not stabilized. Researchers suggest that the brain lays out circuits that are its best guess about what's required for vision, for language, for every function. Now, it is up to neural activity—no longer spontaneous, but driven by a flood of sensory experiences—to take this rough blueprint and progressively refine it.

During the first year of life, the brain undergoes a series of extraordinary changes. Starting shortly after birth, a baby's brain produces trillions more connections between neurons than it can possibly use. Then, through a process that involves competition, the brain eliminates connections or synapses that are seldom or never used. The excess synapses in a child's brain undergo a pruning, starting around the age of ten or earlier, leaving behind a mind whose patterns of emotion and thought are, for better or worse, unique.

Deprived of a stimulating environment, a child's brain suffers. Children who don't play much or are rarely touched develop brains 20 to 30 percent smaller than normal for their age. Rich and stimulating experiences result in many more synapses per neuron.

Experts now agree that a baby does not come into the world as a genetically preprogrammed automaton or a blank slate at the mercy of the environment, but arrives as something much more interesting. Nature is the dominating factor during this phase of development, but nurture plays a vital supportive role.

To relate this research to what was discussed earlier, changes in the environment of the womb—whether caused by maternal malnutrition, drug abuse, or a viral infection—can wreck the clockwork precision of the neural assembly line. Also, the instructions programmed into the genes can affect this developmental process.

What this research makes clear is that the genes control the unfolding of the brain. However, as soon as the neurons make their connections and begin to fire, what they do begins to matter more and more. Experience becomes critical. There is a wealth of new knowledge on the importance of this experience on the developing brain. Those wires that are stimulated persist. Those wires that are not used disappear.

For example, when a baby is born, it can see and hear and smell and respond to touch, but only dimly. Over the first few months of life, the brain's higher centers explode with new connections. By the age of two, a child's brain contains twice as many synapses and consumes twice as much energy as the brain of a normal adult. Experience influences this wiring process. Each time a baby experiences something (like a sound or touch or sight), tiny bursts of energy shoot through the brain, weaving neurons into integral circuits. Decreased experience or lack of experience can result in a brain that is less developed or worse.

Where all of this research will lead us is mind-boggling. Certainly, it raises questions not only about child-rearing but about the critical role of day care centers. How it might clarify issues relating to ADHD or learning disabilities is not known.

We do see one possible clinical problem that might best be explained by this new developmental knowledge. A higher percentage of children with language disabilities had a history of frequent ear infections over months or years of early childhood. Is it possible that reduced hearing during certain critical periods of early development influenced the brain's ability to develop the sites needed to distinguish the subtle differences in sound we discussed earlier, the phonemes? Might this impact on development have resulted in language problems? We do not know the answer yet.

### Other Possible Factors

Studies to date have not shown a consistent relationship between ADHD and such variables as birth order, number of siblings, times the family moved, family income, mother's age, mother's educational level, father's age, or father's educational level.

It is suggested that there may be cultural factors involved in the development of ADHD. It is true that there are cultural and bilingual factors that might influence the quality of education a child receives or the level of academic accomplishment he or she reaches. It is important to realize that these difficulties related to cultural, bilingual, or socioeconomic factors are not the result of processing problems. There is no underlying neurological dysfunction resulting in difficulties processing and using information.

### In Summary

We know a lot. We also know very little. We understand many possible causes of ADHD. We do not have a definite answer yet. Until we do, we cannot speak in terms of prevention or cure, only of hope for preventive efforts and better treatments.

ADHD does appear to be the result of a neurotransmitter deficiency in a specific area of the brain. At this time, we cannot correct the nerve cells involved and cause them to start to produce more of this neurotransmitter. But, as will be discussed in Chapter 16, we do have medications that increase the level of this neurotransmitter in this area of the brain and thus decrease the level of hyperactivity, distractibility, and/or impulsivity.

# 4

## Behaviors That Would Suggest Attention Deficit Hyperactivity Disorder

As will be discussed in the next chapter, the official definition of attention deficit hyperactivity disorder (ADHD) describes the essential features as a persistent pattern of inattention and/or hyperactivity-impulsivity that is more frequent and severe than is typically observed in individuals at a comparable level of development. These problems have to be chronic; that is, they must have existed before age seven. They must also be pervasive, occurring in two or more settings (home, school, work).

Individuals with ADHD usually show some difficulties in each of these areas, but to varying degrees. It is important to understand that some children and adolescents will have one, some two, and some all three of these behaviors. *It is not necessary to have all three behaviors to have ADHD.* A child can be relaxed, even lethargic, and have ADHD if he or she shows inattention or distractibility.

If your son or daughter is hyperactive and/or inattentive-distractible and/or impulsive and if he or she has displayed these behaviors for most of his or her life, you should consider the possibility of ADHD. Let me review in more detail these three behaviors.

# What Are These Behaviors?

The three behaviors characteristic of ADHD are hyperactivity, inattention, and impulsivity.

## Hyperactivity

A child need not run around in circles or up or down the hall to be hyperactive. There are such children. However, for most kids, we are talking about fidgety, squirmy behaviors. In the 1960s, the focus for ADHD was on hyperactivity. Physicians were taught, "If you went out to your waiting room and it was in a shambles, you knew you had a hyperactive child." We now understand that most children with ADHD are more likely to be fidgety or restless. If you look, you will see that some part of their body is in motion, often purposeless motion. Their fingers are tapping, or they are playing with their pencil. They may be sitting, but their legs are swinging or they are twisting or squirming in their chair. Teachers report that these kids sit with one knee on the floor or rock their chair. You may notice that your child has never sat through a whole meal without getting up and moving around. Some children appear to be verbally hyperactive, talking constantly.

As children move toward adolescence, the more obvious high activity level may be less apparent. However, they remain fidgety, especially with their hands. They might stand or pace when they are doing their homework. If the ADHD continues into adulthood, adults seem to work at controlling their activity level by selecting careers that allow for movement. They might avoid jobs that require sitting at a desk all day. But you might see them sitting in a chair, both feet on the ground and their knees moving up or down. Or their legs might be crossed with one leg swinging.

## Inattention

Prior to the most recent change in the diagnostic criteria, physicians used the term *distractibility* to describe kids who have a short attention span and have difficulty staying on task. The terms *inattention* and *distractibility* are similar. An individual with ADHD will be inattentive because he or she is distracted.

For children and early adolescents, the most frequent problem is blocking out unimportant stimuli in their environment. They are distracted by auditory and/or visual stimuli. If the person is auditorily distracted, he or she will hear and respond to sounds that most people would hear and tune out. Teachers report that if someone in the back of the room is tapping a pencil or whispering or if someone is walking in the halls, others will ignore the sound but this child must turn and listen. If someone is talking in another room or a basketball is being dribbled on the playground, this student looks up and notices. At home, he or she might react to minor sounds like a floorboard cracking, the dog's tail wagging, traffic outside, or someone on the telephone. If a person is visually distracted, she or he might pay attention to the design on a rug, or a picture or poster.

You leave your child in the morning to get dressed. When you return, he is playing with a toy. He saw the toy and became distracted from dressing. You send this child upstairs to do something, and he never returns. On the way, he saw something and began to play with it, then moved on to something else and began to use it. Outside, this child will notice birds flying, clouds going by, the leaves on the trees moving; he won't stay focused on the appropriate activity.

By later adolescence or adulthood another form of inattention or distractibility might arise. Some have difficulty blocking out their internal thoughts in order to focus on what they should be attending to. In general, there are two types of internal distractibility. Some complain that their mind *drifts*. They daydream all the time. They'll be talking to someone and suddenly realize that their mind has wandered and they weren't paying attention. It is clear that they're not avoiding something stressful because this drifting occurs all the time, even when they're relaxed and with friends. Others complain that their mind *jumps*. They describe having many thoughts at once and not being able to block out the unwanted ones. They are trying to listen or do something and thinking of two or three other things at the same time. Sometimes they make a comment that springs from one of their internal thoughts, and people wonder why they changed the subject. Some adults describe how they'll be doing something, then, another thought will occur and they'll drop that and move to something else. Then another thought and another jump to another activity. Their life is full of incomplete piles of unfinished activities.

Some children and adolescents with auditory or visual distractibility appear to be able to attend to certain tasks for long periods of time. You question if they are really distractible if they can spend hours watching television or playing a video game. These tasks are usually ones that the kids find enjoyable and are highly motivated to do. To attend, these kids must learn to hyperfocus. They often appear to be in a trance. You cannot reach them unless you touch or shake them or stand between them and the activity they are focused on. Some adolescents with auditory distractibility seem to study best with music playing in the background. You wonder how they could be distractible if they can do their homework with the stereo blasting. Many will tell you that the music is like white noise. This steady sound blocks out all of the small sounds that distract them (people talking, phone ringing).

Young children with auditory and visual distractibility might show *sensory overload* when in a busy, noisy place (shopping mall, birthday party, circus). They become irritable and upset and complain about the noise. They may hold their ears and want to leave.

## Impulsivity

Individuals with impulsivity appear not to be able to reflect before they talk or act. Thus, they do not learn from experience, since they cannot delay action long enough to recall past experience and consequences. They may call out without raising a hand or may blurt out something or interrupt the teacher while he or she is working with another student. At home, they might interrupt when their parents are on the phone or talking to someone else. They may say something before thinking and hurt someone's feelings.

Actions may be impulsive as well. He gets upset and pushes or hits. She wants something and grabs for it. This child acts quickly and may run into the street or away from mother in a busy shopping center. Adolescents may use poor judgment in their actions. Adults might buy something without thinking if they can afford it or quit one job before finding another. The hallmarks of impulsivity are poor judgment and being accident-prone.

## How Do Professionals Observe These Behaviors?

It is difficult for clinicians to observe these behaviors in their office. Most general physicians or pediatricians see a child for five to seven minutes. This child may have learned to be very alert in this office or run the risk of being stuck, gagged, or poked. Thus, he or she may be quiet and very attentive. If the child is going to see a general psychiatrist, child and adolescent psychiatrist, or other mental health professional, the office is likely to be quiet and the child will have a one-to-one interaction with the adult. It is important to understand that if the clinician doesn't observe hyperactivity, distractibility, and/or impulsivity in this setting, this professional should not conclude that they do not exist.

The best source of observational data is from real-life situations. Professionals must learn from parents, teachers, tutors, and other adults who interact with the child or adolescent and who can describe what he or she is like in structured and unstructured situations. Each can describe the child's behaviors at school, in the home, and with friends. Each can describe whether the behaviors exist all of the time or only during certain activities or tasks. It is most important that the clinician explore what you as parents live with.

It is usually not realistic for the clinician to visit the school or observe the child at play. It becomes critical, then, that he or she obtain behavioral descriptions from teachers. There are rating scales and other informational forms that might be given to parents or teachers to complete. Such data are helpful. I'll discuss these instruments as well as other methods of collecting behavioral data in Chapter 5.

# Not All Behaviors
# That Look Like ADHD
# Are ADHD

The most frequent cause of hyperactivity, distractibility, and/or impulsivity with children, adolescents, and adults is anxiety. When you are anxious, you cannot sit still or pay attention. You might be irritable and snap at people. The second most frequent cause for any age group is depression. Like adults, children might be restless and unable to stay focused. The third most common cause of these behaviors is a learning disability. Here, the child or adolescent may not finish class work, may have difficulty doing homework, or may appear not to be listening because of the underlying learning disability. The least most common cause of hyperactivity, distractibility, and/or impulsivity in any age group is ADHD.

Thus, it is critical to differentiate the cause for the behaviors. Not all children and adolescents with one or more of these three behaviors has ADHD. A teacher might report that a child cannot sit still or stay focused in class. This observation is important but should not lead to the diagnosis of ADHD. These described behaviors might be due to anxiety, depression, a learning disability, or even pinworms.

# In Summary

It is possible that some children and adolescents are improperly diagnosed as having ADHD. With the increasing knowledge and skill of physicians to understand and apply the diagnostic criteria, this is less likely to happen than twenty years ago. Now, if a teacher describes a child as fidgety or inattentive and the parent goes to the family physician, this physician is more likely to know that more data are needed.

It is equally possible that too many children and adolescents who are hyperactive, distractible, and/or impulsive are not diagnosed properly as having ADHD. The clinician may see the presenting emotional, social, and/or family problems and establish a psychiatric diagnosis without considering whether these problems might be caused by or made worse by ADHD. In the next chapter, I review how ADHD is diagnosed.

# 5

## The Diagnosis of Attention Deficit Hyperactivity Disorder

At this time, there are no formal tests to establish the diagnosis of ADHD. Unfortunately, there are no specific physical examination findings or blood, urine, brain imaging, brain wave, or other neurological findings that establish the diagnosis. There are excellent psychological tests, computer-based tests, and rating scales in use today. These evaluation approaches might clarify whether a child or adolescent is hyperactive and/or inattentive and/or impulsive. However, none of these evaluations will clarify why this individual has one or more of these behaviors. The only way we currently can do this is to take a clinical history. It is this information obtained from parents, teachers, and previous records along with information learned from the person being evaluated that leads to the diagnosis. This chapter will help you make more sense out of the diagnostic process and will help you participate in it more effectively.

As I've noted, some say that ADHD is the "disease of the nineties." Everyone seems to have it, thinks he or she has it, or wishes he or she had it so there would be an explanation for his or her problems. It is true that the number of individuals diagnosed with ADHD has increased significantly over the past ten to fifteen years. However, the reasons for this are consciousness-raising and education. Through the effort of parent organizations, the print and electronic media, and a plethora of books, more parents and classroom teachers have learned about ADHD and which behaviors suggest that the child or adolescent might have this disorder. Thus, more students have been recognized and referred for evaluation. More physicians have learned about ADHD and make this diagnosis rather than a behavioral diagnosis. Further, in the past ten years, the concept that adults can have ADHD has been communicated to professionals. Thus, more adults are now diagnosed.

In the last chapter, I emphasized that the most common reason for hyperactivity, distractibility, and impulsivity is anxiety, followed by depression and then learning disabilities. A child with sensory integration disorder and tactile sensitivity might be fidgety and squirmy. A child or adolescent who has obsessive-compulsive disorder might be distracted by her or his intrusive thoughts or behaviors. *Remember: The least common cause of hyperactivity, distractibility, and/or impulsivity in any age group is ADHD.*

Perhaps the reason some children and adolescents are misdiagnosed with ADHD is that the clinician involved does not know of this differential diagnostic issue and does not use the appropriate approach for making the diagnosis. A teacher tells a parent that his or her child cannot sit still and pay attention. This parent goes to the family doctor and repeats these concerns. The family doctor promptly prescribes Ritalin. I often ask family doctors, If a child came in with the complaint of lack of energy and listlessness and you noticed that the inner lining of his eyelids were pale, would you conclude that the child was anemic and start treatment? No, you would get the necessary blood and other studies done first so that the correct diagnosis could be made. The same approach must be taken with the child or adolescent who comes into the family doctor's office with the complaint that he or she is overactive or inattentive or impulsive. This information is only the start of the diagnostic process. It is necessary to collect other essential information before making the diagnosis.

I want to explain first what the official criteria are for diagnosing ADHD. Then I will review the differential thinking to clarify if the person with these behaviors has an anxiety disorder, depression, another neurologically based disorder, or ADHD.

# The Official Criteria for ADHD

The official guidelines used by physicians and other professionals to diagnose ADHD are found in the official classification guide, the *Diagnostic and Statistical Manual of Mental Disorders,* published by the American Psychiatric Association. This manual is now in a fourth edition; thus, the brief name for it is DSM-IV.

Don't let the title of the manual upset you. ADHD is identified as a psychiatric disorder, thus listed in this publication. Perhaps you would like to know how this happened. The World Health Organization has members from each nation. One of the goals of the organization is to have a common definition of all medical disorders with specific criteria for diagnosing each. In this way, there can be uniformity around the world in diagnosing diseases; thus, there can be uniform data collected on diseases. These guidelines are developed and finalized by committees made up of representatives from around the world. Once they are agreed upon, each member nation must follow these guidelines. About every ten years the World Health Organization publishes an updated set of guidelines called the *International Classification of Diseases.* The current form is the tenth edition, ICD-10. Once published, each nation must modify its own classification system to conform with the ICD. In the United States, the American Medical Association is given this task. The modified form of the ICD for the United States is called the *International Classification of Diseases—Clinically Modified,* or ICD-CM. The current one is the ICD-CM-9. The American Medical Association assigns different parts of the diagnostic system to the appropriate specialty organization to prepare the revised publication. The World Health Organization defines what is a "mental disorder." The American Medical Association assigns these disorders to the American Psychiatric Association to update the existing guidelines to conform with the new guidelines. These changes are published as the *Diagnostic and Statistical Manual of Mental Disorders.*

Much of what we knew and practiced in the past when working with mental disorders was based on our understanding of the mind. Knowledge of the brain was not yet available. With the major explosion over the past twenty to thirty years of knowledge of the brain and of the mind-brain relationships, many mental disorders once thought of as psychologically based are now understood to be neurologically based with possible psychological consequences. ADHD is one of these disorders; Thus, it may not be inappropriate to have ADHD listed in this manual.

In the DSM-IV, ADHD is clarified using five major steps, each with specific criteria:

A. Presence either of (1) or (2) as listed below:
  1. Six (or more) of the following symptoms of *inattention* have persisted for at least six months to a degree that is maladaptive and inconsistent with developmental level:

  INATTENTION
  a. Often fails to give close attention to details or makes careless mistakes in schoolwork, work, or other activities.
  b. Often has difficulty sustaining attention in tasks or play activities.
  c. Often does not seem to listen when spoken to directly.
  d. Often does not follow through on instructions and fails to finish schoolwork, chores, or duties in the workplace (not as a result of oppositional behavior or failure to understand instructions).
  e. Often has difficulty organizing tasks and activities.
  f. Often avoids, dislikes, or is reluctant to engage in tasks that require sustained mental effort (such as schoolwork or homework).
  g. Often loses things necessary for tasks or activities (e.g., toys, school assignments, pencils, books, or tools).
  h. Is often easily distracted by extraneous stimuli.
  i. Is often forgetful in daily activities.
  2. Six (or more) of the following symptoms of *hyperactivity-impulsivity* have persisted for at least six months to a degree that is maladaptive and inconsistent with developmental levels:

HYPERACTIVITY

a. Often fidgets with hands or feet or squirms in seat.
b. Often leaves seat in classroom or in other situations in which remaining seated is expected.
c. Often runs about or climbs excessively in situations in which it is inappropriate (in adolescents or adults, may be limited to subjective feelings of restlessness).
d. Often has difficulty playing or engaging in leisure activities quietly.
e. Is often "on the go" or often acts as if "driven by a motor."
f. Often talks excessively.

IMPULSIVITY

g. Often blurts out answers before questions have been completed.
h. Often has difficulty awaiting turn.
i. Often interrupts or intrudes on others (e.g., butts into conversations or games).

B. Some hyperactive-impulsive or inattentive symptoms that caused impairment were present before age seven years.
C. Some impairment from the symptoms is present in two or more settings (e.g., at school [or work] and at home).
D. There must be clear evidence of clinically significant impairment in social, academic, or occupational functioning.
E. The symptoms do not occur exclusively during the course of a pervasive developmental disorder, schizophrenia, or other psychotic disorder and are not better accounted for by another mental disorder (e.g., mood disorder, anxiety disorder, dissociative disorder, or a personality disorder).

In DSM-IV, there are three types of ADHD. The clinician needs to clarify which type the individual has:

*Attention Deficit Hyperactivity Disorder, Combined Type:* Both Criteria A1 and A2 are met for the past six months.

*Attention Deficit Hyperactivity Disorder, Predominantly Inattentive Type:* Criterion A1 is met, but Criterion A2 is not met for the past six months.

*Attention Deficit Hyperactivity Disorder, Predominantly Hyperactive-Impulsive Type:* Criterion A2 is met, but Criterion A1 is not met for the past six months.

One word of caution before moving on. There are many books available today for parents to read about ADHD. Most are good. Some are excellent. However, popular books do not have to meet the same standards as professional books. Thus, you might read a book that uses the terms *attention deficit hyperactivity disorder* or *attention deficit disorder* in which the author presents his or her own criteria for this diagnosis. Some let you know in the beginning that the author does not follow the DSM-IV guidelines; some do not. Parents often come to me because they've read one of these books and concluded that they or their son or daughter has ADHD. The individual meets the characteristics described in the book but does not meet the official criteria; thus, I cannot make the diagnosis.

## Diagnosing ADHD

The only approach we have to the diagnosis of ADHD is the clinical history. If the child's behaviors started at a certain time or occur in certain situations, we must think of anxiety, depression, or another neurologically based disorders first before considering ADHD. Billy was first described as hyperactive and impulsive in third grade. We learn that his parents separated during the summer before and a favorite grandmother died. Allison is only inattentive/distractible in her reading group or when sitting at her desk working on a report. She is very attentive when there is class discussion. José seems to be distracted when doing homework but at no other home time. None of these children has ADHD.

ADHD is present at birth or during the early years of life. Thus the history of the behaviors is both *chronic* and *pervasive*.

This makes sense. The child is born with the problem and the brain is with him or her throughout life; thus the behaviors are pervasive—seen year after year. This brain is with the child every minute of every day; thus, the behaviors occur all day.

The history is chronic. A mother might say that her child was particularly active in utero or has been active all of his life. "He started walking at ten months, and at ten months and one minute my life became hell. He never stopped running." At a school conference for a third grade girl, the teacher comments that she doesn't stay in her seat or pay attention. The mother says, "You think you have problems. Her second grade teacher complained. Her first grade and kindergarten teachers complained. She was kicked out of nursery school because she would not sit in circle time and pay attention." Adults with ADHD will describe their problems as being present since adolescence or childhood. With some effort, the clinician can usually find evidence to support the chronic nature of the problems.

The problems are pervasive. The morning teachers complain about the behaviors. The lunch room monitor complains as do the afternoon teachers. The tutor complains. The piano teacher complains. The soccer coach complains. Sunday school teachers are not allowed to complain, but they let you know. These behaviors are not just school problems. They interfere with friends, family life, and after-school activities.

To make the diagnosis, then, the clinician must take the following steps:

1. Confirm the presence of the criteria in DSM-IV to establish the presence of one or more of the three behaviors.
2. Show through the clinical history that these behaviors have been present throughout life—they are chronic.
3. Show through the clinical history that these behaviors are present throughout the person's present life—they are pervasive.

DSM-IV requires this chronic and pervasive history. The behaviors identified must have been present before age six. And, these behaviors must interfere with functioning in two or more areas of the person's life.

# Test Instruments Used as Part of the Diagnostic Process

There are written rating scales and computer-based tests that assist in the diagnosis of ADHD.

## Rating Scales

Rating scales are popular when assessing children's behaviors. These behavioral rating scales might be completed by parents, teachers, and/or the child or adolescent being evaluated. The results can be analyzed and compared to established norms. Important information can be obtained in an efficient way. These findings provide a baseline to which any changes can be compared.

The difficulty is in using the results to make the diagnosis. The results will clarify if the individual is hyperactive, inattentive/distractible, or impulsive. However, the results will not clarify the reason for these behaviors.

My bias is not to use rating scales. I have great respect for them. However, I learn more by spending time with the parents and child or adolescent and then talking to the teacher or teachers by phone. This process might take more time, but it's worth it. I can learn more by talking with a teacher for five minutes than I can learn from any rating scale.

Rating scales are two-dimensional. The results are reported as a behavior or behavioral cluster being present at a significant level or not. When I talk to the teacher, I can pick up more. For example, the teacher might report to me that the child is hyperactive and inattentive and would have marked the rating scale accordingly. But, as we discuss the child, I learn that these behaviors are only noticed during certain activities and not during others. Or they occurred after something happened at home, or they are more likely to be seen when the child is at one parent's home than at the other's home. I can also pick up the teacher's affect. How upset or angry is he or she about these behaviors? "He is so disruptive that I can't teach my class!" tells me more than a check on a rating scale saying the child is impulsive.

I must admit that I am in the minority. Most professionals like rating scales and use them as part of the diagnostic process. The Conners series of parent and teacher rating scales are probably the most popular. There are other behavioral rating scales in use. New rating sheets are developed all of the time, and some professionals have their own. Some school systems use standard rating scales that have been modified to fit the school's needs. If your professional uses a rating scale, ask her or him to explain what it screens for and how to interpret the results.

## Computer-based Tests

Several tests have been developed using the computer to assess the child's or adolescent's ability to pay sustained attention. The results will suggest that an individual has difficulty sustaining attention or that he or she shows evidence of impulsivity.

There are professionals that insist that they can make the diagnosis of ADHD based on the results of these studies alone. They cannot. The results should be used as one part of the diagnostic process. The results might provide an excellent baseline to be used later in assessing the impact of medication on these behaviors.

The Continuous Performance Test (CPT) and the Test of Variables of Attention (TOVA) are the most frequently used. For each, the child's vigilance is assessed by having him or her respond to an auditory or visual stimulus by pressing a button. The stimulus is in the background of similar signals. For example, letters appear on a screen and the child is asked to push a button when a certain letter appears. The task is monotonous and requires constant attention. The speed or complexity of the task can be increased. ADHD children or adolescents perform more poorly than normal children. They might make more errors of omission (missed signals) and errors of commission (pressing the button in error). Errors of omission are seen as reflective of inattention. Errors of commission are seen as reflective of impulsivity.

## In Summary

Not all children, adolescents, or adults who are hyperactive, inattentive/distractible, and/or impulsive have ADHD. In reality,

ADHD is probably the least most common cause for these behaviors. A clear differential diagnostic process that takes into account all possible causes for these behaviors is needed before a diagnosis can be made. There must be a chronic and pervasive history of the hyperactivity and/or inattention/distractibility and/or impulsivity.

Because individuals with ADHD have a higher likelihood of having learning disabilities than other children and adolescents, if someone is diagnosed with ADHD, the possibility of a learning disability must be considered. So, too, the possibility of one of the modulating disorders or a tic disorder must be considered.

If there are emotional, social, or family problems, the clinician must help in clarifying if these problems are causing the behaviors or if these problems are secondary to the ADHD and the resulting emotional and behavioral problems.

# PART THREE

## The Associated Neurologically Based Disorders

# 6

## The Specific Learning Disabilities

All of us have areas in which we readily learn. A few of us even seem to excel in limited areas with very little apparent learning—thus, the "natural" athlete, the musical "genius," the "gifted" artist. All of us also have areas in which our abilities will never be more than average and a few areas in which we cannot seem to learn anything. Children, adolescents, and adults with learning disabilities have areas of strength and average ability, too. These individuals, however, have larger areas, or different areas, of learning weakness, than most people. Each person with a learning disability displays a different pattern of strengths and weaknesses. You must learn as much as you can about the whole pattern that your child displays—the disabilities, of course, but also the abilities. What your child can do, and may indeed do well, is just as important as what she or he cannot do, because it is these strengths upon which you must build.

You may have suspected a learning disability before your child entered school. This concern became real when he or she failed to learn the basic skills taught in first or second grade. Depending on the types of learning disabilities, some students will do well until third, or fifth, or sixth grade. Only then will their disabilities interfere with academic success.

Your child may have read letters backwards or confused certain letters or numbers. Or he or she may have misunderstood what you said or been slow in developing speech or muscle coordination.

To help you understand learning disabilities, let me outline a simple scheme describing what the brain must do in order for learning to take place. The first step is *input*—getting information into the brain from the eyes and ears primarily but, as I will discuss later, from other senses as well. Once this information arrives, the brain needs to make sense out of it—a process called *integration*. Next, the information is stored and later retrieved— the *memory* process. Finally, the brain reacts through talking or using our muscles—*output*.

The brain does a great deal more than this, of course. Any learning task involves more than one of these processes. However, this simplified scheme will do for our purpose.

## Input Disabilities

Information arrives at the brain as impulses, transmitted along nerve cells called neurons. This information comes primarily from our eyes and ears. This input process takes place in the brain. It does not pertain to visual problems, such as nearsightedness or farsightedness, or to any hearing problems. This central input process of seeing or hearing or perceiving one's environment is referred to as perception. Thus, individuals who have perception disabilities in the area of visual input are labeled as having *visual perception disabilities,* and those with disabilities in the area of auditory input as having *auditory perception disabilities.* Some children have problems with one area of input; some have both kinds of perception disabilities; and some may have problems when both inputs are needed at the same time. An example would be seeing what the teacher writes on the blackboard while listening to the explanation of what is being written.

### Visual Perception Disabilities

Your child may have difficulty in organizing the position and shape of what he or she sees, perceiving letters or numbers to be reversed or rotated. A *u* might look like an *n;* an *E* might look like a *W,* a *3,* or an *M,* or a *6,* like a *9.* The child may confuse similar looking letters because of these rotations or reversals: *d, b, p,* and *q* may be confused with one another. All children show this problem until age five and a half or six. This confusion with position or input becomes apparent when the child begins to read, write, or copy letters, numbers, or designs.

Another child might have what is called a *figure-ground* problem—that is, difficulty in focusing on the significant figure instead of all the other visual inputs in the background. Reading requires focusing on specific letters or groups of letters, then tracking from left to right, line after line. Children with this disability may have reading difficulties. They skip words or lines or read the same line twice. Many life situations require figure-ground ability. For example, a child might be told to pass the salt shaker but have difficulty finding it among the many dishes and platters on the table.

Judging distance is another visual perception task. Information is received from each eye and combined to create three-dimensional vision. Some individuals have a *depth perception* problem. Your child may misjudge depth, bumping into things, falling off a chair, or knocking over a drink because the hand got to the glass before expected. What you see as carelessness may in fact be just this type of perception error.

There are other types of problems associated with visual perception disabilities. These occur when several areas of perception are needed at the same time. While playing in an open field or gym, your child may become confused and disoriented because of trouble organizing his or her position in space. Or perhaps the child may have difficulty understanding left and right or up and down.

One very common type of visual perception disability relates to doing activities when the eyes have to tell the hands or legs what to do. This is called a *visual-motor* task. When such information is unreliable, activities like catching a ball, jumping rope, doing puzzles, or using a hammer and nail become difficult or impossible. To catch a ball, the eyes must first focus on the ball (that is, visual figure-ground). The child must then keep his or her eyes on the ball so that the brain can use depth perception to perceive the correct position, speed, and path of the ball and then tell the various parts of the body exactly where and when to move. A child who has difficulty with figure-ground or who misperceives distance or speed may have difficulty catching, hitting, or throwing balls. Thus, he or she may not do well with sports that require such quick eye-hand coordination (baseball or basketball). For similar reasons, this child might have difficulty with jump rope, four-square, or hopscotch.

## Auditory Perception Disabilities

As with visual perception, your child may have difficulty with one or several aspects of auditory perception. A child with an auditory perception disability may have difficulty distinguishing subtle differences in phonemes. He or she might confuse words that sound alike: *blue* and *blow, ball* and *bell, can* and *can't.* I might ask a child, "How are you?" and she may answer, "I'm nine." This child may have thought I said "old" instead of, or in addition to, "are."

A child may have difficulty with auditory figure-ground. For example, he might be watching television in a room where others are playing or talking. When you call out to him from another room, you might be into your third thought before the child realizes that it is important to distinguish your voice (that is, the figure) from the other voices and sounds (that is, the background). With this disability, it appears that the child never listens or pays attention. Intuitively, you might have learned early that it helps to have eye contact before speaking. You would have gone into the room, called the child's name, waited until there was eye contact, and then begun to speak.

I recall observing Mary in her fourth grade classroom. She had been evaluated and found to have learning disabilities, one of which was an auditory figure-ground problem. What I observed didn't make sense to me until later when she helped me understand what happened. She was at her desk reading a book. Other children were talking in the back of the room. There was noise of movement in the hall and the usual noise of recess through the open window. The teacher suddenly said, "Children, let's do our math. Open up your book to page thirty-eight and do problem five." Mary looked up to listen to her teacher as she heard "problem five." She looked around and saw the others take out their math books. So she did the same. She then looked over the shoulder of her friend in front of her to see on which page she could find problem five. Mary thought she was being a good student. At that moment her teacher shouted, "Mary, stop bothering Jan and get to work." The teacher then looked at me sitting in the back of the room and said, "See what I mean? She never pays attention." Mary was confused and hurt because she didn't know what she had done wrong. (How many times has your child done something to upset you and then said in all sincerity, "I didn't do anything.") This was the only brain Mary had ever had, and she didn't know that it was different. She only knew that she was trying hard and suddenly the teacher was angry with her. The teacher was frustrated with Mary because she did not yet know of her disabilities. Later, I explained the problem to the teacher and suggested how she could use Mary's strength (visual figure-ground) to compensate for her weakness (auditory figure-ground). When the teacher wanted to give the class instructions, she would first say, "Class, may I have your attention." (She did not want to embarrass Mary by calling out only her name.) She watched until Mary was looking at her. Then she gave the instructions. She was building on Mary's strengths to compensate for her weaknesses. This approach is called accommodation.

Some children cannot process sound inputs as fast as other people can. Most special education professionals call this problem an *auditory lag*. A speech-language therapist might call this problem an *auditory processing* problem or a *receptive language* problem. It is as if this child has to concentrate on what he or she is hearing for a fraction of a second longer than expected before understanding it. Then, he or she must refocus on what is being said. Only, by now, the child has missed a word or phrase. Soon, the child cannot keep up and becomes lost. For example, a teacher might explain something in class. This child misses part of what was said and is confused, so the child asks a question. The teacher becomes annoyed and says, "I just explained that. Why don't you pay attention?"

## Sensory Integration Disorder

How does the brain know how to orchestrate muscle activities? For example, when a person is tying a shoe or writing on a page or hopping, how does the brain know exactly which muscles or joints to use in what way in the proper sequence? We call this ability motor planning as different from muscle strength. There are four basic sensory inputs needed to provide the brain with the information needed. If these sensory inputs are not performing correctly or the brain has difficulty integrating these inputs, the individual has a *sensory integration disorder*. These four inputs are:

> Visual perception (which I've just discussed)
> Tactile perception
> Proprioception perception
> Vestibular perception

### Tactile Perception

There are nerve endings in our skin that relay information about touch. Some are near the surface and respond to light touch, and others are deeper and respond to deep touch or pressure. Some children misperceive messages from these nerve endings and have a *tactile perception* disability. They are tactilely defensive. Such a person is sensitive to touch and may perceive it as uncomfortable or even painful. From early childhood, he or she will not like being touched or held. The tighter you cuddle, the more the child cries. This is frustrating to the parent and to the infant. Later, the child may complain of the tag on the back of a shirt, only like to wear soft and loose clothes, say the elastic in his or her underwear or belt is too tight. This child might wear socks inside out, complaining that the seam bothers his or her feet or might prefer to keep shoes off. He or she sits in class but fidgets, rearranging clothes or tags or taking shoes off. The scalp is very rich in these nerve endings. This child might cry and be upset when you wash, brush, cut, or comb his or her hair. These children seem crazy, and their behaviors are hard to understand until the reason for the behaviors is explained.

Parents learn early that they cannot grab, hold, or touch such a child without warning. If the child volunteers to climb into your lap it is okay. If you want to touch him or her, you have to announce your intention and approach face-to-face so the child can prepare. If you come up from behind and touch the child, he or she might jump away. You might have learned that such children prefer deep touch. You squeeze hard and rub deep when you hold them.

Some children with tactile sensitivity feel defensive and try to avoid people getting too close. They walk around the edges of groups, don't like to sit with the class during circle time, lag at the back of lines. They might be walking down the hall when another child accidently brushes against them. These sensitive children might respond as if the touch were a major blow and hit the other child.

Some children with tactile defensiveness feel deprived of touch. Thus, they might seek touch when they are in control. They might go around the room hugging or touching other children. This is not to say that all young children who do this have sensory integration disorder, but such a possibility must be kept in mind, especially when the other behaviors associated with this disorder are noted.

### Proprioception Perception
There are nerve endings in our muscle fibers, ligaments, and joints that tell us which muscle groups are relaxed or contracted and which parts of which joints are bent or extended. These proprioception nerve endings inform the brain of muscle tone, muscle and body movement, and body position. These inputs help individuals adapt to their environment and hold their body upright. This information also helps the brain orchestrate complex motor planning activities such as writing. A child or adolescent having difficulty with this sensory input may be confused with his or her body in space and may have difficulty with muscle tone and maintaining posture. The child will have difficulty maintaining balance. He or she might have difficulty with motor planning involving groups of large muscles (gross motor activities) such as running, jumping, hopping, climbing. Or he or she might have difficulty with motor planning involving groups of

small muscles (fine motor activities) such as buttoning, zipping, tying, or writing.

Some children with this disability feel deprived of proprioception input. They might seek such input by jumping, stomping their feet, or bumping into the wall.

### Vestibular Perception

There is an organ system in each inner ear called the semicircular canals. The nerve endings in these systems inform the brain of head position, thus body position in space. This information is essential to handling the impact of gravity and to maintaining the correct position in space. It allows you to balance on one leg or to ride a two-wheel bicycle. An individual who has a *vestibular perception* disability will have difficulty with body position in space. These problems may result in difficulty climbing on a jungle gym or riding a two-wheel bike. He or she may become anxious or uncomfortable with sudden changes in body position. It is this system that helps the brain maintain the necessary tone to maintain body posture against gravity. Thus, some children with this disability have weak upper back muscles and prefer to rest their head on the desk or to lie down from time to time.

Some children with this problem feel deprived of vestibular stimulation. They might try to create such stimulation by spinning in a chair or swinging in a swing. Some may sit or stand and rock their body back and forth.

### The Integrated System

*Sensory integration disorder* refers to combinations of the above-described problems. The gross and fine motor planning problems may be most obvious. The other problems are more difficult to observe unless you know to look for them. An occupational therapist can evaluate this individual, clarify the problems, and provide the essential therapeutic interventions.

## Other Sensory Inputs

Children and adolescents with learning disabilities might show difficulty with other sensory inputs. There is no research yet to validate this, but the clinical observations are there.

Some seem very sensitive to taste. Food tastes different or funny to them. They are picky eaters and complain about foods most others like. Others may be sensitive to smell. They complain of smells you do not pick up. They avoid a certain area because "it smells funny."

Some children seem not to be as sensitive to temperature as others. They go outside in the middle of a cold winter without a coat and seem to be fine. Some may be less sensitive to pain. They hurt themselves and appear not to notice.

Children with these sensory sensitivities were not put on this earth to drive you crazy. Their problems are real and must be understood and accepted.

## Integration Disabilities

Once information coming into the brain is registered, it has to be understood. This is a complex process. Let me try to explain it before I go into the specific integration disabilities. To do this, let me ask you to do something for me. I want you to print the following three symbols in your brain:

d  o  g

No problem with visual perception; so it is correctly printed in your brain. There are at least three things you would have to do to make sense out of, that is, to integrate, these three symbols. First, you would have to place the symbols in the right order, or sequence the inputs. Is it

d-o-g or g-o-d or o-g-d

or what? Second, you have to infer meaning for the word from the context in which it is used. For example, "the dog" and "you dog" have very different meanings. In one case, you're naming a pet, and in the other case, you're insulting someone. Thus, you have to abstract meanings in these words. Finally, you have to take this word, now that it is recorded properly and you know what it means, as well as take in all of the other words that are pouring into your head plus the many memory tracks being stimulated by these words and pull them all together or organize them in a way that can be understood.

The process of integrating inputs, or of understanding what your brain has recorded, thus requires three steps: sequencing, abstraction, and organization. Your child might have a disability in one or more of these areas. Since inputs are processed through both the visual and the auditory pathways, some children might have a *visual sequencing disability* or an *auditory sequencing disability*. So, too, the other integrative tasks might involve one input mode and not the other.

## Sequencing Disabilities

A child with such a disability might hear or read a story; but in recounting it, he or she may start in the middle, go to the beginning, then shift to the end. Eventually the whole story comes out, but the sequence of events is wrong. Or a child might see the math problem as $16 - 3 = ?$ on the blackboard but write it on the paper as $61 - 3 = ?$ Or a child might see $2 + 3 = ?$ And write $2 + 5 = 3$. The child knows the right answer but gets the sequence wrong. He or she knows the math concepts but makes careless errors in calculation. Spelling words with all of the right letters but in the wrong order can also reflect this disability.

A child might memorize a sequence—the days of the week or months of the year or the times table—and then be unable to use the sequence. He or she can recite the months of the year; however, if asked what comes after August, the child pauses before answering "September." When asked why the pause, the child explains that he or she had to go back to January and move forward month by month to get the answer. Using the dictionary can be very frustrating. The child has to return to *a* each time to know if the next letter means going up or down the column to follow the alphabet sequence.

A child with a sequence disability might hit the baseball, and then run to third base rather than to first or might have difficulty with board games that require moving in a particular sequence. When setting the dinner table, he or she might have difficulty remembering where to properly place each item. The child may also have difficulty with the sequence of dressing. A mother walks into her child's bedroom in the morning and doesn't know whether to laugh, cry, or bite her tongue. The boy may have his pants on but be holding his underpants. Or the girl might have her blouse on but be holding her undershirt.

## Abstraction Disabilities

Once information is recorded in the brain and placed in the right sequence, one must be able to infer meaning. If children with learning disabilities have abstraction difficulties, they usually have only a mild form. Abstraction is such a basic intellectual task that if the disability were too great, the child might function below normal level.

Children with abstraction problems take things very literally. For example, the teacher might be reading a story about a police officer, then begin a discussion of police officers in general. The children are asked if they know any men or women who are police officers in their neighborhoods, and if so, what do they do? A child with an abstraction disability may not be able to answer such a question. She or he can only talk about the particular officer in the story and can't generalize to all law officers.

I remember observing a teacher working with four children at one table, one of whom had an abstraction disability. The rest of the class were at their seats doing independent work. Two children in the back of the room began to whisper to each other. The teacher looked up and said, "Class, will you please be quiet." The child with the abstraction difficulty looked up, seemed annoyed, and complained, "I wasn't talking." The teacher agreed and explained that she knew he wasn't talking but that she was referring to the class in general. He became more upset. He had taken her statement literally. If the class was talking and he was part of the class, she meant that he was talking. And he was not talking. He would not stop as he continued to protest about being accused of doing something he did not do.

An older child, adolescent, or adult with abstraction problems may not understand jokes. He or she won't know what's so funny and when to laugh. This individual may be confused by puns or idioms. He or she seems to take things literally and to misunderstand what is said.

## Organization Disabilities

If your child or adolescent has difficulties with organization, you will not need a formal evaluation to know. Look at his or her notebook and papers, locker, desk, or bedroom. He or she is "disorganized" in all aspects of life. The notebook will be a mess with papers in the wrong place or shoved in or falling out. He or she will lose or forget things like books or coats or pencils. The homework gets done but somehow gets lost or forgotten and isn't turned in. The bedroom is a disaster no matter how many times you have cleaned it or told your child to keep it clean. This child might have difficulty allocating the time needed to do homework or planning ahead to be on time.

This student never seems to bring home what he or she will need to do for homework. Even if the teacher uses an assignment sheet, it doesn't help this child. There is chaos in the morning as the child or adolescent tries to get everything together to take to school.

Information, once recorded, sequenced, and understood, must be integrated with a constant flow of information and related to previously learned information. Some students with organization disabilities have difficulty breaking a whole concept down into its parts; other students have difficulty pulling pieces of information into a whole concept. An example of difficulty going from the whole to its constituent parts is the child who reads a book, can discuss the book in general, giving good information, but be unable to answer specific, detailed questions about it. The child with difficulty going from parts to the whole might read this book and provide great detail about everything that happened in the story. However, when asked what the theme of the book was or who the lead character was, this same child might not know. Students who have no difficulty going from the whole concept to parts often do well with essay examinations. Students who have difficulty taking pieces of information and recalling the whole concept may have difficulty with multiple choice examinations. (The student who does very well in high school, writing beautiful papers and essays, may bomb on the SAT examination, which is multiple choice.)

Some individuals have difficulty organizing their thoughts before speaking and seem to ramble. Others have difficulty organizing their thoughts on paper. They explain what they want to write in great detail; then they write a confusing paper with all of the facts but in the wrong order or disconnected.

## Memory Disabilities

Once information is received, recorded in the brain, and integrated, it must be stored so it can be later retrieved. This storage and retrieval process is called memory. For most students with learning disabilities, we can consider that there are two types of memory—short-term memory and long-term memory.

*Short-term memory* is the process by which you store and hold information by the method of concentration and repetition. The information is available while it is being attended to but might be lost once this attention is removed. For example, when you call the information operator for a long-distance telephone number with the area code, you get a ten-digit number. Most people can retain this number long enough to dial it if they do so right away and nothing interrupts their attention. However, if someone starts to talk to them in the course of dialing, they might forget the number. Similarly, someone might go to the store with five items in mind to buy. No list is needed. They know they will remember. But by the time they get to the store, so many different impressions may have intervened that they forget some of the items. Remember in high school or college when you studied for the mid-term examination by "cramming"? You shoved all of the facts into your head by reviewing over and over. You studied up till the minute the exam started. You probably did well. Then, weeks later, you started to study for your final. You looked at your notes and reacted as if you had never seen them before. This is short-term memory.

*Long-term memory* refers to the process by which you store

information that you will use often. You can retrieve this information quickly by thinking of it. For example, you can come up with your current home address and telephone number quite readily by merely thinking about them.

If your child or adolescent has a memory disability, it is most likely a short-term one. Like abstraction disabilities, long-term memory disabilities interfere so much with intellectual functioning that a child who has such a disability is more likely to be functioning below normal.

It may take ten to fifteen repetitions throughout several days for a child with a short-term memory problem to retain what the average child might retain after three to five repetitions on one occasion. Yet, this same child might have no problem with long-term memory. He or she will surprise you at times by remembering things that happened years ago in great detail that you have forgotten.

A short-term memory disability can occur with information learned through what one sees, a *visual short-term memory disability,* or with information learned through what one hears, an *auditory short-term memory disability.* Some may have one form of the disability; others may have both.

This child might read through a spelling list one evening and really seem to know it (because he or she is concentrating on it). The next day, he or she has lost most or all of the words. Similarly, a teacher might review a math concept in class until the child understands and remembers it (because she or he is concentrating on it). Yet, when it is time to do the math homework that night, this child has forgotten how to do the problems. If a parent does the first problem, bringing the memory back, the child can then do the rest. Likewise, this student might read a page and remember it, read the next page and remember it, and the next and the next page. Then, he or she gets to the end of the chapter and doesn't remember anything he or she just read.

If your daughter or son has this disability, you learned the hard way that you cannot give more than one instruction at a time. If you say "Go upstairs, wash up, get into your pajamas, then come down again for a snack," forget it. He or she will not remember that many instructions at once.

Your son or daughter might make you angry by constantly

stopping in the middle of a sentence and saying, "Oh, never mind" or "It's not important." If your child does this a lot, it's possible that she or he has a short-term memory disability. This individual starts to speak, knowing what he or she wants to say. However, partway through, he or she forgets the flow of ideas. It is embarrassing to say, "I'm sorry. What was I saying?" It is easier for the child to say, "Oh, forget it."

## Output Disabilities

The brain communicates information either by means of words (language output) or through muscle activity such as writing, drawing, or gesturing (motor output). An individual with a learning disability might have a *language disability* or a *motor disability*.

### Language Disability

For our discussion, let's focus on two types of language used in communication—spontaneous language and demand language. You use *spontaneous language* in situations where you initiate whatever is said. Here you have the luxury of picking the subject and taking some time to organize your thoughts and to find the correct words before you say anything. In a *demand language* situation, someone else sets up a circumstance by asking you a question or by seeking a comment. You then must respond quickly. Now you don't have as much time to organize your thoughts or to find the right words. You have only a split second in which you must simultaneously organize, find words, and answer more or less appropriately.

Children with a language disability usually have no difficulty with spontaneous language. They do, however, often have problems with demand language. Special education professionals usually call this a demand language disability. Speech-language therapists call this problem an *expressive language disability*. This inconsistency between spontaneous and demand language can be striking and confusing. A youngster or adult may initiate all sorts of conversations, may never keep quiet, in fact, and may sound quite normal. But put into a situation that demands a response ("What did you do today?" or "What is the answer?"), the same person might answer "Huh?" or "What?" or "I don't know." Or she or he might ask you to repeat the question to gain time or may not answer at all, appearing not to be paying attention. If forced to answer, his or her response may be so confusing or circumstantial that it is difficult to follow. She or he may sound totally unlike the person who was speaking so fluently just a minute ago. This confusion in language behavior often puzzles parents and teachers. A teacher might put a child down as lazy or negative because he or she speaks all of the time in class; however, if the teacher calls on this child to answer a question, he or she often will say, "I don't know."

## Motor Disabilities

We discussed motor output problems earlier in another context. Let me review again. The individual with a learning disability might have difficulty coordinating groups of large muscles (arms, legs, trunk), called a *gross motor disability*. Or he or she might have difficulty coordinating groups of small muscles (like those in your hands), called a *fine motor disability*.

Gross motor disabilities may cause your child to be clumsy, stumble, fall, bump into things, or to have trouble with generalized physical activities such as running, climbing, jumping, or riding a bike.

The most common form of a fine motor disability shows up when the child begins to write. The problem lies in an inability to get the many muscles in the dominant hand to work together as a team. His or her handwriting is poor. The child holds a pen or pencil awkwardly and writes slowly; thus, his or her hand gets tired. The child seems not to be able to get his or her hand to write as fast as the head is thinking. Watch your dominant hand as you write something. Notice the many detailed fine muscle activities that it takes to write legibly. Writing requires a constant flow of such activities. Now place your pen in your nondominant hand and try to write. You suddenly have a writing disability. If you go very slowly, it is tedious but your handwriting is legible.

But how frustrating it is for your mind to be so far ahead of what you are writing! If you go at a regular pace, your hand aches and your handwriting immediately deteriorates. Shape, size, spacing, and positioning—everything about the handwriting looks awful no matter how hard you try. A child with a fine motor disability goes through this all of the time. How many times have you said to your child, "If you take your time, your handwriting will be better? When you rush, it becomes too sloppy." How did it feel for you when you slowed down to compensate?

Some may only have this fine motor problem with writing. Usually, however, the child has a broader problem called a *written language disability.* In addition to the problems with the mechanical aspects of writing, he or she has difficulty getting thoughts out of the brain and onto the paper. He or she may have difficulty with spelling, grammar, punctuation, or capitalization. The child seems to know more than he or she shows when writing. Often, once they've written something, those kids can edit and correct their own errors. The difficulty is in the outflow of information. The same child who gets 100 on spelling tests may misspell the same words or simpler words when writing.

A written language disability is very frustrating and can be very serious. Most schools do not grade you on what you know but on what you put down on a piece of paper. If you cannot copy from the board fast enough, take notes when the teacher is talking, or write in class, you have a problem. Of necessity, homework requires writing. Maybe this is why your child or adolescent resists doing homework. Think of copying from the board. First, you have to look at the word (visual perception). Then, you have to retain the word while you look down to write (visual short-term memory). Finally, you have to copy the word on the paper (fine motor). Children with disabilities in these areas may have to copy one word or letter at a time, never finishing the work.

## Establishing Your Child's Profile

Although the learning process is much more complex, this simple input-integration-memory-output model for describing learning disabilities should help you understand the many problem areas. When you read reports or sit in on conferences regarding your child, these are the terms you'll see used.

The important thing is that you must know your son's or daughter's specific profile. Look at the checklist of learning disabilities that follows. Do you know where your child's disabilities lie? Where are his or her strengths? You must know this information in order to learn how to build on your child's strengths rather than magnifying weaknesses when selecting chores, activities, sports, or camps. You must know this information and how to best help your child with his or her homework. If you cannot complete your child's profile, ask the special education member of the school team to help. Or ask the individual who did the testing to help you translate the results into this type of information.

### LEARNING DISABILITIES

INPUT
Visual perception
Auditory perception

INTEGRATION
Sequencing
    Auditory
    Visual
Abstraction
    Auditory
    Visual
Organization
    Auditory
    Visual

MEMORY
Auditory short-term memory
Visual short-term memory

OUTPUT
Demand language
Motor
    Gross motor
    Fine motor

In Chapter 1, I noted that for about 50 percent of children and adolescents with learning disabilities, such disabilities appear to be a familial pattern—that is, the problems are inherited. This means that there is about a 50 percent possibility that one parent also will have a learning disability. As you learn about your child, you might say "That's me." This may be the first time in your life that you understand why you have had so much difficulty in school or in life. If so, learn about yourself. The new knowledge will be valuable. It may help you rethink your past and some of the experiences you have had. You may need this knowledge when help for your son or daughter is discussed. As one mother once told me, "You keep telling me that I have to help my son be more organized with his work. But I haven't been organized one day of my life. How can I help him when I have the same problem?"

## Another Perspective on Learning Disabilities

It is helpful to understand the general progression of the curriculum through school. The following overview might explain why some students start to have difficulty in the first grade, others in the third or sixth or ninth. Although each school system establishes its own curriculum for each grade, there is a similiar theme for all.

In first grade, children are taught the basic skills. In reading, the goal is phonological awareness, that is, the ability to attach the correct sound to each symbol and then to blend these individual sounds into a word. It is assumed that between prekindergarten and kindergarten, students will learn the graphic symbols (*A* through *Z* and *1* through *9* plus *0*). In writing, the goal is learning to print each letter of the alphabet, first in lowercase and later in uppercase. In math, it is learning the basic concepts of numbers. First, we use a base 10 system in math. Second, numbers can neither be created nor made to disappear (called the "conservation of numbers"). These concepts lead to addition and subtraction.

Second grade is usually used to consolidate the skills taught in first. Basically, no new skills are taught. Thus, if a student is not fully at grade level at the end of first, second might be used to improve these skills.

Third grade is very important because a major leap is made. The first weeks are spent in review. Then it is assumed that you know your basic skills. Thus, the focus shifts to using these skills. It is no longer, Can you read? but What have you read? Read a book and explain what you read. It is no longer, Can you write? but What have you written? Students write journals and book reports. Spelling, grammar, punctuation, and style of writing become important topics. It is assumed that you know the conservation of numbers. Multiplication and division are introduced. Thus, a student who enters third grade without solid basic skills will start to struggle by November, following the review period. The year will become more and more difficult.

Fourth and fifth grades are spent expanding on the use of skills. Gradually, having and using the skills are not the issue. These abilities are employed to study subject matter—history, science, geography, and so on. If the abilities needed in third grade are not solid, fourth and fifth will be difficult.

Sixth, seventh, and eighth grades—middle school—focus on subject content. It is assumed that each student has both skills and the ability to use these skills. The student who is weak in one or more of these skills will struggle. In general, the subjects are taught in a structured way, focusing on teaching learning strategies and study skills. Because there are now five to seven teachers and subjects, students who have problems with organization may have difficulty managing the classes and assignments.

In high school, the focus continues to be on topic areas. The material is presented with the assumption that the student knows good learning strategies and study skills. Thus, students with organization or executive functioning disabilities may struggle.

One can see why some students who have learning disabilities that interfere with mastery of basic skills may begin to have difficulty in first and second grade. Others may have the ability to learn the skills, but the areas of disability might interfere more with reading comprehension, written language, or higher math concepts. They will struggle in third grade. Students with learning disabilities that primarily interfere with organizational skills might not struggle until middle school. Students with difficulties in the executive functioning areas might do well until high school.

# In Summary

Each individual will have his or her specific profile of learning disabilities and learning abilities. This chapter provides parents with the knowledge and vocabulary to understand their son's or daughter's learning disabilities. It is essential that parents fully understand the areas of disability and the areas of ability.

# 7

## The Modulating Disorders and the Tic Disorders

### The Modulating Disorders

In Chapter 1, I introduced the concept of problems with modulation. To function, it is important that the brain be able to modulate, or regulate, specific functions in order to maintain a balance, or equilibrium, and to avoid extremes. These modulating tasks appear to be regulated using the same areas of the brain and the same neurotransmitter, serotonin.

These areas modulate anxiety, anger, and mood. Thus, difficulties in modulation will result in difficulties with one or more of these feelings. The individual might feel anxious, have difficulty controlling anger, or feel depressed. With obsessive-compulsive disorder, the person has difficulty modulating or regulating specific thoughts or behaviors. These modulating disorders are chronic. That is, they have been there since early childhood. The modulating disorders appear to have a high frequency of a familial pattern, often up to 50 percent. Parents or closely related relatives have or have had the same problems.

Since children and adolescents with ADHD and/or learning disabilities have a higher likelihood of having one or more of these modulating disorders than the normal population, it is important for parents to understand each. By knowing what it is, how it is recognized and diagnosed, and how it is treated, par-

ents can be sure that their daughter or son sees the right professional and receives the right help.


## Problems Modulating Anxiety

Anxiety is that emotional uneasiness associated with the anticipation of something bad happening or of danger. We distinguish
it from fear, the emotional response to real danger, although the
body's response to each is the same. Anxiety is a common life experience. You are driving down the highway and notice a flash-
ing red light in your rearview mirror. Your first response may be
to feel anxious, your heart may start to pound, and you may
begin to sweat. Then, the police car passes you and drives on and
you relax. The anxiety was that you might be pulled over for
speeding. Anxiety is a normal feeling prior to taking a test or
being examined by your family doctor. However, anxiety also
can be part of many psychiatric and other medical disorders.

Each person might experience anxiety differently. The most
common responses are listed here:

### BEHAVIORS EXPERIENCED WHEN ANXIOUS

*Related to the heart:* palpitations, rapid heart beat, increase in
blood pressure, flushing or pallor.

*Related to breathing:* feeling of shortness of breath, increased
rate of breathing.

*Related to the skin:* blotching, rash, increase in skin temperature with sweating, funny sensations felt in the skin.

*Related to the muscles:* mild shaking (tremor), muscle tension,
muscle cramps.

*Other physical behaviors:* headache, chest pain, overalertness,
startling easily, insomnia, nightmares, dizziness, fainting, uri-
nary frequency.

*Other psychological behaviors:* talk of fears; feeling scared, tense, nervous, upset, stressed, fretful, restless; can't think clearly.

*Other social behaviors:* appearing clingy, needy, dependent, and/or shy; being withdrawn; uneasiness in social situations.

Children and adolescents might show a *generalized* feeling of anxiety. They have excessive and unrealistic worries about competence, approval, appropriateness of past behavior, and the future. Others might show a *specific* feeling of anxiety. They might have a separation anxiety, feeling anticipatory uneasiness about separating from parents or other loved ones. Or they might develop a phobia, a specific fear that results in avoidance behaviors and functional and social impairment. Common phobias seen with children and adolescents include animals in general, cats, dogs, blood, fire, germs, dirt, height, insects, small or closed spaces, snakes, spiders, strangers, and thunder.

There are other types of anxiety disorders seen with youths. Some may develop a *social phobia,* showing significant anxiety that is provoked by exposure to certain types of social or performance situations, often leading to avoidance behavior. Following a traumatic experience, children or adolescents might develop a *posttraumatic stress disorder.* They are anxious and overly cautious, and often reexperience the feelings associated with the extremely traumatic event accompanied by symptoms of increased arousal and by avoidance of stimuli associated with the trauma.

For some, the anxiety level gets so high that a fight-or-flight response is triggered. This is called a panic attack and is seen with *panic disorders.* The individual experiences a sudden onset of intense apprehension, fearfulness, or terror, often associated with feelings of impending doom. During these attacks, the body responds with such symptoms as shortness of breath, palpitations of the heart, chest pain or discomfort, choking or smothering sensations, and fear of "going crazy" or of losing control.

If a child or adolescent develops a high level of anxiety or one of these anxiety disorders at a specific time in her or his life, it is important to explore what is causing it. The anxiety might be understandable. For example, many children with learning disabilities begin to show anxiety in late August as they realize school is about to start again. The anxiety might relate to family stress such as the illness or death of a close relative or tension between parents. Sometimes the cause is not readily apparent.

The difference with children and adolescents who have a modulating disorder manifested by anxiety or panic attacks lies in its chronicity. These children are described in early childhood as more tense and anxious. They have always been more fearful. The current set of problems is only the latest example of a long-term problem. At an earlier age, they were afraid to be separated from their mother or afraid to go to sleep alone. Later, they might have frequent nightmares, wake up, and need to sleep with their parents. Now they might be afraid to be in a part of the house (another floor) if no one else is there or might be afraid to play outside because there are bees. Or now they are afraid to be around crowds or noisy places or to play sports.

If your son or daughter shows evidence of generalized or specific anxiety, it is important to speak with your family doctor or to a mental health professional. Reflective therapy, behavioral therapy, and/or family therapy might be very helpful. However, if you are aware that the current picture of a problem with anxiety is part of a chronic pattern for your child or adolescent, stress this theme to the professional. A modulating disorder related to anxiety is often treated in a different way. I will discuss these treatment approaches later in this chapter.

## Problems Modulating Anger

Anger, like anxiety, is a normal feeling. What is important is how the child or adolescent handles or shows this anger. Parents usually role-model acceptable ways of showing anger. Thus, some youths will show anger by being negative, walking off stomping their feet, yelling, or slamming doors. Others may throw a pillow or bang their fists. Some learn that in their family there is no acceptable way to show anger as a child or adolescent. They may go to their room and beat up their pillow or stuffed animal.

Youths with a problem modulating anger show a very different picture. They explode. As with the other modulating disorders, there is a chronic history of difficulty regulating anger. Parents might note that this child had terrible temper tantrums as an infant, violent tantrums lasting a long time as a younger child, and now has explosive behaviors.

These explosive behaviors are called *intermittent explosive disorder*. They are manifested by a sudden onset of explosive behavior. The "fuse," or threshhold point for controlling anger, appears to be so short that often it may not be possible to figure out what caused the explosion. Once the child or adolescent explodes, there is no reasoning or controlling him or her. He or she will scream, yell, curse, throw things, hit, break things. During the episode, he or she may sound paranoid: "Everyone hates me" or "You're trying to hurt me" or "Don't hit me." The episode lasts from three to five to twenty minutes or more with most children and adolescents. Then, it stops as quickly as it started. Once it's over, the person may be so tired he or she wants to rest or sleep. There might be some show of remorse for what happened. More often, the child or adolescent doesn't want to talk about it, preferring to watch TV or do something else neutral.

These explosive outbursts are frightening and difficult to handle or tolerate. When they occur each day or several times a day, everyone becomes overwhelmed and nonfunctional. Parents feel helpless. Siblings are afraid and avoid this person.

Usually, children and adolescents with anger-regulation problems only explode at home with parents or with other significant adults. It is not clear if they know they have to "hold it in" at school or over at a friend's house or if the stresses that cause the anger are more associated with family issues. Occasionally, they may explode with peers. Less so, they may do so at school.

The treatment for intermittent explosive disorder goes beyond talking or behavioral therapy. The specific treatment approaches will be discussed later in this chapter.

## Problems Modulating Mood

Depression is also a normal feeling. Each major growth step experienced by a child is associated with some anxiety and depression. He or she learns to walk and can get about without help. There is the anxiety of moving out alone and there is the sadness or depression of leaving behind a special kind of closeness and dependency that will no longer exist. Adolescents can feel the same way. They are anxious about growing up and becoming an adult and they feel the sadness or depression of giving up the special experiences and safety of childhood.

A child or adolescent who is depressed might show one or more of the behaviors below:

## BEHAVIORS ASSOCIATED WITH DEPRESSION

1. Depressed or irritable mood
2. Diminished interest or loss of pleasure in almost all activities
3. Sleep disturbance
4. Weight change or appetite disturbance
5. Decreased concentration or indecisiveness
6. Suicidal ideation or thoughts of death
7. Agitation or slowness of thinking
8. Fatigue or loss of energy
9. Feelings of worthlessness or inappropriate guilt
10. With children, irritability and increased anger

So that you can be familiar with terms used by psychiatrists and other mental health professionals, I need to mention two specific types of depressive disorders. When the child or adolescent shows a depressed or irritable mood that lasts a year or longer and is never symptom-free for more than two months, the depression is called *dysthymia*. He or she may show appetite changes, sleep changes, decreased energy, low self-esteem, difficulty making decisions or poor concentration, and/or feelings of hopelessness. If the individual shows depressed mood or the loss of interest or pleasure in activities; evidence of changes in appetite or weight, sleep patterns, or clearness of thinking; decreased energy; feelings of worthlessness or guilt; problems with concentrating or making decisions; or recurrent thoughts of death or suicidal ideation for a period of at least two weeks, it is called a *major depressive episode*.

Some individuals who show a major depressive episode might have difficulty modulating the "upswing" of affect as well. They might go into a hypomanic (excited) state manifested by an abnormal and persistently elevated, expansive, or irritable mood. They might have an inflated self-esteem or grandiosity, decreased need for sleep, pressure to speak nonstop, flight of ideas, high distractibility, increased involvement in goal-directed activities, or psychomotor agitation. This hypomanic state might last a week or more if not treated. If a person experiences both major periods of depression and hypomania, he or she has a *bipolar disorder* (formerly called a manic-depressive disorder). If the person only experiences periods of normalcy and depression, he or she has a *unipolar disorder*.

We do not yet know the exact clinical picture of these depressive disorders in young children. Often what we see is irritability and anger. The mood swings might be less going from normal to sad and more going from pleasant to angry. Thus, the younger the child is, the harder it is to make the diagnosis of a depressive disorder (dysthymia or major depressive episode) or a mood disorder (unipolar or bipolar).

However, we do know that children or adolescents can become depressed. The cause might be apparent or unclear. A youth with a modulating disorder has had the problem chronically. Parents report that this child was always moody or sad or unhappy. He or she rarely showed happiness or enjoyment in relationships or activities. The current problem is only the most recent picture of this chronic problem. Treatment for these depressive disorders will be discussed later in this chapter.

### Obsessive-Compulsive Disorder (OCD)

Obsessions are unwanted thoughts, images, or impulses that the individual realizes are senseless or unnecessary, intrude into his or her consciousness involuntarily, and cause functional impairment and distress. Despite this lack of control, the sufferer still recognizes that these thoughts originate in his or her own mental process. Since they arise in the mind, obsessions can take the form of any mental event—simple repetitive words, thoughts, fears, memories, pictures, or elaborate dramatic scenes.

Compulsions are actions that are responses to a perceived internal obligation to follow certain rituals or rules. They also cause functional impairment. Compulsions may be motivated directly by obsessions or by efforts to ward off certain thoughts, impulses, or fears. Occasionally, children report compulsions without the perception of a mental component. Like obsessions, compulsions are often viewed as being unnecessary, excessive or senseless, and involuntary or forced. Individuals suffering from compulsions will often elaborate a variety of precise rules for the chronology, rate, order, duration, and number of repetitions of their acts.

A person with OCD may have obsessions, compulsions, or both. These behaviors result in difficulty functioning. Individuals feel that they are being forced or invaded by the symptoms, and they possess insight into the senselessness or excessiveness of their thoughts or acts. They might try to ignore or suppress these thoughts or actions; however, the anxiety builds and the behaviors break through.

Common behaviors seen with individuals who have OCD are listed here.

## BEHAVIORS SEEN WITH OBSESSIVE-COMPULSIVE DISORDER

1. *Counting or repeating behavior:* the need to touch something a certain number of times or an even/odd number of times; the need to repeat a specific behavior or pattern of behaviors; the need to count certain things until finished.
2. *Checking or questioning behavior:* the need to check and recheck something (front door is locked, stove is off, car keys were brought in, closet light is off); the need to ask a question a specific number of times or until the person answers in the exact way it is needed to be heard.
3. *Collecting or hoarding behavior:* collecting matches, rocks, pieces of glass, pieces of paper; hoarding newspapers or other items and becoming upset if they are thrown away.
4. *Arranging and organizing behavior:* the need to tie shoes or to dress or undress in a certain sequence or way; the need to organize toys or dolls or other items in a certain way; becoming upset if anything is changed.
5. *Cleaning and/or washing behavior:* the need to lather and rinse an exact number of times while showering or to brush the hair a certain number of times in a certain pattern; the need to wash hands repeatedly.

These obsessions and/or compulsions may begin to appear at age six or seven. If someone has OCD, he or she clearly reports that the behaviors were causing frustration and difficulty by early adolescence.

## Treatment for these Modulating Disorders

The research of the mid- and late 1990s has begun to clarify these modulating disorders. The common theme appears to be that the areas of the brain involved use the same neurotransmitter, serotonin. The modulating disorders appear to be due to a deficiency of this neurotransmitter. This deficiency had already been observed with depression and with OCD, and medications that increase the level of serotonin in these areas of the brain have already been established as the best treatment. Recently, these same medications have been used for children and adolescents with a chronic pattern of anxiety and/or anger-regulation problems. Current studies strongly suggest that they help. As the level of serotonin goes up, the anxiety and angry outbursts decrease or stop. Much more research is needed in these areas. But, for now, the clinical treatment for each of these modulating disorders is to use medications that increase the level of serotonin in these areas of the brain. In addition to the medications, cognitive behavioral therapy is important. In some situations, reflective therapy or family therapy will be recommended as well.

The medications used are called selective serotonin reuptake inhibitors because they appear to increase the level of serotonin by decreasing the reabsoption of this neurotransmitter at the nerve ending. At this time, there are four SSRIs available.

### The SSRIs

| Trade Name | Chemical (Generic) Name |
|---|---|
| Prozac | Fluoxetine |
| Paxil | Paroxetine |
| Zoloft | Sertraline |
| Luvox | Fluvoxamine |

The current availability of information on the use of SSRIs by children and adolescents does not show clear guidelines for choosing one over the other. Each clinician might prefer to start with one, then, if needed, move on to another.

This book focuses on ADHD. It is important to understand that these modulating disorders might exist along with ADHD. It is beyond the scope of this book to go into more detail on the medication treatments for the modulating disorders. If your son or daughter is recommended for one of the medications, the physician prescribing it should explain the actions, potential side effects, and other important information.

## The Tic Disorders

A tic disorder is not a modulating disorder. However, tic disorders are frequently found as part of the neurological continuum discussed in Chapter 1. Most of the studies showing that these disorders are frequently seen together focus on one type of tic disorder, Tourette's disorder. Of all children and adolescents with Tourette's disorder, about 50 percent will have ADHD. About 60 percent of individuals with this disorder will have a learning disability, and 50 percent will have OCD.

A tic is a sudden, repetitive movement, gesture, or utterance that typically mimics some aspect of normal behavior. Usually of brief duration, individual tics rarely last more than a second. They tend to occur in bouts and at times have a paroxysmal character. Tics can occur singly or together in an orchestrated pattern. They can vary in their frequency and forcefulness. Although many tics can be temporarily suppressed, they are often experienced as being involuntary.

Muscle or motor tics vary from simple, abrupt movements, such as eye blinks, head jerks, or shoulder shrugs, to more complex, purposeful-appearing behaviors, such as facial expressions or gestures of the arms or head. In extreme cases, these movements can be obscene or self-injurious (hitting or biting). Vocal tics can range from simple throat-clearing sounds to more complex vocalizations and speech.

## Types of Tic Disorders

It is important for parents to know the types of tic disorders and the terms used for each. If the motor or vocal tics begin before age eighteen and last for more than a month, but less than a year, the disorder is called a *transient tic disorder*. This problem is not uncommon with young children. If left alone, the tics go away and are never seen again. If the motor or vocal tics begin before age eighteen and last for more than a year, the disorder is called a *chronic motor* or *vocal tic disorder*. If the person has a chronic motor or vocal tic disorder where the tics occur many times a day nearly every day or intermittently throughout a period of more than one year with never a tic-free period of more than three consecutive months and where the disturbance causes marked distress or significant impairment in social, occupational, or other important areas of functioning, the disorder is called Tourette's disorder. Individuals with Tourette's disorder frequently have a family history of other close relatives with this disorder.

Most individuals with either a chronic motor or vocal tic disorder or Tourette's disorder will first begin to have tics between the ages of seven and twelve. Most adults with these disorders report that their tics began during this time.

## Treatment for the Tic Disorders

Tic disorders are not treated unless the motor and/or vocal tics create a psychological or social problem for the child or adolescent or these tics are so severe as to cause muscle soreness. If it is necessary to treat the tic disorder, certain medications can decrease or stop the tics. The most frequently used medications today are listed here.

## MEDICATIONS FOR TIC DISORDERS

| Trade Name | Chemical (Generic) Name |
|---|---|
| Haldol | Haloperidol |
| Orap | Pimozide |
| Catapres | Clonidine |
| Tenex | Guanfacine |

As I mentioned with the modulating disorders, it is beyond the scope of this book to go into detail on the medication treatment for the tic disorders. If your son or daughter receives treatment for a tic disorder, the physician prescribing the medication will inform you of the actions, effects, and side effects.

# PART FOUR

# Social and Emotional Disorders Associated with Attention Deficit Hyperactivity Disorder

# 8

## Normal Psychosocial Development

A mother called me about her child. Her son refused to leave her and began clinging and crying if she tried to walk away. If she left him with someone else, he threw a tantrum. What should she do with him? I couldn't say anything until I found out her son's age. If he was one year old, this behavior could be quite normal. If he was two, I would be slightly worried. If he was four or eight, I would be very concerned. If he was fifteen, I would be alarmed. Normal behavior has a great deal to do with your son's or daughter's age and the stage of development that the child is in at the time.

All children go through stages of psychological and social development, and most do so with minimal difficulty. They may occasionally face a stressful situation—being in the hospital, getting used to a new baby brother or sister, or coping with their parents' divorce—and briefly retreat to earlier behaviors. But ordinarily they soon rally and move ahead again. Growth means many steps forward with occasional steps backward.

Much of this psychological and social—psychosocial—growth interweaves with stages in physical growth. As the brain and body mature, the child develops new abilities with which to handle problems. This same growth, however, also introduces new problems.

Most children go through the various stages of development without serious problems, while some progress with a few obvious difficulties. Some children and families find certain stages of growth more difficult than others. The child with ADHD or learning disabilities, however, may have trouble with some or all of the stages of psychosocial development. First, I'll review what is understood to be normal development. This knowledge will help you see the ways in which ADHD or learning disabilities inhibit or alter this development.

## Normal Child Development

The newborn infant functions initially as a physiological being— the brain receives messages from the body and environment and responds. During the early weeks and months, the baby begins to recognize sounds and some visual inputs. He or she begins to become aware of certain significant people, recognizing, for example, the mother's or father's voice, image, or smell. As the infant begins to relate to his or her world, he or she is unaware of any distinction between his or her body and objects in the environment—a baby has no sense of any boundaries. People, pets, food, furniture, toys—all objects outside of the self appear to be merely extensions of the child. For now, the infant and his or her world are one. This stage of development is depicted in Fig. 8-1.

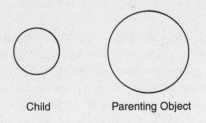

Child          Parenting Object

FIG. 8-1

### Basic Trust

Gradually, the infant begins to discover that objects have extensions and limits to them as well. The child discovers his or her fingers and hands, toes and feet, and finds that these objects belong to the same body that he or she has begun to experience. By about three months, the infant can recognize certain pieces of the external world and relates to these "part objects" in special ways that acknowledge their importance. Now, for the first time, the "social smile" appears. The child looks at a familiar face and smiles. This social smile is an early psychological landmark of normal development.

By about nine months, the infant has completed the process of discovering where he or she leaves off and the world begins. Having learned to associate pleasurable experiences with certain "human objects," the baby begins to comprehend that these specific human objects are very important—that they are absolutely necessary, in fact. Thus, the baby learns to place *basic trust* in these key people and becomes totally dependent on them.

With the establishment of basic trust, the infant masters the first major step in psychosocial development. But now the baby becomes upset if he or she is left alone. The child fears separation and strangers. Before this stage, anyone could pick up the baby and get a smile. Now if someone unknown or not very well known picks up the baby, he or she starts to cry. This fear, which normally appears at around nine months, is another psychosocial landmark. This stage of total dependence, manifested by separation anxiety, is depicted in Fig. 8-2.

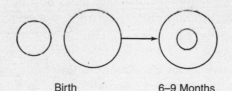

Birth          6–9 Months

FIG. 8-2

## Separation

The next task in psychosocial development is mastering *separation*. The infant must realize that he or she can separate from these significant people and still survive, and then learn how to do that. Mastery of this stage of development involves several steps that start at about nine months and usually finish at around three to three and a half years. (Many children today are placed in day care during the early months and seem to master separation much earlier.) Until mastered, separation from the significant people in his or her life results in anxiety— separation anxiety. This accomplishment of separation, which leads to a sense of an autonomous self, is illustrated in Fig. 8-3.

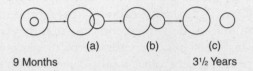

(a)          (b)          (c)

9 Months                          3½ Years

FIG. 8-3

Initially (see *a* in Fig. 8-3), the infant must have some form of sensory connection with the significant person. The baby cries, hears a parent's footsteps in the hall, and stops crying. This auditory linkage is enough. Or the infant crawls behind a chair, loses sight of a parent, and cries. When the parent moves into view, the child stops crying. This visual link, the sight of the parent, reestablishes the necessary contact. For example, the baby cries at night. When the mother or father picks him or her up in the dark and holds the child, the crying stops. The touch, smell, and voice of the parent reassures the infant that the intimate connection is not broken.

Beginning at about eighteen months, the child slowly learns to separate for longer and longer periods of time (see *b* in Fig. 8-3 ). However, the toddler still must frequently return to the parent to "refuel" or "tag up." A hug or a kiss or a cookie will do, and the child is off again. Some children find these early efforts at separating easier if they can take something that reminds them of a parent along with them. Children usually select these favorite items, which are commonly called "security blankets" or, more properly, transitional objects, because the items have a familiar smell, soft touch, or the cuddly feel that they have learned to associate with the parent.

By about three, the child can usually separate from his or her parents with no discomfort (see *c* in Fig. 8-3). Again, children who are placed in day care settings early in life might master separation earlier than age three. This full mastery of separation is yet another landmark in psychosocial development.

Two major psychological events take place during this stage of mastering separation, one internally motivated and the other externally caused. Each aids in mastering separation and in establishing autonomy, and each has a major influence on personality development. The internal event is negativism, beginning at about age two. During the "terrible twos," the child responds to most requests or comments with "No" or "No, I do myself." The child is beginning to separate and to show that he or she has a mind of his or her own. Although exasperating to parents, this healthy step toward separation and autonomy is a very necessary one.

The other event that occurs at age two to three is toilet training. In learning to accede to this requirement of the outside world, the child confronts two new tasks that have to be mastered. First, the child must alter his or her concept of love and relationships. Until now, the child has perceived the whole world as being there to take care of him or her. Love and caring were automatic and free. Suddenly, the child faces a situation in which love appears no longer to be free and available on demand. Now, if the child wants love, he or she must do something to get it. Loving relationships no longer center totally around one's wishes and needs; now the child must learn to participate in a give-and-take process. Urinate in the potty and mommy loves you; urinate in your pants and mommy frowns. Getting love sometimes requires doing what is wanted. To receive pleasure requires pleasing. This forces the child to make a revolutionary shift in his or her concept of the world, people, and relationships. He or she must move from a self-centered world (primary narcissism) to a world where he or she is aware of his or her own needs as well as those of others.

Toilet training introduces a second new concept that provides the child with a new way to handle angry feelings. For the first time, the child has an active weapon in the battle to get what he or she wants. Prior to this, the child could cry or have a tantrum, but the parents could choose to ignore the behavior. Prior to this, the child experienced anger and expressed it openly by crying, screaming, kicking, or hitting. Now the child begins to realize that there are different ways to express anger and that the way one does express anger has a great deal to do with getting and keeping love. Direct expressions of anger don't work. The price one has to pay may be too great. A child now learns that more indirect expressions of anger work somewhat better than hitting and yelling. Now, when angry with Mom or Dad, the child can squat right in front of the parent, preferably when company is around, and, with a big smile, "make" in his or her pants. When the child is pleased with Mommy and Daddy, he or she will "make" on the potty. The child begins to learn the importance of controlling anger, or more precisely, of learning subtler, more ambiguous, and therefore more acceptable ways to express anger.

These issues—the reciprocal nature of loving and being loved and pleased, and handling angry feelings—are struggled with individually and together. The two themes often interrelate. At this age, one can readily love and hate the same person at the same time or hurt and care for the same person at the same time.

## Individuation

When the child has mastered the first major task of development, establishing basic trust, and the second major task, handling separation, he or she is ready for the third task, *individuation*. This task involves asking and trying to answer the question "Who am I?" Now that the child knows that he or she is a separate person who can survive without being totally dependent on important people, what kind of person is that child? The struggle to answer these questions usually takes place between three and six years of age.

At this age, the brain is still immature, and not all thinking is based on reality. Fantasy, which seems as real as what is real, forms one basis for a lot of the child's thinking. If the child thinks something is so, it may as well be. A child at this age, then, can have opposite beliefs and feelings simultaneously, with no notion that a contradiction exists or that only one of two or more different possibilities can come true. For example, loving and hating, wanting and not wanting, going to a movie and at the same time going on a picnic—the child excludes nothing and sees no problem with believing in all possibilities coming true at the same time.

The child also tries out many roles. If the child pretends to be Superman, he or she is Superman. What is it like to be big? little? aggressive? submissive? a boy? a girl? Children play "house," "school," or "doctor," exploring various roles and different situations. One day your daughter may act like a boy, the next day a girl, or a mommy, a daddy, a teacher, a cartoon hero. Your daughter or son tries to learn about people and how to do activities, and attempts to master those concerns through repetition in play. For example, children must learn to listen to adults other than their parents. When they play school, they take turns being the teacher who gives instructions and orders, and then the pupil who must listen and obey. When they play doctor, they take turns being the doctor who explores and the patient who is explored.

Whenever a child tries to "be" someone else in the family—for instance, mother or father—he or she may feel the need to compete with siblings who may also want to be that parent. The child also has to try to attract the attention of the other parent. So another characteristic of this age period is the child's tendency to cause splitting and tension between parents as well as among siblings. Children learn with remarkable aptitude how to divide parents, getting one closer to them and pushing the other away. Thus, on one day a child may seem close and loving, yet on another day he or she is irritable and hostile.

For the first time, in Fig. 8-4, the diagram of the child's relationships must include both parents.

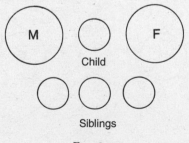

FIG. 8-4

If the boy or girl wants to play "being mother," then the mother must be pushed away, along with any siblings who might compete for her role, as in Fig. 8-5.

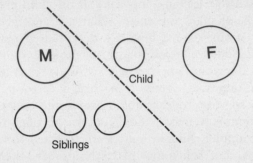

FIG. 8-5

If the child wants to play "being father," then the father has to be pushed away, along with any siblings who might want that role, as in Fig. 8-6.

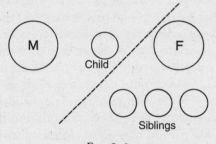

FIG. 8-6

Because both splits occur from time to time, the diagram of the child's relationships has to look like that which is depicted in Fig. 8-7.

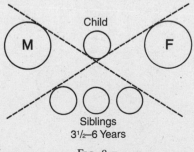

FIG. 8-7

A child's thoughts at this age are magical—that is, they are not reality-based—and the child often has trouble distinguishing among his or her actual feelings, thoughts, and actions. The child's thoughts, especially angry thoughts, scare him or her. Nightmares are common. A child worries that others, like parents, know what he or she is thinking and that they will retaliate. This magical fear of retaliation causes the child to worry excessively about body integrity and body damage. Any cut or scratch is a disaster. This is why this age is often called the "Band-Aid" stage.

During these frustrating fours and fives, most children and their parents do have a lot of fun. The child is animated, uninhibited, and imaginative and enjoys interacting and playing. However, the child can cause stress between parents and among siblings and have trouble sleeping, have nightmares, or want to sleep with parents. One minute you love and cuddle the child, the next you feel like giving him or her away to one of your neighbors. All of this is normal.

By about age six, most children begin to find preliminary answers to the question "Who am I?" Little girls begin to learn that they are to become "just like Mommy" and enjoy playing this role. They give up wanting Daddy all to themselves and look forward to some day having someone just like their father. Little boys begin to learn that they are to become "just like Daddy." They give up wanting Mommy all to themselves and settle for the idea of having someone just like their mother some day. Although some of these self-assessments may later change, it is through this process of identification that children learn to become more or less like the parent of the same sex. (The child in a single-parent family may have more difficulty working through this stage of development. Most make it through, but if you think that consulting a mental health professional would help, don't hesitate to get advice yourself and perhaps for your child.)

During this time, between about three and six, most children are struggling to establish basic assumptions about themselves. It is then that parents and other significant adults often introduce concepts of stereotypical sex-role behaviors. If a boy reaches for a doll to play with, he may be brusquely told that boys play with trucks or guns, not with dolls. Cultural clichés like this always amaze me—adult men must know how to relate lovingly to their children, among other people, not how to use guns, and adult men know that. Adult women must know how to express themselves productively, not just how to use eye makeup, and adult women know that. Still, many continue to teach little girls that they play with dolls and do tasks in the kitchen; they do not work with tools or excel in sports. Many girls are taught that it is acceptable to express love and sadness, but not self-assertion or anger. Many boys learn that it is acceptable to express anger, but that "big boys don't cry."

Fortunately, the consciousness-raising efforts of the women's movement have helped to free more and more families from the need to pass along these stereotypes. Children must feel free to explore and to learn many roles to become fully developed males or females. They must learn that true maleness and femaleness has nothing to do with the things one does or how one expresses different emotions, but instead with the kinds of resources and experiences one has, the kinds of relationships one can sustain, and the respect developed toward oneself and others.

Toward the end of this stage, at about age six, two changes take place that help the child master the process of individuation. The central nervous system takes a large maturational leap forward, and this helps the child to move from nonreality-based thinking to reality-based thinking. Contradictory feelings and thoughts can no longer coexist with equal power. The child begins to understand that feeling or thinking one thing means not believing in its opposite at the same time with equal conviction; for example, loving and hating the same person at the same time. In other words, the realization dawns that one cannot do or be two (or more) things at the same time. The child can now distinguish between reality and fantasy. For example, the child might pretend to be Superman, but he or she now knows it is only pretend.

The other change during this stage involves the child's emerging awareness of the various accumulated values and value judgments that he or she has learned. At about this age, the child fuses these beliefs into an established conscience called the *superego*. This "voice," or conscience, stays with one throughout life and becomes increasingly significant. It "tells" the child which thoughts, feelings, and actions are acceptable and which are not. Initially, the parents teach these values, and the child usually adopts them fairly automatically. He or she may rebel, but this is more because the child wants his or her own way, not because any serious questions about moral or intellectual validity come up. In adolescence, as we shall see, these values are routinely reviewed and reconsidered.

## Latency

Once the child has mastered the third task of development, individuation, he or she moves into a period of consolidation. Sometime around age six, the child becomes free to move out of the family and into the community. With the major psychological work of childhood done, the child's energy is freed to range more widely, in school and other learning activities, and in expanding relationships. This period, which lasts about six years, is called the *latency* period, illustrated in Fig. 8-8.

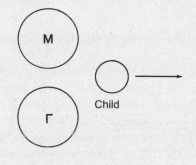

FIG. 8-8

During the latency period, the child learns to relate to adults other than his or her parents and to children other than his or her siblings. The child begins to focus on relationships with children of the same sex and may ignore or move away from peer activities that include children of the opposite sex. Most boys prefer boys and often don't like girls. Most girls prefer girls and may avoid boys. Very intimate "chum" or "best friend" relationships develop, and the child's behavior that you got used to during the individuation stage changes completely. A boy will shrug and push his mother away if she tries to hold or kiss him. Two boys or two girls may walk down the street arm in arm. During this period, children explore and learn the ability to relate to

people of the same sex and form both intimate and casual friend-
ships with them.

The latency period usually covers grades one through six.
Massive knowledge must be learned and mastered, from reading,
writing, and arithmetic to subject information and study skills. A
child who does not resolve or master each stage of psychosocial
development before entering these grades can have difficulty
functioning in school or mastering the required tasks.

By the age of twelve to fourteen, this period of consolidation
ends. Adolescence arrives and, with it, new tasks to master.
Everything is about to change—possibly for the worse, but eventually for the better. Each stage of psychosocial development for
the child must be mastered, and he or she must feel comfortable
entering adolescence. If any previous developmental stage was
not resolved, the child might have more difficulty with adolescence.

## Normal Adolescent Development

Adolescence is a difficult time for almost everyone and for almost all parents. The period of adolescence prepares a person to
move out of childhood and into adulthood. This transition has
to be unique for each generation. Parents often rely on their
own models and experiences, responding to their teenage children as their parents did to them or as they think they should
have been responded to. The difficulty is that these role models
and experiences more or less successfully prepared today's parents for the last third of the twentieth century. Today's adolescents have to learn to live in the twenty-first century. You will
have to speculate right along with your teenage child on the
strengths, attitudes, and skills needed for adulthood. Many of
your own life experiences will be out of date and probably too
restrictive.

As parents of an adolescent, you must teach your youth the
values that you believe are important, but you must also take
into account the unique issues that your teenager struggles with
in the world as it is now and it will be for him or her. You have to
give your teenager roots and wings at the same time. The adoles-

cent will need the roots—the security that comes with a solid foundation—in order to spread his or her wings and fly.

The adolescent must rework most of the psychosocial tasks of childhood. Physical growth still plays a major role in the stages of psychological growth. Some adolescents go through these stages with little or no difficulty; other have problems with a stage, then regroup and move forward.

## Problems with Physical Changes

It is useful to distinguish between puberty—the period of physical changes—and adolescence—the period of psychosocial changes. Ideally, the two occur hand-in-hand. However, with some teenagers, these processes get way out of sync. When one is out of phase with the other, the person has to cope with even more stress than usual.

Think of a girl who, at ten or eleven, is taller than all of the other girls, full-breasted, and already menstruating, or the seventeen-year-old boy who is five feet tall, with peach fuzz and a high voice. Both are physically normal, but each is at a different end of the normal growth curve. And each has additional stresses with which to cope. The reverse can be equally stressful. For example, consider the boy in sixth grade who is already almost six feet tall and growing a beard, or the short, flat-chested young woman who still looks like "a little girl" as she graduates from high school. Each must cope with more than his or her share of the stress that adolescence normally brings.

Just as children do, adolescents have feelings and thoughts that cause conflicts and tension. However, their physical growth gives them capacities for action and reaction that no child has. When a six-year-old boy cuddles with his mother, he feels pleasant sensations; when a fourteen- or fifteen-year-old boy does so, he may be embarrassed when he has an erection. A little girl can thoroughly enjoy sitting on her father's lap, but a thirteen-year-old girl who does so may have physical sensations that worry her. Wrestling with or tickling a sibling of the opposite sex can become both sexually stimulating and distressing. These new reactions that come with physical maturation may be so upsetting that the adolescent feels forced to transfer the relationships that cause these feelings to "safer" people outside of the family.

The same is true for angry feelings. For example, it is one thing for a little boy to feel rage at his mother when his eyes are at the level of her kneecaps. However, it is another situation when the angry adolescent realizes that he is taller and bigger than his mother and that he could really hurt her.

The distress and loss of confidence caused by these physical and emotional changes encourage the early adolescent to become more dependent on home and parents. But the same newly discovered emotional feelings and physical reactions make it more difficult to explore and work out relationships and problems with parents and siblings. Thus, there is conflict—within the adolescent and eventually within the family. The adolescent pushes to become more dependent and childlike while at the same time, he or she pulls to become more independent and adultlike.

Initially, the early adolescent may attempt to cope with all this by using fantasy, choosing to relate to people who are unavailable and therefore safe. For example, boys and girls have "mad crushes" on movie stars, rock musicians, and sports heroes. The probability of a rock music star suddenly knocking on the door of an adolescent girl and asking her for a date is remote enough to allow her to safely fantasize a relationship with him. Gradually, however, the young adolescent will begin to explore relationships with real, potentially available people. At first, these interactions are likely to occur within groups, then within smaller groups, and finally with individual people. Very early dating is usually narcissistically motivated; the adolescent wants to date someone who makes him or her *look* good—the cheerleader, the football hero, someone whom everyone thinks is desirable. Often a boy behaves toward his date much as he would toward a boy friend, clowning around, showing off, or hitting. Later on, both adolescent girls and boys will date someone who makes them *feel* good. Looks are still important, but less important than personality.

## Issues of Psychological Changes

The psychological phases each adolescent goes through as he moves toward adulthood can be seen as occurring in three stages:

> Independence
> Identity
> Intimacy

### Independence

The first task of adolescence is to move from being a dependent person to being an independent person. The initial struggle often revolves around the concepts of sex roles and identification. The old techniques that the child used to master separation at age two may turn up again.

Negativism reappears—"No, I can do it myself," "Don't tell me how long my hair can be," "Don't tell me how short my skirt can be." This negativism is a renewed attempt to tell first you and then the world that this growing person has a mind of his or her own. And again, it becomes an active verbal way of expressing anger. An adolescent seizes almost any opportunity to exploit an issue that shows that he or she has a mind separate from his or her parents. Parents and adolescents may argue about the choice of friends and peer groups, school plans and courses, points of philosophy, religion, and etiquette. Clothing, hair styles, and jewelry have always been favorite issues with which to prove one's independence. The casual or unisex theme of today resembles the "cause" of every other generation—the flappers, the zoot-suiters, the rockers, the hippies, and so on. Remember how you showed your parents that you had a mind of your own? Each generation recalls how they used clothes, hairstyles, and other external badges (for example, earrings for boys; multiple earrings for girls; piercings on different parts of the body), the more shocking the better, to show their parents that they had minds of their own.

All the old struggles over expressing love and anger reappear as new issues. For example: What do you have to do to be loved? to keep love? to show love? What do you do with angry feelings? All of these questions have to be worked through with family and friends. In the process, the adolescent begins to develop more consistent concepts of relationships and styles of expressing feelings. Thus, the adult personality is beginning to form and emerge.

In the process of gaining independence, the adolescent often feels a need to reject the parents' values and to reformulate his or her own value system. Unless this happens, the adolescent's parents remain with him or her forever in the form of the conscience programmed in during childhood. A teenager may need to rework these previously accepted values to fit with the values he or she wishes to adopt for today and tomorrow. The adolescent will probably reject his or her former values at first, pointing out contradictions in the parents' values. He or she may feel that "no one over thirty can be trusted." The adolescent may challenge his or her parents for giving conflicting messages (for example, "What do you mean, all people are created equal—you get mad at me if I date someone who's Jewish [or Protestant, Catholic, Black, White, Hispanic, Asian]"; "Why should I be honest—you cheat on your income tax"; "Why shouldn't I drink [or smoke]—you do").

This interim vacuum, when old values are rejected and new ones have not been established, can be upsetting. Some adolescents temporarily seek a preset "package" of values such as Boy or Girl Scouts with specific oaths and laws. For others, their peer group provides this interim system. Closed cliques (the "in" groups) often set rules about all kinds of behavior—how to dress, whom to talk to, who is "in," and who is "out."

Slowly, the adolescent begins to blend many different values from all kinds of sources into his or her own existing values. By young adulthood, a new conscience, or superego, is established. The compatibility and flexibility of this new superego strengthens one's ability to handle and express feelings and emotions in relationships. All through life one's superego will have to be able to change and grow in order to accommodate new life situations.

As the adolescent begins to feel independent of his or her family, and as the family supports and encourages this emerging maturity, the question of the three- to six-year-old is heard once again—"Who am I?" The answer, of course, can no longer be "just like Mommy [or Daddy]."

### Identity

The second developmental task of adolescence, establishing one's *identity*, begins at this point. Becoming a "chip off the old block" isn't enough and can be too restrictive. Unlike the child, the older adolescent will select characteristics from many people—religious leaders, teachers, neighbors, relatives, parents, friends, maybe even famous people—blending certain of their features with her or his own to become a unique new person. This new person, or identity, is not one's final self, but it forms the basis of what one will become. One's identity must be reworked throughout life as roles change. One must adjust to becoming a graduate, a spouse, a worker, a parent, a grandparent, or a retiree.

Each generation and each culture exerts different social and cultural pressures on human beings. The child growing up in the Victorian era heard very different messages from the outside world than one growing up in the "wild" decade of the post-World War I twenties did. The adolescent growing up in the post-Vietnam War world of the eighties and nineties experienced different social and cultural standards than her or his parents did. So, too, adolescents of today struggle with different issues of relationships, careers, and futures than did the adolescents even twenty years ago. Let me note again that it is crucial for parents to understand and accept that their adolescent lives in a different world than they did as adolescents and that their child's adulthood will be different from their own.

The total developmental process that begins at birth culminates in an identity for each person. If your child masters all of these tasks, he or she will have a successful, functional identity with healthy and positive feelings about himself or herself. If any tasks are not successfully mastered, this identity can be restrictive or dysfunctional.

### Intimacy

The adolescent has one remaining task to master. Until this time, relationships have been primarily based on a child-adult model. Now the adolescent or young adult has to learn to relate successfully to other people, and eventually to one other person, as an equal, on a one-to-one basis. This kind of relationship is often referred to as *intimacy*. This task starts in late adolescence, but it is not complete until young adulthood.

When people relate in a dependent-independent mode, they need and depend on significant and more powerful people, like parents. When you are young, you may very well feel as if you and your parents are one. This is intimacy, but not a workable kind of intimacy in an adult world. In an adult intimate relationship, in the independent-independent mode, each person depends on the other. However, even though each loves, leans on, and needs the other for his or her emotional well-being, neither loses his or her boundaries. At all times, each can still function well independently. This is a goal that most of us work on all of our lives and few of us achieve with total success. But because it represents the best that human beings can make of their adult relationships, it makes a fitting close for the discussion of normal development from childhood to adulthood.

# 9

## The Secondary Emotional and Social Problems of Children with Attention Deficit Hyperactivity Disorder

The key to understanding the emotional and social problems of children and adolescents with ADHD is to see the behaviors as messages. It is often the task of parents to figure out what these messages mean. Sometimes the help of a mental health professional is essential. If the child shows emotional problems such as sadness, anxiety, or fears, our task is to find out what these emotions mean and why they exist. If he or she is aggressive with siblings and peers or into power struggles and defiant, again, our task is to find out what these behaviors mean and why they exist.

Being hyperactive, inattentive, distractible, and/or impulsive can make a student less available for learning or for playing successfully with others. These behaviors do not automatically result in emotional or behavioral problems. They are caused by the frustrations and failures these children and adolescents experience. It is constantly getting feedback that they are unmotivated or bad, getting into trouble and not knowing what they did wrong that may lead to difficulties. Thus, it is the secondary consequences of ADHD that lead to the emotional and behavioral problems in most children and adolescents.

All too often, it is these emotional and behavioral problems that result in the individual being referred to and evaluated by a mental health professional. It is critical that this professional clarify if the emotional and/or behavioral problems are causing the hyperactivity, inattention/distractibility, and/or impulsivity or vice versa. As we have discussed, children or adolescents who are anxious or depressed can look as if they have ADHD. Individuals who act out—getting into trouble in school, at home, and with peers—may appear as if they have ADHD.

This chapter is about these secondary emotional, behavioral, and social problems of children and adolescents who have ADHD. It is about difficulties that are the result of ADHD. It is not about emotional and behavioral problems that might look like ADHD.

When I prepared the first edition of this book, I used the case example of Bobby to illustrate these secondary problems. Since then, I have seen far too many Bobbys. But his story remains representative.

Bobby's parents came to see me because he had just been suspended from the fourth grade because of fighting. He was ten years old. On the phone, his mother commented that he had been a problem all of his life.

I met with Bobby's parents first. They reported no problems during pregnancy or delivery. The first three months of life were described as impossible. Bobby had colic. He did not sleep well and would wake up crying about every three hours. After several changes in formula, he improved. By about three months he was eating better and crying less. Sleeping at night was still a problem.

His motor and speech development were normal. He began to walk at ten months and "at ten months and one minute he took off." He ran about the house and ran away from his parents when outside. Toilet training was started at age two. He remains a bed wetter at night.

At age three Bobby entered a part-time nursery school. He ran around the room and refused to sit during story time or rest period. Parents were told that he was not ready for nursery school. They were not surprised since they experienced the same behaviors at home. They described him as very active, unable to listen to stories or entertain himself, and having a "short fuse" with his sister.

When Bobby was four they entered him into another nursery school. Throughout this year his teachers complained that he would not sit still during circle time or pay attention to the group activities. Often, he would get up and wander about the room. If another child didn't do what he wanted, he would hit the child.

Although kindergarten was no better, his parents felt there was some improvement. He went to first grade where he had a firm but caring teacher who "stayed on top of him." She allowed him to walk around if he wanted. The next year was not a good one. He was in second grade, and his teacher complained that he would not stay on task or complete his work. He got into trouble with the other children, especially during unstructured and less supervised times. His third grade behavior was the same. He "distracted" the class by the noises he made or the tapping with his pencil. He called out in class and forgot to raise his hand. He often got up to "do something."

Bobby started fourth grade promising his parents that he would be a good boy this year. By the end of October, his parents were called to school for a conference. Bobby's teacher told them he was moving about the room and bothering the other children. His calling out or interrupting her disrupted the other children who were trying to work. He did not complete his class work and appeared to be daydreaming. His parents were told that Bobby was immature and required constant attention. The other children did not like Bobby and avoided him during lunch and recess. The parents were told to talk to Bobby about the need to "grow up" now that he was in the fourth grade. His parents knew what the teacher was describing because he was the same way at home. They had tried everything they knew without success. They wondered what they were supposed to do now.

In late December Bobby hit a boy who was teasing him. This boy's mother called the principal to complain, and Bobby was suspended from school for three days. His parents were told to get help "before he grew up to be a delinquent."

Bobby's parents reported that he had been active and fidgety all of his life. They commented that he had difficulty paying attention. It was necessary to bring him back to task constantly when he did his homework. He always interrupted them when they were talking or on the phone. He hit his sister, grabbed toys, screamed, and threw tantrums whenever he didn't get his way. They were clearly frustrated and overwhelmed with his behaviors. On specific questioning I learned that over the past year he had begun to steal money from them. On a few occasions they found him with matches, lighting paper in his room.

I met Bobby. He was a delightful, pleasant boy. During the ses-

sion, he sat quietly. He did show a short attention span when moving from one play activity or game to another. I did not observe the
Bobby described by his parents or teachers. (It is not unusual to see
no hyperactivity or distractibility during a quiet, one-to-one session.)

Yet it was clear that Bobby was not functioning in school. He
had poor peer relationships, and his behavior at home resulted in
constant yelling, fighting, and punishment. Both his teacher and his
parents were overwhelmed and felt helpless.

Bobby's problems are not unique. The common theme is a
chronic and pervasive history of hyperactivity, distractibility, and
impulsivity. An early history of difficulty with eating, sleeping,
and irritability is not uncommon among children with ADHD.
Year after year, the teachers correctly identified the behaviors,
but no one recognized the probable cause. Each projected his or
her frustration and anger onto the child and the parents. By the
time Bobby came to see me, there were emotional, social, and
family problems. However, these problems were secondary to the
unrecognized and untreated ADHD. If individual and family psychological interventions were started, Bobby might have improved for a short period of time. However, his hyperactivity,
distractibility, and impulsivity would have persisted. By treating
the ADHD in addition to providing the needed individual and
family help, the total clinical picture could be improved.

Recently, I evaluated an eleven-year-old boy very similar to
Bobby. He experienced years of behavioral problems in school
and with the children in the neighborhood. At home he was negative and everything was a power struggle. His chronic and pervasive history of hyperactivity, distractibility, and impulsivity
were described year after year. When I explained to the parents
why I thought their son had ADHD, they expressed surprise that
their pediatrician or the school professionals had not thought of
this possibility. Then, the father began to share that he thought
he had the same problem He described being a major behavioral
problem throughout school. He barely finished high school and
did not go on. His wife added that her husband was impulsive
and explosive at home. The father asked to see me on his own.
During our meeting alone, the father described being dis-

tractible and impulsive at work, at home with the family, and with friends. To establish if these behaviors had been present throughout his life, I asked him to contact his mother for her recollections or school reports. Two weeks later, he came in with every report card from kindergarten through twelfth grade. The teacher comments were consistent. He was described each year as inattentive, calling out in class, and a troublemaker. His second grade teacher called him immature. His third grade teacher referred to him as unmotivated to learn. His fifth grade teachers described him as a trouble maker who disrupted the class. During middle school and high school, he was constantly in trouble and frequently in detention. As he read these comments with me, he became sad. The pain of his past was still there. Finally, he added that he wanted his son to get help now so the boy wouldn't have to repeat the life he had led.

Each time I feel we are making progress in educating teachers to recognize ADHD and to recommend that a student be evaluated, I meet another child like the two described above. We are making progress, but not fast enough with enough teachers.

## Secondary Emotional and Behavioral Problems

When children experience stress, they usually react with anxiety and/or depression. This stress might reflect a normal development. For example, when a two-year-old begins to master separation and moves out into "the world," he or she naturally feels anxiety about this unknown experience. There is also sadness about leaving the comfort of a closer, more consistent attachment to mother or father. So, too, with the kindergartner starting school, who feels the excitement and anxiety about this new adventure and sadness at not being home or in a known and comfortable preschool program.

The child with ADHD and possible learning disabilities begins to feel the stress of school with academic struggles and inappropriate behaviors. This child might react with anxiety that he or she cannot perform as expected, or with depression, the sadness of not being able to please the teacher and parents by doing what is expected.

When the stress a child experiences becomes too great, he or she must do something to cope. In general, we see children taking one of four possible approaches to coping:

> Internalizing the stress
> Externalizing the stress
> Somatizing the stress
> Using other approaches to cope with stress

## Internalizing the Stress

Some children become very aware of their problems and feel anxiety or depression or both. They have these feelings at school and at home. The feelings often lift and lessen or disappear during the summer and on school vacations.

### Anxiety

Such children might focus their anxiety on school, showing a fear of going to school (school avoidance) or a fear of doing schoolwork. This anxiety might expand into a generalized anxiety disorder. They might become afraid of sleeping alone or of being in a part of the house alone. They might be afraid to ride on the school bus. Some might become so upset when doing homework that they will not start, or they become upset as soon as they have any difficulty doing the work. Others might become fearful in the classroom and appear to withdraw from any potentially frustrating or uncertain situations by getting upset, resisting the work, or pulling back and becoming passive. They become unavailable for learning.

Eight-year-old Mary had these problems. She was described at home and with her friends as being a "lovely child." Yet at school she constantly got into difficulty. She called out answers before being called. She spoke to her friends while the teacher was talking. She often did not finish her class work because she was "daydreaming." Everyone described her problems, but no one tried to figure out why there was such a contrast between her behavior in school and out of school. She did poorly academically and was currently starting second grade for the second time. When I asked her what she did in school when the teacher became angry with her or she did not finish her work, she replied, "I don't mean to be bad. I try to be good and to do my work." She often was afraid to go into her classroom and described being nervous all day that she might "get into trouble." She did not know why she called out or seemed not to pay attention.

### Depression

Some children with ADHD do not develop the ability to cope with the pain of frustration and failure experienced at school and experience a true sense of depression. Failures, inadequacies, and poor interactions with peers and significant adults leave the child feeling angry and devalued. Younger children who are often unable to experience the depression internally may express their feelings by being irritable and aggressive toward everyone. Older children may exhibit classic symptoms of depression. They appear to be sad, cry easily, and may have trouble sleeping and eating. Sometimes they turn so much anger inward that they become self-destructive or speak of "life not being worth living" or have thoughts of killing themselves.

Some depressed children feel so bad about themselves that they cannot accept praise. They feel that they are too bad to deserve such praise. If a teacher compliments a piece of work, the child may feel compelled to destroy it. If a parent compliments the child, he or she might act terrible until the parent yells or enacts a punishment.

After repeated lack of success in school, some children develop a feeling of worthlessness, resulting in a poor self-image and low self-esteem. These children see themselves as inadequate, bad, worthless people who can't do anything right. Feedback from the outside world often encourages this self-image and, at the very least, does nothing to help correct it. Ronnie, a markedly depressed ten-year-old boy with such feelings had been hyperactive since birth. Ronnie was always all over the place. His mother reported, "All he ever heard from me was 'no' or 'don't' or 'bad boy.' " Ronnie was kicked out of nursery school for being a "monster." He grew even wilder in kindergarten and was no better in first and second grade. Still undiagnosed, he repeated second grade, started third, and was then suspended from school. He had never known himself to be anything but bad, unlikable, inadequate, and stupid. The fact that he was finally found to be very bright and to have ADHD didn't change his self-image.

No one can talk these children out of their self-assessments because their self-image results from a collection of real experiences. They can improve, however, when they begin to see the changes that come with appropriate help and when they begin to master learning and behavioral tasks.

Depression with the resulting poor self-image or low self-esteem might be apparent in the child's comments. This child says that he or she is "bad," "stupid," or "dumb" or "not as smart as the other kids." Classwork and homework challenges are met with "I can't do that. It is too hard." There is a sense of sadness about this child. Not infrequently, the child will say that he or she feels sad and unhappy.

This depression might lead to regression. The child retreats to an earlier stage of psychological or social development. Earlier behaviors or immature, infantile interactions, things you think the child has completely outgrown, recur. For example, the parents of seven-and-a-half-year-old Debbie complained that their daughter had been happy and "normal" until she entered kindergarten. As her mother explained it, at this point "she had a change of personality." "She had trouble keeping up with the other children," the mother said, "In first grade she just didn't learn much so now she's repeating first." The father added, "Home life is terrible. We yell at her all of the time. Since school began this year, she's gone backwards, acting like a baby and talking like a baby. She's impossible. She won't listen and tunes me out. She's begun to wet her bed for the first time since she was three. She even eats with her fingers." At a therapy session, Debbie talked about school. "I have trouble because I can't pay attention and I don't understand the work. The teacher talks, and I am listening to the kids in the next classroom. The teacher gets mad at me, and I start to hate myself."

## Externalizing the Stress

Some children find the discomfort and pain of stress with the resulting anxiety and depression too much to cope with. They decide not to cope with the stress by "getting rid of it." They externalize the anxiety and depression. To do this, they project all of their problems onto others, accepting no responsibility for the problems. Suddenly, the behavioral or academic problems are because this kid did this and that kid did that. They get into three fights at school in one week and insist that each was the result of someone else's behavior. "Billy started the fight . . . don't blame me. I didn't do it." "Mary made a face at me and got me mad." So, too, it becomes the teacher's fault or a parent's fault.

By projecting all of the blame onto others, this child does not have to accept responsibility for any problems. The child is in the principal's office because of getting into trouble twice in the same day. He or she is sitting back, not upset. "I didn't cause the problems. The first time my teacher didn't listen to me and then got angry. It was her fault." The other time "the teacher did not see that John kicked me under the table. I just told him to stop and the teacher accused me of talking. John should be in here, not me."

The characteristic of children who externalize their stress, then, is that they accept no responsibility and appear not to be anxious or depressed. All of the meaningful adults in this child's life—parents, teachers—feel anxious and depressed about the child. This is a difficult child to help. Since he or she accepts no responsibility for poor behavior, the child doesn't see a need to be in therapy or insists that there is nothing to talk about.

Under the current mental health guidelines (listed in the *Diagnostic and Statistical Manual for Mental Disorders, Fourth Edition,* or DSM-IV), there are two diagnostic labels for children who externalize their problems. If they externalize primarily within the family—challenging rules, getting into difficulty and then blaming others, being oppositional and defiant—we label the child as having *oppositional defiant disorder* (see Chart 1). If the behaviors expand beyond the family, leading to challenging school and society rules—fighting, stealing, breaking rules—we label the child as having a *conduct disorder* (see Chart 2). In reality, these two diagnostic groups are only ways of describing the areas in which the child externalizes stress. Neither diagnostic label explains the cause of the stress.

It is not uncommon for a child who is initially described as being anxious or depressed to be seen later as having an oppositional defiant disorder, and still later to begin showing types of problems that lead to being seen as having a conduct disorder. It is important to understand that these diagnostic categories for externalizing behaviors do not explain the cause for the behaviors, only the style the child uses to cope. For the children we are discussing, the most frequent problem is that the frustrations and failures experienced in school, the family, and with peers lead to significant stress. It is this stress that might be externalized as an oppositional defiant disorder or a conduct disorder. Children with behavioral problems at school along with school failing experiences often develop one of these disorders. It is critical to understand the probable causative impact of ADHD.

## CHART 1
### DIAGNOSTIC CRITERIA: OPPOSITIONAL DEFIANT DISORDER

1. A pattern of negativistic, hostile, and defiant behavior lasting at least six months, during which four (or more) of the following are present:

    Often loses temper.
    Often argues with adults.
    Often actively defies or refuses to comply with adults' requests or rules.
    Often deliberately annoys people.
    Often blames others for his or her mistakes or misbehaviors.
    Is often touchy or easily annoyed by others.
    Is often angry and resentful.
    Is often spiteful or vindictive.

2. The disturbance in behavior causes clinically significant impairment in social, academic, or occupational functioning.

## CHART 2
### DIAGNOSTIC CRITERIA: CONDUCT DISORDER

1. A repetitive and persistent pattern of behavior in which the basic rights of others or major age-appropriate societal norms or rules are violated, as manifested by the presence of three (or more) of the following criteria in the past twelve months, with at least one criterion present in the past six months:

a. *Aggression to people and animals*
Often bullies, threatens, or intimidates others.
Often initiates physical fights.
Has used a weapon that can cause serious physical harm to others (e.g., a bat, brick, broken bottle, knife, gun).
Has been physically cruel to people.
Has been physically cruel to animals.
Has stolen while confronting a victim (e.g. mugging, purse snatching, extortion, armed robbery).
Has forced someone into sexual activity.

b. *Destruction of property*
Has deliberately engaged in fire setting with the intent of causing serious damage.
Has deliberately destroyed others' property (other than fire setting).

c. *Deceitfulness or theft*
Has broken into someone else's house, building, or car.
Often lies to obtain goods or favors or to avoid obligations (i.e., "cons" others).
Has stolen items of nontrivial value without confronting a victim (e.g., shoplifting, but without breaking and entering; forgery).

d. *Serious violations of rules*
Often stays out at night despite parental prohibitions, beginning before age thirteen years.

Has run away from home overnight at least twice while living in parental or parental surrogate home (or once without returning for a lengthy period).
Often truant from school (beginning before age thirteen years).

2. The disturbance in behavior causes clinically significant impairment in social, academic, or occupational functioning.

## Somatizing the Stress

Some children focus their anxiety on bodily functions. A child may develop stomachaches, lower abdominal cramps, headaches, diarrhea, or frequency of urination or bowel movements. These complaints often occur only in the morning of a school day and rarely on weekends, holidays, or during the summer. These children have to leave class to go to the school nurse or to go home. As with any physical symptoms, the discomfort is real. The pain goes away when the child is allowed to stay home, not because she or he was faking, but because the stress of going to school is reduced when the child is able to stay home.

Katie, who was about seven at the time, once explained, "Sometimes I get into trouble because I forgot to do what the teacher said or I erase too much. . . . The teacher yells at me and I get scared . . . Then my stomach starts to hurt, and I have to go to the nurse." Similarly, Franklin woke up each school day with severe stomach cramps and vomiting. His mother kept him home from school, and the pains usually disappeared by noon. A complete medical workup found Franklin perfectly normal. He must have guessed why he was brought to see me. His first words were "I know my stomach trouble is because I'm afraid of school. Only it really does hurt, no kidding!"

Other children may explain their anxiety by focusing on their increasing awareness that something must be wrong with their bodies. They have heard parents, teachers, and doctors talking about their brain or their "nervous system," and they have been through countless examinations and tests, so they express their worries by being hypochondriacal: "My back hurts," "My head aches," "My knee feels funny." Sometimes this concern with their body extends into a general concern with body image or body damage. At times these complaints become a complete rationalization for failure. "I can't help it if I made a mistake. My arm hurts today."

## Using Other Approaches to Cope with Stress

Some children cope with the stresses of school by being the class clown or by using other methods to handle anger.

### The Class Clown

Clowning can be very successful. The child learns what to do to the wrong person at the wrong time to disrupt the lesson plan or to be kicked out of class. Clowning serves several functions. It can be a way of controlling feelings of inadequacy—the child clowns around to cover up feelings of worthlessness and depression. By playing the clown or freak, the child seems to be saying "They call me a clown, but that's only because I choose to be one. I really can turn it off if I want to, but it's too much fun this way." If the child succeeds in this behavior, he or she disrupts the lesson plan or is told to leave the group, thus avoiding the academic work, and therefore the potential failure. Clowning behavior may win a certain measure of peer acceptance. Suddenly, the child everyone teases becomes the class hero because of what he or she did. The clowning behaviors are reinforced.

In some schools, the "punishment" of being sent to the principal's office is well worth the effort—doing no schoolwork, talking to the secretary, delivering messages, or playing with the computer. After four years of special education and psychotherapy, Jack returned to regular classes and was doing well. He saw me, and I asked him to describe what he remembered about his previous experiences in regular classes. "Boy, were those teachers stupid. Anytime it was my turn to read or to do anything I had trouble with, I would tease another boy or joke around. It worked great. I got sent out of the room." Then he added, "Only you got me to see that I was the stupid one . . . You can't get help if you're not in class, and I sure didn't want to spend the rest of my life in a special class."

### Handling Anger

When some children have difficulty dealing with anger, they may choose an indirect way of showing it. One such style is called *passive-aggressive*. The child's behavior is not actively aggressive in and of itself, yet the child seems to make everybody angry with him or her much of the time. While supposedly getting dressed, for instance, the child may play with his or her clothes or with toys until the parent becomes furious. The child then looks up in bewilderment and says, "Why are you so mad at me? I didn't do anything." A special education teacher once said to me of such a child, "He was so cooperative and helpful and sweet that I felt like hitting him."

Other children become *passive-dependent*. Initially, the child avoids failure and unpleasant feelings by staying out of the situations that could result in failure. But this passivity can expand into a veritable lifestyle. He or she avoids taking any initiative in anything and minimizes getting involved in everything. A truly helpless child arouses sympathy in adults. The passive-dependent child's behavior often makes people angry because the helplessness appears to be deliberate and contrived.

Occasionally, children appear to act in an *overly mature* way. Faced with feelings of being different and inadequate, and fearful that no one will like them or take care of them, these children decide to grow up quickly. They also sense that they are not making it as a child with other children and guess that it would be safer to be an adult. Often they have a compelling need to be in control and become upset if they cannot control every situation. This controlling behavior might be their way of coping with a world that they experience as out of control. It might be a way of becoming an adultlike person and taking control of the world. They look, act, and relate to others like serious adults. This behavior may pay off. Adults compliment them and spend more time with them. Chuck is an example of overmaturity. His parents described this seven-year-old boy as not needing anyone to take care of him. Chuck was totally independent; in fact, he took care of everyone else in the family and in his school class. He enjoyed most having discussions with the teacher. He had no sense of humor and was described as a "perfect little man," completely self-sufficient. In a psychiatric diagnostic session, Chuck's fantasy and play reflected great concern about dependency needs and a fear that no one would meet them. So he had to take care of himself. Chuck denied his anger and his wish to be taken care of. He used all of his emotional energies to maintain his protective facade.

## Emotional and Behavioral Problems of the Adolescent

How well your adolescent deals with the special demands of being a teenager is based in part on how well he or she succeeded in handling the developmental stages of childhood and in part on how much the behaviors of ADHD interfere with the successful mastery of each phase of adolescence. Another critical factor relates to when the ADHD was recognized and treated. Adolescents whose problems were not recognized until high school have a double problem; they must deal with their existing problems while trying to handle the many problems experienced in childhood before diagnosis and treatment.

Adolescence is a time when being different from peers is painful and peer acceptance is essential. Being a successful adolescent is particularly difficult when the individual with ADHD has poor social skills, difficulty acting like a teenager, or doesn't fit in. Adolescence is also the period when rebelling against authority and rules and trying to "have a mind of one's own" is normal. For some adolescents with ADHD, struggles with separation and becoming independent create an even greater need to challenge authority and rules.

Recall from Chapter 8, on normal development, that the first task of adolescence is to move from being dependent to being independent. The second task is to begin to figure out who one is, forming one's identity. The final task is to learn to relate to adults as an adult, intimacy. Let me review each of these tasks and how having ADHD might add to the difficulty of succeeding.

## Independence

Becoming independent, or moving from being a child toward becoming an adult, means going out from the family and realizing successes and positive experiences on one's own. If the adolescent is insecure, has a poor self-image, and relates poorly to his or her peers, he or she will have difficulty moving away from family and being more independent. Some may cling to their dependency, turning away from outside companions, putting on the appearance that they would prefer to stay home and watch television. Others might find their feelings of dependency unacceptable and fight to deny them or to cover them up. Negativism, power struggles with adults, and unacceptable clothing, hairstyles, and choice of friends are often ways of expressing one's fear of and discomfort with dependency. It is important as parents to be understanding and to maintain communication and availability during these periods.

You might try to help your adolescent gain confidence in the areas where he or she feels most insecure. If relating to peers is difficult, find an acceptable activity for your child to participate in and to practice social skills. Initially, try to find a structured, adult-supervised program with a focus. This activity might be a community service project, a youth club, or another type of club. The focus is on the task rather than on social interactions. Once the adolescent gains confidence, he or she might be willing to try a less-structured activity. If the social problems are too great, consider a social skills group. Whether the task is using public transportation, learning to shop, cooking, handling money or a checkbook, driving a car, or interacting with friends in everyday activities, work with your adolescent to develop strategies for coping and succeeding.

## Identity

Establishing a positive concept of self is difficult at best in our world where value systems change, career opportunities vary, and options for the future are not always secure. The world that today's adolescents face is different from that which you may have encountered. Sexual values and the importance of relationships have changed. College no longer "guarantees" the opportunity for social and economic advancement. Family life has become and will continue to become more mobile. About 50 percent of adolescents today live in single-parent or remarriage families.

As the child moves into adolescence, it is important that he or she has a positive self-image and good self-esteem. It is from this base of feelings that the emerging identity of the adolescent must develop. We know that self-esteem in childhood is based on two major factors—success in school and peer acceptance. Many children with ADHD and possible learning disabilities have been unsuccessful in both areas. Thus, they move into adolescence with a poor self-image and a low level of self-esteem. They need to experience success if they are to rework these views of themselves and develop a positive concept of their identity.

It is important for parents to learn how to advocate for necessary services for helping gain maximum control over the ADHD. It is equally important to find places and opportunities to build successful social interactions.

## Intimacy

As discussed in Chapter 8, this task starts in late adolescence and continues into early adulthood. The high school senior may begin to experience "being in love" with someone who makes him or her feel good and may begin to experiment with interactions in a shared relationship.

If your son or daughter has a poor self-image, low self-esteem, a limited positive sense of identity, or poor social skills, dating and close relationships may not be possible. The longer the limited successes or isolation exists, the greater the problems become. Even if the adolescent is now able to change, his or her past reputation among peers minimizes his chances for being accepted.

There are no simple answers. Sometimes psychological help is needed. You might seek opportunities for social contact that have a potential of being successful. Try finding activities that are centered around a topic or task rather than on social interactions, maybe a computer club, nature club, a volunteer work group sponsored by the school or your religious organization, or working for a political campaign. The focus will be on what is learned or done rather than on talking or interacting. Ideally, this activity is adult-supervised rather than peer-supervised. Your son or daughter will begin to be part of a group activity without having to be accepted or successful with group interactions. By using the adult leader for guidance and his or her own problem-solving abilities, he or she might begin to feel more comfortable and successful around peers. Encourage your child to practice relating to the others in the group. At a minimum, he or she will have something to do and a positive group experience. All the better if he or she gains some confidence and social abilities. At the best, a friendship might be started with someone who isn't from the school where your child's role and reputation are known, or with a schoolmate who is able to revise his or her opinion once he or she gets to know your child.

## Specific Areas of Difficulty

### Resistance to School and Learning

If ADHD and possible learning disabilities have gone unrecognized and untreated or if they were addressed in grade school but not in middle or high school, the adolescent is likely to develop psychological difficulties. Some adolescents begin to resist their education and "fight" being in school and doing classwork or homework. They lie about and avoid homework. Some will try to convince you (and themselves) that they could be successful but that they just don't care about school. You hear that "school is stupid" or "who needs to learn that subject" or "the teacher is terrible." Some will act out in school, cutting classes, or getting into trouble with school rules. Some of these young people who need special help, sadly, resist getting the help or going to the tutor or special education room.

Some get the message that the school doesn't really want them and drop out of school. I call this "school pushout" rather than school dropout. Current statistics show that 50 percent of students identified by the school as having a learning disability quit high school. There are no similar statistics for high school students who have ADHD. I suspect the figure to be at least as high. How could this happen? How was the ADHD or LD missed? Once out from under the pressures of school, the dropouts may settle down, get a job, work toward a high school equivalency, and move on with life. For many, though, without professional help, they will carry their problems and difficulties into adulthood.

## Alcohol and Drug Use

The relationship between substance use and abuse and ADHD is complex. A summary of the many studies done suggests that if the child with ADHD is recognized early and receives all appropriate help, the likelihood of alcohol or drug problems in adolescence is no greater than would be found in the population he or she is growing up with. However, if the child's ADHD was not diagnosed early or not diagnosed at all and if he or she received minimal or no treatments, the likelihood of alcohol or drug problems in adolescence is greater than would be found in the population he or she is growing up with. These findings suggest that having ADHD is not the risk factor. Having unrecognized or untreated ADHD is the risk factor.

I've heard reports of adolescents with ADHD "self-medicating" with drugs. There may be some truth here. Adolescents with ADHD, especially those with hyperactivity and/or impulsivity, might find alcohol or marijuana relaxing and quieting. They report that they like these drugs and often do not like the others because they make them anxious. There are clinical examples of adolescents and adults with ADHD who have been alcohol- or drug-dependent and who are now not drinking or using, reporting that Ritalin or Dexedrine calms them down and helps. They report that it's easier not to return to alcohol or drugs because they "don't need them." The final answer on self-medication is not yet in. However, this possibility must be considered with adolescents who have ADHD.

## Acting Out Behaviors

If an adolescent is insecure with limited academic and peer successes, he or she may have to struggle with becoming independent more than the average adolescent. As this teen struggles with his or her difficulties in being independent, all of the normal adolescent rebellious behaviors may become worse. More negativism and power struggles will arise in an effort to deny dependency needs. Conflicts around clothing, hairstyle, jewelry, or peer groups may be significant.

What happens if even these efforts fail to help the struggling adolescent survive and cope? Some may need to move to a greater level of acting out. The goal here appears to be to numb or deny the feelings of anxiety and depression they are struggling to avoid. These behaviors can be serious, destructive, and possibly life-threatening. Sadly, some of the more common of these extreme efforts to deny or numb the pain are:

1. Alcohol use, misuse, or abuse.
2. Drug use, misuse, or abuse.
3. Running away from home.
4. Cutting classes or skipping school.
5. Delinquent behaviors.
6. Apathy—a state of being where the only motivation is to not "feel" any emotional pain for the next hour or so. The teen is self-destructive but unable to see that what she or he is doing needs to stop.
7. Suicide gestures or attempts, or successful suicide.
8. Increased sexual behavior—for boys as a means of control and power, for girls as a means of gaining attention and acceptance.

If your adolescent is moving into these more destructive levels of defending against pain or is already there, you must seek professional help immediately.

## Social Problems

Children and adolescents with ADHD often do not relate well to peers and may not be accepted by them. They may have problems with classmates and with neighbors. Difficulties can be found in out-of-school activities such as Scouts, organized sports, and religious education. This peer rejection can be devastating and can lead to feelings of loneliness, poor self-image, and low self-esteem. For adolescents, such problems and feelings can also lead to poor school performance, juvenile delinquency, and dropping out of school. Research has shown that the longer-term outcome for children without positive peer relationships can include occupational difficulties, alcoholism, and other emotional problems.

In addition, some children and adolescents feel so out of control that they will try to dominate their environment. When among their peers, they need to control what is done and how it is done. They can be bossy and demanding. For others, their frustration may result in anger. In impulsive children, this anger can result in aggressive behaviors. Adolescents may annoy their friends with their constant activity or with their inability to pay attention.

Many adolescents with ADHD have difficulty with social skills and in correctly reading social cues. They don't recognize the tone of voice or the body language that suggests their behaviors are annoying someone. They may have limited age-appropriate social skills needed to interact in a positive way with peers. If they are impulsive, each of these problems is made worse. They not only do not read the social situation well, they often act or speak before they think, resulting in behaviors that annoy or anger peers and result in peer rejection.

All of these problems are seen in school—in the classroom, in the halls, and on the playground. Each of the ADHD behaviors causes difficulty. These students can be disruptive in the classroom. They may be inattentive and require frequent comments from the teacher to return to the tasks at hand. They may be verbally intrusive, interrupting the teacher or other students. Their voice may be too loud. They might not be aware of space and get too close to others. Their increased activity level—calling out and making noises, increased contacts with classmates, and frequent fidgety behaviors—have a negative impact on everyone.

Students with ADHD often have academic difficulties. Each of the behaviors associated with this disorder can interfere with their success in school. Work may be incomplete or not finished on time. Impulsivity may cause the student to rush through work or put down his or her first thought instead of a more reasoned response. This lack of reflectivity may result in frequent erasures and errors, careless mistakes, and incorrect work. The overall result may be that the student performs below his or her abilities and may even fail. The combination of annoying behaviors in the classroom, frequent corrections by the teacher, and poor academic performance may lead the other students to view these children or adolescents as dumb, thus contributing to peer rejection.

## In Summary

If a child or adolescent is diagnosed as having ADHD, the secondary emotional and social problems must be recognized and addressed along with the ADHD. Approaches to treatment will be discussed in Part Five.

The critical question for parents and for professionals is whether these emotional and social problems are causing the hyperactivity, distractibility, and/or impulsivity or are a consequence of having ADHD. Each conclusion leads to a very different understanding and treatment plan.

# 10

## The Impact of Attention Deficit Hyperactivity Disorder on the Family

*When one member of a family is hurting, everyone feels the pain.* Everyone reacts to the pain—parents, brothers, sisters, grandparents. Everyone in the family needs to understand the behaviors resulting from ADHD and their reactions to these behaviors.

It is not easy to live with a child or adolescent with ADHD. Their constant activity, noise, or getting up and down during meals is annoying. Their short attention span and difficulty staying on task when reading or doing activities is frustrating. Their interrupting, calling out, and inappropriate or potentially dangerous behavior is upsetting. Homework time is a struggle, if not a battle. You watch your son or daughter playing with others and see how different his or her behavior is compared to the others'. Teachers complain about your child's class behavior or the incompletion of tasks. Neighbors call to tell you what he or she did. Your other children are angry with their sibling and want you to "make him stop" or "tell her to be quiet." And since you don't understand what's going on either, you get frustrated and angry. Worse, you feel helpless, not knowing what to do.

All of these experiences will be made worse if each parent reacts to her or his confusion, frustration, and anger in a different way. One parent tries to be understanding and permissive, and the other insists on firmness and punishment. One parent tries to keep the peace, and the other withdraws, using work or some other excuse not to be home in the evening. When home, this parent often handles his or her helplessness by blaming the other parent for all of the problems. Rather than each parent supporting the other through this family crisis, each begins to clash with the other.

The other children in the family have a rough time too. They react with frustration, anger, and embarrassment when their friends are over and see the ADHD sibling acting out. They feel stressed. And they want their parents to "fix the problem." Soon, the whole family is dysfunctional. No one is happy. No one feels like being understanding and nice to the child or adolescent with ADHD.

Parents' and siblings' ill will become so great that everyone forgets that the child or adolescent with ADHD is hurting too. He or she is the direct recipient of the looks and reactions of disappointment, disapproval, and anger. This child has only had one brain all his or her life and doesn't know that it is different. He or she is confused. Why do I always get into trouble? What is everyone so mad about? I didn't do anything!

Often added to these stresses on each family member is the lack of help from others. Numerous complaints to the family doctor are met with "He'll outgrow it" or "You have just got to relax." Grandparents remind you that if you were more strict and firm, there would be no problems. Teachers make you feel as if your son or daughter is "bad" and that you need to make him or her "better." Those looks from others in the grocery store or shopping mall communicate the same messages—the child is bad and the parent does not know how to parent.

Until the ADHD is diagnosed, nothing seems to help. These stresses may overwhelm a parent, a marriage, or a family. Hopefully, a professional finally recognizes the correct diagnosis. Treatments are started. Shortly after the sigh of relief, the work begins. In this chapter I'll discuss the reactions first of parents and later of siblings to their family member with ADHD. In Chapter 15, I'll discuss family interventions that will be helpful.

## Normal Reactions of Parents

It's normal for a parent to have difficulty fully accepting that a son or daughter is different. The idea that something is wrong with your child's brain and that he or she needs medicine to "be normal" is not easy to believe and to accept about your loved one. Often, you will experience a series of reactions not too different from the reaction of grief that people have when someone dear to them dies, although this grief is of lesser intensity. In reality, this reaction is somewhat valid. You might feel that you have to "give up" a part of your child or at least your ambitions for this child that you fear may never be realized. If you see yourself as I review these normal reactions, do not become distressed. These feelings are to be expected, need to be accepted, and must be understood. Later in this chapter, I will discuss the not-normal reactions of parents. If you recognize any of these more serious reactions, you would do well to consult with your family physician or a mental health professional.

Don't be ashamed to discuss these feelings because they seem selfish or unworthy of you. These problems are real, and your feelings are genuine. You must look at them and deal with them. Keeping a stiff upper lip or denying that they exist only makes things worse for you and for your family.

I once evaluated a ten-year-old boy who was a major behavioral problem in the family, neighborhood, and school. When I met with his parents to review my impressions and to make my recommendations, I started by saying "You know, I hate to say this, but now that I have gotten to know your son, I must tell you that if he were my son, I probably would have killed him by now." His mother began to cry. She was so relieved to hear that someone else could be as angry with this child as she felt.

What do I mean by *normal reactions*? Why do parents experience them? It is no surprise to you to recognize that in addition to being mothers and fathers and parents, you are also human beings. You have your own feelings and thoughts, your own lives and career goals. You have your own dreams and hopes. You probably have a mate with whom you enjoy life, closeness, and an intimate relationship, a relationship that is often hard enough to manage successfully without additional family stresses. Having a child with a disability stirs up feelings, fears, and hopes that most people are unprepared for. These reactions affect you both as an individual and as a part of a couple.

At no point is the stress greater than when the diagnosis is made. There is relief that there is a reason for the problems and that something can be done. However, this is also the moment when parents feel the first rush of anguish, fear, helplessness, anger, guilt, and/or shame, all at once. Until the problems are understood and the treatment interventions result in improvement, there is little relaxation of your concerns. If the professional does not fully explain ADHD and the interventions to be used, you're left more confused. If no one explains how medications work, you may be left wondering if you are "drugging" your child. If the family doctor says, "Try this medicine at different doses and let me know what you learn," your anxiety will go up. You don't know how to be a physician. What are you supposed to do?

Once the diagnosis is made, many parents struggle with feelings that are normal and expected. The first reaction is usually denial. Anger or guilt may follow. Why these feelings? When you experience something that is overwhelming, your mind often protects you by using denial. "It just can't be true." "I can't believe it." Remember visiting an older relative who lost a spouse? She or he might have said, "I know it sounds silly, but I still expect him [her] to walk in and say hello." Denial protects you from the overwhelming initial reactions of loss. Later, many people feel so helpless about what happened to them that they try to find a reason for what happened. It is as if knowing the cause might help prevent something terrible from happening again. Some might try to see someone else as the cause. They experience anger. Others might blame themselves. They experience guilt. Slowly, you work through what has happened and come to peace with the realities of life, going on with life. With the loss of a loved one, this full process might take a year or more. With parents of children with disabilities, the time needed is often much less.

## Denial

Upon learning that a child or adolescent has ADHD, a parent might react with denial. "It can't be true . . . the doctor must be mistaken." What follows might be "She only saw him for an hour. I don't believe it." This parent may doubt the competence of the bearer of such news and want to punish him or her. Frequently, parents seek another opinion. Getting other evaluations can be useful. However, "doctor shopping" for one who will tell you what you want to hear does not do anything productive for your child or adolescent.

Another form of denial is the cover-up reaction. One parent, usually the mother, wants to "protect" the other parent by not sharing the results of the studies or by minimizing the problems. Perhaps this parent feels the other parent would not accept the findings. Some parents successfully hide the facts from the other parent, not revealing that the child is in special programs or receives medication. Sadly, the parent who is uninformed about the child's difficulties may continue to build up unrealistic expectations and may demand a level of functioning from the child that is not possible. The child, seeing through this cover-up, perceives the true reason for it. "They can't accept me as I am. They have to pretend that I am different than I really am." This reaction often makes children angry and/or sad. They have difficulty accepting themselves when they do not feel that their parents can accept them.

### Anger

A period of anger frequently follows the denial phase. Parents may direct this anger inward, against themselves, or may project it outward, blaming the other parent or any other outside source. After learning of the ADHD, it is not unusual to feel anger. "Why me?" How could God do this to me?" How could I have done this to my child?" "How could you have done this to our child?" "We should not have had children."

A pattern of blaming or attributing the fault to someone or something else may start. Finding someone who "was responsible" protects you from feelings of helplessness. A parent may blame the physician. "He didn't get to the hospital fast enough . . . I told him I was in labor." "She told me to wait. Then I had to rush to the hospital and delivered in the car." "If the pediatrician had seen my child rather than prescribing over the phone, the fever would not have gotten that high." Some parents might generalize this reaction to all professionals, who then become incompetents. Other parents might generalize this reaction to the school and school professionals. "It's the school's fault." "She's just a young, inexperienced teacher." "He's just an old and rigid teacher." The doctor, teacher, or whoever is the focus of the anger often never hears these complaints. But the child hears them. He or she might lose faith in and respect for the very people he or she must turn to for help and for hope.

## Guilt

If you turn the anger inward, blaming yourself, you feel guilt. Often, doing this results in feelings of depression. It is a short step from "How could I have caused this?" to "It must be my fault." Parents might berate themselves: "God is punishing me because . . ." or "I didn't follow my doctor's advice and . . ." or "I've been given this extra burden to prove my worthiness." Some may feel guilty for the way they treated their daughter or son before they understood the ADHD.

If the feelings of guilt result in depression, the difficulties may become worse. This parent might become isolated. He or she may withdraw from the child or the other parent at just the time that they or other members of the family need that parent the most.

Some parents attempt to suppress their guilt or their need to place the blame on themselves by overprotecting the child. When a child is hurting, the most human response for any parent is to reach out and try to protect him or her. This is necessary and helpful. But a parent's goal must be to protect the child only where she or he needs protecting and to encourage the child to grow where she or he does not need protecting. A blanket of overprotection covers the child's weaknesses, but it also smothers the child's strengths. Not only does overprotectiveness keep a child immature and delay growth in areas where growth is possible, it also makes the child feel inadequate. When everyone else has a chore to do but he or she does not, when everyone takes turns clearing the table but he or she is excused, it is easy to conclude "See, they agree with me. I can't do anything."

Most parents work through these normal reactions of denial, anger, and guilt. They gradually become strong advocates for their children, mobilizing their energy in constructive ways. Some parents may not work through these normal reactions and move into less healthy reactions.

## Nonproductive Parent Reactions

If the initial feelings of denial, anger, or guilt are not resolved, a parent might move into a chronic state of experiencing these feelings and reactions. Whereas the initial reactions are normal and expected, the persistence of these reactions is not normal and proves to be nonproductive. As you read of these reactions, if you feel that the discussions sound like you, it would be important for you to discuss these concerns with your family physician or a mental health professional.

### Chronic Denial

A parent in chronic denial may continue to "doctor shop" in a constant search for the doctor with the magic answer or magic cure or for someone who will say that nothing is wrong with the child. Such a parent often greets the newest professional with flattery and praise, criticizing the many doctors, educators, and others whose opinions he or she has rejected. Ultimately, this new "hope" is also rejected and then attacked. As the parent's frustration grows, he or she moves from one promised cure to another, often becoming the victim of those who capitalize on people in distress. This hopeless "shopping" deprives the child of time that could be spent in constructive programs and the valuable therapy that is needed.

This chronic denial reaction has other potentially serious consequences. Because each "authority" fails, she or he must be downgraded when the parent moves on to the next. The child may pick up the message not to have faith in anybody in any professional capacity. However, this faith and trust is essential if the child is to have hope. It is equally necessary if the child is to work with this teacher or professional. Another possible consequence is the child's concluding that this parent cannot accept the child as he or she is. This parent always seems to be "looking for someone who will say that I am not the way I am."

## Chronic Anger

If the anger is not resolved, a parent may continue to project it. Nothing can go right. "After all the time and money . . . my child is no better." "After all I do for you, why are you not doing better?" Such a parent feels miserable about his or her circumstances. Everyone who interacts with this parent feels the pain, reflected as anger, and must handle it.

People naturally avoid a parent with chronic anger. She or he goes into the school building, and every teacher and administrator hides. Meetings are scheduled, and everyone looks for an excuse not to come. Unfortunately, the very people who are needed to help the child or adolescent with ADHD are chased away.

The other parent reacts to this chronic anger by distancing himself or herself rather than encouraging support and cooperation in helping their son or daughter. The other children feel the anger and wonder why their parent is so upset all of the time. Rather than the family being a place for support and comfort, home becomes a place of conflict and distance.

## Chronic Guilt

When a parent's guilt persists into a chronic pattern, all suffer as well. At times the parent handles the unresolved guilt by becoming overly dedicated to the child or adolescent with ADHD. Not far under the surface is the anger at having to do so much. What comes across in public is the dedication. No task, no trip, no expense is too great to help this child. What comes across in a more subtle way is the anger at having to do all of this and of having to give up so much. Occasionally, this parent might appear to be a martyr. He or she never lets anyone forget how great the effort, how selfless the sacrifice has been. The surface behavior may be sweet and admirable. Somehow, though, the child picks up the bitter parallel message. "Look how much I do for you, you ungrateful child. You show no appreciation for my sacrifices."

Some parents might handle the unresolved guilt by withdrawing from other social and/or family contacts and by totally dedicating themselves to the child. Some parents carry this to the point where they have almost no energy left for relationships with the other children in the family or with their partner. Taking care of their child's needs becomes so demanding and taxing that they are too worn out, too weary, to meet the needs of others or for social activities or for sharing an intimate relationship with their mate. The result is a dysfunctional family and a strained marriage. It may be that the anger is never openly discussed between the parents but displaced onto the child who is seen as the cause of it all.

For other parents, the normal initial reaction of overprotecting the child might become a lifestyle. This lifestyle prevents growth for both the child and the parent and increases the child's or adolescent's feelings of worthlessness. Under these circumstances, this son or daughter can easily become immature or infantilized. Occasionally, this overprotective behavior may stem from a parent's attempt to cover up feelings of inadequacy as a person and a parent. If a parent feels low self-esteem and feelings of worthlessness, he or she might achieve feelings of being wanted and needed by believing that she or he is "all the child has in the world."

A self-defeating cycle begins. The child, now acting immature with feelings of incompetence, is unable to be successful and retreats into the home. The overprotecting parent sees the failures and feels even more justified in moving in and protecting. The child now increasingly realizes that she or he is helpless without the parent. The parent reinforces this idea that the child cannot survive without this parent.

## Reactions of the Other Family Members

*When someone in the family is hurting, everyone feels the pain.* This means siblings too. Hopefully, once a diagnosis of ADHD is made, a professional explains to parents what it is, what causes it, and how it is treated. Hopefully, too, someone explained all of this to the child or adolescent. However, rarely, if ever, are the issues discussed with the siblings. Yet they are part of the family, and they need to know. If they do not know, they will merely react to the problems. With knowledge, they can become positive helpers within the family.

The reactions of your other children might be made worse because you expect more of them than you expect of yourself. The child or adolescent with ADHD may be very good at getting parents frustrated and angry. One parent may yell or hit; another parent might cry, withdraw, or pout. Your other children get just as frustrated and angry. Yet if these siblings yell or hit or cry or withdraw or pout, they are often punished and told they may not act this way. They are human, too. They are entitled to the same feelings you have. You cannot tell them that they cannot have these feelings. They have as much difficulty controlling their frustration and anger as you sometimes do. You cannot tell them not to model their behaviors after their parents. You must acknowledge that they have normal and expected feelings and help them learn what to do with these. You must teach them acceptable ways of expressing these feelings within the family.

If two parents disagree on parenting styles or discipline methods, the conflicts between the other children and the child with ADHD can cause major stress between the parents. This stress can be even worse if these parents are divorced and the children spend time in two different families, each with a different style of responding.

Your other children and adolescents struggle with many different feelings as they live with and try to cope with the sibling who has ADHD. I'll review the more common reactions. In Chapter 15 I'll discuss ways of addressing these problems.

## Anxiety

Some siblings of kids with ADHD become worried and feel anxious. This feeling is especially common in families where little information, if any, is shared. "What's wrong with Jimmie?" they ask. Their parents say nothing or might say "Oh, nothing special . . . it's okay." Yet they see their parents taking Jimmie from one place to another, and they hear phrases like "brain problems" or "chemical problems in the brain" or "Where are we going to get the money for all of this?" They see their sister or brother take medicine but are not told why. They see their mother or father upset, maybe crying, maybe angry. Aware that something is wrong but not knowing what it is, their imaginations may take over. Frequently, they fantasize that things are worse than they really are, and then they worry. I have heard siblings say, "Is he going to die? or "Will it happen to me?" or "If it's not important, why all the whispers and secrets?" Your other children need to have clear information at a level that they can handle.

### Anger

Sisters and brothers may become angry, often fighting with the child or adolescent with ADHD. If double standards are in effect, you can be sure that they will notice them and become angry. "How come I have to make my bed in the morning, and she doesn't?" or "He broke my toy, and you didn't do anything" or "Why is it that when I do something, I get punished and when he does the same thing, I am told that I have to be more understanding?"

Another source of anger is the amount of time and energy that parents spend with the child who has ADHD, causing jealousy. The entire morning might be spent getting this child up, dressed, fed, and out the door, leaving little time for the others. Evenings might be spent helping with this child's homework to a greater extent than with others. So much money may have to be spent on this child or adolescent that everyone else has to do without or vacations have to be compromised. You can't really blame the siblings for complaining.

I sometimes find another source of anger. A sibling may have to take being teased at school. "Hey, how's your spastic brother?" or "Your sister acts funny . . . She's gross . . . Is she a mental case?" or "Why does your brother take medicine? Is he weird or something?" Anyone, especially a child, is embarrassed by such comments and may react with anger. Even at home, the other children in the family may not feel safe. Their parents insist that they let the sibling with ADHD who has no friends play with their friends when they come over. This child acts silly or is hyper and embarrasses the sibling. This brother or sister might stop bringing friends home for fear of what will happen. Some will do everything possible not to rush home after school, preferring to go to a friend's house.

## Guilt

Sisters and brothers may feel guilty, too, especially guilty when they are angry and the message from parents is "He can't help it" or "It's not her fault." This is a hard message to swallow for someone who has not yet gained a lot of perspective on life. Another source of guilt might be a sibling thinking normal thoughts but not knowing that they are normal—"I'm glad I don't have ADHD" or "I wish she lived someplace else."

## "Acting Out"

Because of feelings of anger or guilt, a brother or sister might act out these feelings against the sibling with ADHD. They might tease and provoke this child or encourage misbehavior. They might do something themselves and then set up this child to be a scapegoat. Because they are so frustrated and angry and are told that they cannot show their feelings, they get even in subtle ways that may go unnoticed. As the parent punishes the child with ADHD, this sibling smiles and gets a feeling of revenge.

## Covering Up Success

It seems the plight of children with disabilities that a younger brother or sister is not only supernormal and delightful but precocious, quickly passing him or her socially and academically. These siblings have lots of friends. They are praised for their behavior. They excel in school. The contrast may create a conflict with parents. On one hand, these parents are delighted and proud. On the other hand, these successes make the child or adolescent with ADHD look even worse. The successful sibling must be praised and encouraged. Do not ask that he or she be quiet about grades or accomplishments so that the child with ADHD does not feel bad. This is not appropriate or fair. The child with ADHD will have to learn to cope with reality.

## In Summary

There are no easy ways to prevent some or all of the feelings described above from surfacing in your family. None of your children were born as self-denying, altruistic models of charity. Besides, all of these feelings, provided that they are kept within limits, are normal and can be handled. The more you are aware of your behavior and the more you try not to have double stan dards or expect more from your children than they are capable of doing, the fewer difficulties you will have. The only way to forestall the worst of this anger and frustration among your other children is to keep them informed, let them know that it is safe and acceptable to discuss with you what they are thinking and feeling, and, finally, to answer their questions reasonably and as honestly as you can.

None of this is easy. But you are their parents as well. In Chapter 15 I'll discuss models for minimizing family problems and ways of handling difficult behavior within the family. If you see that you need help in explaining your situation or if you feel that the family is not functioning well, do not hesitate to ask someone for help. Join a support group. Let other parents help you help yourself and your family. If necessary, seek the help of a mental health professional.

## An Example of These Normal Family Reactions

I first met Danny for an evaluation at age three. I followed his progress and worked with the family off and on for the next ten years. I still keep in touch with the parents. Danny is now an adult. Shortly after the initial evaluation, his mother began a diary. Initially she tried to reconstruct her experiences with Danny from the time of his birth. I have interwoven Danny's clinical picture with excerpts from that diary. His mother writes exceptionally well, often eloquently, but don't mistake this for a fictional account. Her words suggest that she read this chapter before she started her diary; this wasn't the case. As she confronts and finally begins to bring the various stages of her despair under control, you will be struck by the truth and validity of her account. Perhaps you will share her tears and pain because you are there in your own life or you have been there.

## Pregnancy

Mrs. S's third pregnancy, after two sons (one four years old, the other two) went without complication. Her comments reflect the anticipation with which both parents greeted this child.

A third son? What a joy, what a delight, such pride for the father—what pleasure for the only woman—the queen in a household of adoring men. The other two are dark-haired and dark-eyed like mom and dad. The third is a unique one with his blue eyes and strawberry blond hair. Grandma says he was meant to be a girl. Everyone agrees, "Well, if you had to have a third son, at least he's different." We didn't realize at that time just how different he was.

Danny had the advantage of being the third child. By the time a third is born all of the anxieties implicit in the care and handling of a normal infant have vanished. No more fits of panic when the baby cries unexpectedly. No more wringing of hands at the first sign of a sniffle or loose bowel movements . . . just a placid, cool, nonchalant parent juggling baby on one arm, holding middle brother with the right hand, pulling the wagon laden with sand box toys with the other, calling to the oldest son to look both ways while crossing the street on his bike. The combination of self-confident mother and animated, stimulating surroundings are calculated to make this third baby so happy, so comfortable, with none of the pressures or tensions that the other two had to endure.

"They bring themselves up, these third children do. He'll be your easiest," assured our pediatrician.

## Delivery and the First Year of Life

Danny's delivery was normal, with no reported difficulties, and his physical examination prior to discharge from the hospital was also normal. Mrs. S quickly noticed, however, that he was different from the other children—irritable, overactive, unable to focus. Feeding him was a problem, and he vomited often. The pediatrician treated him for colic. Danny also had trouble getting to sleep, and he often slept only three to four hours at a time. Sometimes he cried and thrashed about for thirty minutes to an hour. Holding him did nothing to comfort him. Several other early suggestions of neurological difficulties were present. Danny's skin was overly sensitive to touch, and he responded to being held by pushing the mother away.

Mrs. S reported that from the start, Danny didn't like her. When she picked him up, he cried; the more she cuddled him the more he cried (the tactile sensitivity). When she turned his head toward her nipple, he pushed her away (probably a reflex called a tonic-neck reflex that should have stopped by this age). She felt helpless, inadequate, angry, and guilty. She did not yet understand, so she blamed herself.

Well, then, why did he cry so much? Why did he squirm in your arms as if pleading to be released to the security of his crib? Why the endless bouts of vomiting before, after, during his meals? Why not the same show of pleasure at being rocked and played with like his brothers? Why no "coos" or "goos" or babbles or giggles? Where was this joyous, relaxed, happy third baby syndrome?

By the end of Danny's first year of life, I attempted to review all of these statements regarding the easy routine with the third baby— the enjoyment I was supposed to be savoring through him—the idea that "he's your last so lap it up" sort of notion. All I could come up with was a dull ache in the pit of my stomach. Why isn't he fun for me? Why doesn't he return my love? Why no give-and-take between baby and anyone? His constant crying and whining, his discontent and apparent discomfort, convinced me that he must be in some physical distress. That question, along with his persistent vomiting, brought me to the pediatrician who assured me that he was fine. I must relax and learn to loosen up. That along with a little sympathetic support was supposed to reassure me.

But the dull ache in head, heart, and stomach persisted. Why the relief for me at Danny's bedtime? Why the feeling of incompleteness when he was around and the feeling of solidarity and wholeness without him?

My growing conclusion was that there must be something wrong with me to result in this personality conflict. I was perplexed by my feelings of guilt in relation to this child, because if that were my pattern, why wasn't I feeling guilty in relation to my other children? I realized later that my guilt originated from ambivalent feelings toward him—feelings of love and hate, of sympathy and anger, of concern and fear. The insecurity that my relationship to him created inside of me resulted in feelings of self-doubt about my capacity as Mother and in regard to my own emotional stability which had never been in question.

My loneliness while submerged in these feelings was intense. In spite of a good marriage and a loving husband, I was alone. Many of these feelings and observations were not shared by my husband who wasn't with Danny as much as I, who never saw him vis-à-vis his age peers, and who by virtue of a very placid, calm nature had a greater capacity to accept a wide diversity of behaviors. Every attempt I made to acquaint him with my concerns was met with assurance that Danny was fine—perhaps a little immature, but fine. The family reminded me that I was older when I had him—perhaps two kids had been enough, all of this being after the fact. All I was left with were doubts, fear, and anger directed toward myself and toward this creature who was the source of all of my problems.

In looking back over Danny's first year of life, as well as those of others like him, it is difficult to pinpoint just what impact his neurological disabilities had. He was later diagnosed with auditory perception disabilities. What effect did they have on his orienting to sound or on his learning to relate to or attach to his mother? What effect did his auditory figure-ground disability have? Could Danny orient at all to his mother's voice? What must the world be perceived as when being held is experienced as uncomfortable or painful? Mrs. S describes her frustrations, confusions, and ambivalent feelings toward the developing relationship with her infant son. Could Danny's feelings have been any less troubled?

## Years One and Two

Danny's language development was delayed. On top of everything else, he now became frustrated by his inability to communicate his needs. His gross motor development was delayed also, resulting in very slow mastery of sitting, standing, walking, and running. He was hyperactive and distractible. He did not outgrow his tactile sensitivity and became defensive to touch, avoiding too much body contact. Possibly because of these neurological problems, he had trouble dealing with separation. Both parents found handling Danny overwhelmingly difficult. With no information and no reassurance from her pediatrician, Mrs. S continued to search within herself for an explanation.

By thirteen months of age, a lock on his bedroom door was required to keep Danny protected from his own enormous fund of aimless energy which was consistently directed toward destructive pursuits. Perhaps his resentment at being locked in or an increasing hyperactivity was the cause of the extreme havoc he wreaked on his surroundings. Linoleum was lifted up off the floor of his room. Pictures in their frames were torn down from the walls, window shades were replaced because they were ripped up. A rocking chair was used to bang against the wall, thus creating dents in the plasterboard. A harness held him down in his high chair, and one was used in the stroller when he was reluctantly wheeled away from his exhausted mother by an equally reluctant baby-sitter. And all the time I'm thinking what is wrong with me that I have created this child who I wish I never had.

The more I disliked him, the more he clung to me, the less able he was to let me go, thus causing horrendous scenes at my departures, serving to increase my guilt and self-blame. "When I leave he gets so scared. Therefore, I shouldn't leave. But, if I don't I'll go mad. So, I'll leave but he'll scream and I'll feel so awful." This internal dialogue characterized every separation we were ever to endure.

His constant aimless running resulted in many falls and bruises, the worst of which was a collision with Danny's nose and the dining room table. Sutures were required for that accident, which was followed by several other close calls, all a result of his hyperactivity and poor coordination. Along with this went the assaults by Danny upon anyone who dared get physically close. Once he was seated on my lap I would in a five-minute period of time receive several blows to my jaw from the unpredictable banging of his head. His frantic squirming discouraged me from holding him or cuddling him. Kicks on knees and in stomach, little hands pushing my face away from his—so many efforts to keep me away—all added up to one conclusion. He doesn't love me and I don't love him, and it's my fault and it's unnatural and wrong, and I wish I didn't have him and I've ruined my life forever. And yet, there he sat with his sad blue eyes and his confused forlornness. He was as unhappy as I was and I had to find out why.

## Year Three

Danny's gross motor problems persisted. He showed difficulty with fine motor control of his hand activities. He began to develop language, but he often appeared to misunderstand or to respond in ways that made little sense. His parents felt that his thinking was more concrete than his brothers' had been at the same age. He developed fears of unknown places and of new objects. His separation problems persisted. Although toilet trained for bowel functioning by age two and a half, he still wet the bed at night. Danny started nursery school.

At last Danny was three. A new era was ushered in by his enrollment in a nursery school—relief for mommy and some friends (please God, some playmates) for Danny. But more important, at last some objective feedback from emotionally uninvolved teachers who see normal three-year-old kids all the time. No more would I have to rely on Dad's calm assurances, upon Grandmother's accusations, upon my own frantic self-inquiry.

Several months passed before the teachers decided that it was time to confront me with reality. Danny was not involved with the other children, they reported. Furthermore, he was tense, frightened, highly distractible, and most of all, very unhappy. It was with mixed feelings that I received this news. On the one hand I was very upset to hear my worst suspicions confirmed. On the other hand I was relieved to hear that someone else saw the same thing—that my sanity and clear vision need not be held in doubt any longer. Most of all, I was grateful for the sense of purpose and motivation that this shared awareness endowed me with.

It was at this point that the parents brought Danny in for consultation. In the course of the evaluation, his pediatrician and a pediatric neurologist, as well as a special education professional, occupational therapist, and a speech and language therapist, saw him. I did the child psychiatric and the family evaluations. The concluding diagnoses included:

1. Specific learning disabilities, manifested by auditory perception, sequencing, abstraction, auditory memory, gross motor, fine motor, and demand language disabilities.
2. *Hyperkinetic reaction of childhood* (the term in use then for what would now be called ADHD), manifested by hyperactivity, distractibility, and impulsivity.
3. Sensory integration disorder, manifested by tactile sensitivity and defensiveness, gross and fine motor planning diffi culties, and vestibular confusion.
4. Emotional problems, manifested by separation anxiety, fears, and poor peer relationships.
5. Family problems, manifested by overwhelmed, frustrated, helpless-feeling parents.

Also noted were perseveration and bedwetting. These were seen as another reflection of a dysfunctional nervous system.

The following treatment plan was recommended and implemented:

1. Special education, speech-language, and occupational therapy as part of a therapeutic nursery school for children with learning and language disabilities.
2. A trial on medication to minimize the hyperactivity, distractibility, and impulsivity.

3. Preventive family counseling focused on educating the parents about their child's disabilities and their role in helping.

The medication, Ritalin, significantly decreased Danny's hyperactivity, distractibility, and impulsivity. The bedwetting stopped, possibly because of the decrease in impulsivity. Parents learned to use deep touch stimulation when holding Danny, lessening his tactile sensitivity and, thus, his tactile defensiveness. He adapted to the new therapeutic nursery, and slowly his language improved. The long process of special education therapy began.

Mrs. S describes the evaluation and its impact. Her awareness of her feelings and the shift in her ways of handling them reflect the counseling she began to receive.

It was these feelings that enabled me to have Danny evaluated. He was seen by many specialists, each seeming to focus on one part of his problem. By the end, all the parts came together and presto—a diagnosis—something to grab hold of—something to explain it all and most of all a means, a method, a way to help.

Danny's neurological impairment caused perceptual problems which resulted in learning difficulties, we were told. His restlessness, his dislike for being touched and touching, his chronic unhappiness and frustration all could be explained. The cause of it was unknown. So who could be blamed? There was a way to help him . . . please tell us how? There is a way to handle him at home that will make him feel good and happy and worthwhile . . . please tell me and I'll try. It will take time but he'll get better . . . or will he??? How great!

So, with all this, I gazed upon my neurologically impaired Danny, lifted my eyes to the heavens and whispered, "Thank you. It's not as serious as I thought. Thank you. There is help available. Thank you. He will in time get better. Thank you, again. You are not a crazy, unlovable, unnatural Mother. Thank you; thank you; thank you!"

But if that's the case, why didn't anyone believe or support me? Why was I kept in this state of anxiety and fear all these years? Where were the experts or even the loved ones? Why didn't they trust me? Why didn't they hear? And so once again I was angry—a state that was becoming second nature to me—descriptive of my mood and personality. The anger directed itself inward; then because it was futile and uneconomical to express it, I became sad, depressed, forlorn. In short, I felt pity for myself. Why did it have to happen to me? What did I do to deserve this? How will I ever find the strength to endure? How can I be a mother to this poor, defenseless child? Days of brooding were to follow. I was caught up in a grief reaction that was all-consuming. I accused everyone of being unable to understand what I was going through. In a way I was trying to say, "Look how I am hurting. Won't someone take care of me and see how much I am caring?" The only problem with this behavior, I soon determined for myself, was that it accomplished nothing positive nor worthwhile, and, furthermore, it led me to feel unattractive and selfish.

As soon as this awareness surfaced, a new era dawned. Self-indulgence, once completed, paved the way for the realization that Danny and I were going to be involved with one another for many years to come and that I'd better come to terms with the problems and begin to work on it with him so that both of us could be happier than we were. Thus, I allowed myself to become informed by the professionals, comprehending the "whys" and learning the "how-tos." With this knowledge came understanding, and with this understanding came coping, and with this coping came a growing sensitivity toward his positive changes and progress. This encouraged me to continue with renewed courage and with expectations for Danny, based on the reality of the situation.

No longer was there room in my rationale for unproductive self-pity, brooding, or accusations. I realized that the effects of this attitude would result in more problems. Let's then acknowledge that we have a problem. Let's not be afraid to label it, to explore it, to learn about it, and to accept it.

## Years Three Through Twelve

Although Danny remained in special education programs through the fifth grade, by the fourth grade he was in a regular education program, receiving special education and language therapy one hour a week each. He remained on Ritalin. His parents worked closely with his school programs and his teachers throughout the years. They carefully selected those peer activities and sports that tended to build on his strengths rather than to magnify his weaknesses. Each year brought successes and new challenges. Mrs. S reflected on these experiences:

But, does acceptance defend a mother against uncomfortable feelings? Does she ever adjust to the situation and simply continue her day-to-day existence, giving minimal thought or worry to this part of her life? The answer for this mother is a resounding *no!*

The process of adjustment is an ongoing one. On his bad days I feel bad. Back creeps the old sense of fear and foreboding. On good days I feel hopeful and perhaps a trifle excited at the glimpse of health and wholeness I see under the surface. On most days I feel the responsibility of another day. I decided that I will try to begin at his beginnings—to love him, to accept him right where he's at. I realize I must plan according to his needs at that moment and with this comes the task of ignoring some of my own. No one can do that without feeling some anger.

And what about the feelings of deprivation when you see how poorly he measures up to his age group, and, as he grows older, how poorly he stands in relation to children even younger than him? What of the feelings you get when you see him rejected by children and adults alike because he can't relate in the expected, conformist manner? What of the embarrassment you feel when his problems result in antisocial behavior in public? What kind of excuses do you force yourself to fabricate to ease your self-consciousness? What do you say to family when they assure you that all he needs is some discipline and he'll fall into line? The disruption he causes in the tempo of family life—the interference with certain pleasures arouses anger, deprivation, and guilt. And how about the emptiness in your gut when you catch a glimpse of his inner world of confusion and loneliness? How does that make you feel?

With all of these feelings resurfacing with every new situation, how can one ever expect to be adjusted? The only answer I have found is to make room for the feelings, to accept them—not to luxuriate in them, but not to deny them . . . to say them out loud to yourself or to whoever is unafraid to hear them. This paves the way for a stronger, more positive relationship with Danny.

The way I relate to Danny becomes reflected in the way he sees himself. If I allow his problems to scare me, he too becomes scared. Communicating to him that he is worthwhile and lovable and that I have hopes for him enables him to face his future with hope and courage. This places a great responsibility on me, but it is the only chance any of us have for a good life. If we have hope for Danny, he will have hope for himself.

I still wish I had three perfect sons. I occasionally indulge in that "Wouldn't it be lovely" fantasy. I have come to treasure in the other two what many people take for granted. I have a great investment in them but I do in Danny, too. It is an investment imbued by the implicit faith I have encouraged myself to have in him and in me. It will take a long time and it will be difficult, but I have hope that it will work.

## Follow-up on Danny

Mrs. S stopped writing her diary when Danny was in the fifth grade. With her permission, I included her diary and my comments in the first edition of this book, when Danny was in the eighth grade. Academically he was doing well. His peer relationships were limited and best handled one at a time. He related well to his parents and brothers but was described as a "little aloof" with others. He continued to need the medication. Danny had no apparent psychiatric problems.

As I prepared the second edition, I called Danny's mother. He was about to enter his senior year at an excellent college. Academically he was doing very well, and he had a B-plus average. He learned to be very organized and efficient. His major was music. Danny's mother reflected that music had always been his "salvation." He was good, and he could escape into playing for hours at a time. He played the keyboard, composed, and recorded his music. He was well respected as a musician.

He still had social difficulties. He had friends, but no special friend. He still did not have a sense of humor, and although much improved, he did not pick up many social cues. Yet, he had completed three years of college and was comfortable.

She ended this conversation by saying, "He's a real sweetheart, a lovely person. Yet, he is never going to be perfect . . . I hope he will not be a lonely person." Although she agreed that he had accomplished far more than any of us dared to wish for when he was three, four, or five, the worry about his future never ended.

Recently, I again called Danny's mother. Danny had graduated from college and was living on his own. He had a job and also worked as a musician. He had a small group of friends and appeared to be happy. Danny and his brothers had a good relationship with each other and kept in touch. She added, "I wish he would meet a nice girl who would understand and take care of him, but I don't think this will happen. He is on his own, supporting himself, happy, and comfortable with his small group of friends. What more can I ask for?"

# PART FIVE

# Treatment of Attention Deficit Hyperactivity Disorder

# *11*

## Basic Concepts of Treatment

The treatment of ADHD must be multimodal—involving several approaches. These approaches include individual and family education, individual and family counseling, the use of appropriate behavioral management programs, and the use of appropriate medications. Each approach requires working closely with the school. In this chapter, I'll focus on an overview of the treatment for ADHD. In the following chapters I'll address each part of this multimodal approach.

As discussed throughout this book, children and adolescents with ADHD usually have a cluster of clinical difficulties. They might have a learning disability or one of the other neurological disorders. They often develop secondary emotional, social, and family problems. Thus, it is important that each of these possibilities be considered. Your child's or adolescent's primary physician might be able to assess for ADHD. Often, several professionals are needed to do a more comprehensive assessment. If the professional seeing your son or daughter does not explore all possible related difficulties, it would be helpful to discuss this concern. If other professionals are needed, your family physician might coordinate this evaluation process or might refer you to others to do the fuller assessment.

Once the evaluation is complete, it is important that someone integrate the information into a comprehensive diagnostic profile, such as the following.

Clinical Impressions:
1. Attention deficit hyperactivity disorder, combined type
2. Learning disabilities
3. Anxiety disorder, considered secondary to the above disabilities

Once this comprehensive picture of the child or adolescent is known, a treatment plan can be developed that addresses each problem identified. For example, with the above impressions, a treatment plan might read:

1. Parent conference to review clinical impressions and proposed treatment plan. If necessary, a family session will be scheduled later.
2. A trial on Ritalin, starting at 5 mg three times a day.
3. A conference with school professionals to review the special education needs and to develop appropriate accommodations.
4. Cognitive behavioral therapy to address the anxiety with the possibility that an anti-anxiety medication might be used later.

## Implementing the Treatment Plan

When you meet to review the findings of the evaluation, the professional or group of professionals should explain each diagnostic impression and how this specific conclusion was reached. The proposed treatment plan should follow from the impressions. Each treatment intervention should be explained thoroughly enough that you understand what is to be done and why. If the professionals talk over your head, back them up and make them explain things more clearly.

If the professional doing the evaluation feels that a parent needs individual help, that the couple needs parenting or marital counseling, or that the family needs to be seen for counseling, the reasons should become clear. If the professional doesn't bring this up and you feel that such help would be meaningful, this is the time to speak up and express the need.

If your child needs medications, each should be explained in detail. What's the starting dose, and how will follow-up monitoring be done? Don't accept your family physician saying "Try different doses and let me know what works best." You are not a physician and need guidance at each step in the process. Learn how to contact the physician if you notice any side effects. Don't leave this meeting without clear plans on each step of establishing the proper medication, dose, and timing. Further information on medication management is discussed in Chapter 16.

What roles will the school need to play? What accommodations or services are needed? If your son or daughter has a learning disability or is suspected of having such, be sure the next steps are clarified in doing the necessary diagnostic studies or in implementing the appropriate interventions. Who will communicate with the school system? What should you ask of your school professionals? Someone should explain your rights and how to negotiate for what is needed. Information on these issues will be discussed in Chapter 19.

Who will explain ADHD and the impact your son's or daughter's ADHD has had on him or her and on the family? If your child or adolescent will need individual help, how will this be planned and started? If a parent or the couple needs help, what are the next steps? These needs will be discussed in Chapter 13.

Don't be afraid to be assertive about each of the areas of concern noted. You need the information discussed above in order to proceed with the treatment plan. If you leave this interpretive or wrap-up session without a full understanding of the full clinical picture, contact the professional or professional team and ask for clarification.

A brief evaluation resulting in the conclusion that the problem is ADHD and the writing of a prescription are not acceptable. If your family physician can't do more than this, you will have to seek out others to complete the assessment.

Since parents often see mental health professionals to have their son or daughter evaluated, it is important to understand the differences between these professionals and their qualifications. Should a form of psychological therapy be recommended, it is also important for parents to understand these treatment approaches.

## The Mental Health Professionals

There are several professional groups providing mental health services—psychiatrists, psychologists, social workers, psychiatric nurses, and mental health counselors. These professionals might be in private practice, be part of a mental health organization, or be part of the public school system. Each has a core of common knowledge and skills in diagnosis and treatment as well as unique areas of expertise. Each requires different levels of training and certification. Being an intelligent consumer requires that you learn all you can about the qualifications of any clinician who is going to work with your child and your family. All mental health professionals are not equally competent to help children and adolescents, even if within the same profession. Don't be any less concerned about seeking the best qualified person in the mental health field than you would be in selecting the best person in the health field.

### Psychiatry

A psychiatrist is a medical doctor, a physician. A *general psychiatrist* has completed the medical education and training required to become a physician. He or she then does four or five more years of specialized training in psychiatry. Part of this training includes experiences working with children and adolescents. A *child and adolescent psychiatrist* has completed medical education and training required to become a general psychiatrist and then taken two additional years of training in child and adolescent psychiatry. Because of her or his medical training, the general or child and adolescent psychiatrist is familiar with the biological and the psychological aspects of diagnosis and treatment. Of all the mental health professionals, only psychiatrists can prescribe medication or admit patients to the hospital. All psychiatrists are trained to do psychopharmacological treatments as well as individual, group, or family work. The child and adolescent psychiatrist, because of the additional training, may be most qualified to assess and treat the individual with a mixture of neurological, psychological, and social problems.

## Psychology

A psychologist might have a doctorate or a master's degree. Most states require a person to have a doctorate to be licensed to practice. This degree may be in clinical, counseling, school, or developmental psychology, although there are other possible areas. The doctorate-level psychologist has completed four to six or more years of graduate training beyond college, including a year of special clinical training called an internship. Because one can be trained in so many areas and because there are so many different types of internships available, any specific psychologist might have differing skills with different age groups or types of therapy. The depth and variety of training with children or adolescents also may greatly vary. The master's-level psychologist has completed a two-year graduate program beyond college. Because training and experience vary so widely, you may want to discuss the background and training of your psychologist before starting any evaluation or therapy. Psychologists have the unique skill of being able to administer psychological and educational tests.

## Social Work

A social worker has completed college plus a two-year master's degree program in a graduate school of social work. Following graduation, he or she must work under supervision for several years before being eligible to take a clinical certifying examination. A candidate who passes this examination becomes a licensed clinical social worker (LCSW). The level of diagnostic and treatment skills in working with children and adolescents depends on the social worker's additional experience following graduation or as part of other postgraduate training. The kinds of therapies offered will also be based on this required experience or other experience. Thus, being a social worker does not necessarily mean that the individual is experienced in working with children and adolescents. Parents need to learn what training and experience the social worker has had since graduation.

## Psychiatric Nurse

A psychiatric nurse may have completed a training program leading to a certificate as a registered nurse or may have a bachelor's degree in nursing. Some also have a two-year master's degree in psychiatric or mental health nursing. To be certified as a clinical specialist in psychiatric nursing, a nurse must have a master's or doctor's degree in psychiatric or mental health nursing or an acceptable equivalent and must pass a national certifying examination. The psychiatric nurse with graduate school training has core knowledge and skills comparable to those of the other mental health professionals with a similar master's level of training but with a special focus based on training in nursing in a medical setting. Many focus on family therapy, but many are also skilled in other forms of therapy. As with the social worker, parents need to know if the nurse has had special training experience with children and adolescents.

## Mental Health Counselor

A mental health counselor is more difficult to define clearly. Many have completed a two-year graduate degree in counseling followed by several years of supervised experience. These individuals take a clinical certifying examination following this training. If they pass, they are certified as mental health counselors. The licensing laws in some states permit individuals with less to much less training and experience to identify themselves as "counselors." Thus, it is critical that parents clarify the level of training, the type of certification, and the amount of formal training and experience with children and adolescents.

## General Comments

You can see that there are several professional groups within the mental health field. Within each professional group, practitioners have widely different levels of training and experience.

Not all are equally well trained to work with children and adolescents. Not all can do psychological testing or prescribe medications. Not all will be familiar with school systems and such problems as learning disabilities or ADHD.

I continue to be upset and surprised at how people choose a mental health practitioner. They may search the country to find the "best" surgeon for a specific procedure or the "best" physician to treat their specific physical disorder. They might spend hours on the phone or computer tracking down "the best." Yet, these same people will take a family member to the most convenient local mental health practitioner without asking about training, qualifications, and experience. Are the mind and brain any less important than the body?

Be an intelligent, informed consumer. It is not inappropriate to discuss a person's training, experience, and specialty. Parents often ask me about my background. I am not offended. If anything, I respect the parents for caring that much about their child or adolescent. You are entrusting your son or daughter and possibly your family to this clinician. Be sure you have someone qualified to address the diagnostic or treatment concerns you have.

## The Types of Therapy

A child's social, behavioral, or emotional problems must be seen as clinical clues These clues along with other observations and evidence lead to a diagnosis. The diagnosis leads to a treatment plan and to treatment interventions. Thus, it is important that the diagnostic process be done by a competent clinician or a team of competent clinicians. These interventions might be with the individual, with the family, or with the individual in a group setting. Such interventions might include medications, individual therapy, group therapy, or family therapy. Within each of these types of therapy there are several approaches to be considered. If the child or adolescent has a learning disability and/or ADHD and/or any of the other related disorders discussed in this book, these problems must be addressed. To treat a secondary emotional problem without treating the underlying cause will not succeed. Blowing away the smoke does not put out the fire. If the child has a poor self-image because of academic frustration and failure, psychotherapy will not improve his or her self-image unless or until he or she receives the proper special education services.

Sometimes several treatment approaches will be used at the same time or one following the other. For example, the family might be in such a crisis that they start family behavioral therapy immediately. Once the family is more stable, the underlying reasons for the dysfunction might become clear and other treatment approaches will be used.

## Psychoanalytic Psychotherapy

The professional does an evaluation for a "dynamic" or "intrapsychic" problem by talking with the child or adolescent. For younger children, play materials may be used as a vehicle for communicating. The professional looks at the interactions between internal thinking processes (basic wishes and needs, conscience or value system, and the ability to assess the realities of the outside world). The clinician explores the relative strengths of each process, the coping skills available to handle any conflicts between these processes (called defense mechanisms), and whether the conflicts and strategies are age-appropriate and successful. The goal of psychoanalytically oriented psychotherapy is to help the child or adolescent better understand his or her concerns and conflicts and to help him or her develop better methods of coping.

## Behavioral Therapy

Behavioral observations and observational data might clarify that the inappropriate or unacceptable behaviors have been learned and reinforced. If the problems parents are dealing with are seen as a reflection of learned patterns of behavior by the individual or by parents, behavioral therapy might be initiated. Different approaches will be used to help to increase more healthy or acceptable behaviors and to decrease unacceptable behaviors. This therapy might be with the individual, with the parents, or as part of work with the family.

Another form of behavioral therapy might be directed toward helping the individual control anxiety. The child may learn specific behavioral techniques such as relaxation therapy. Similar approaches might be used to help the individual better control anger.

Our behaviors can be seen as consisting of feelings, thoughts, and behaviors. If the individual can't see the influence one of these three experiences has on the others, cognitive behavioral therapy might be used. The goal is to help the child or adolescent to become more aware of the relationship between feelings, thoughts, and behaviors. He or she will learn techniques to become more aware of inappropriate feelings, thoughts, or behaviors and how to gain better control over the inappropriate interactions.

## Group Therapy

If the child or adolescent is having difficulty interacting successfully with peers, group therapy might be considered. In the therapeutic group setting, patterns of behaviors and interactions can be observed and pointed out. New approaches and strategies can be taught and tried out. For younger children, role playing and practice might be used to learn more acceptable styles of interaction.

## Family Therapy

If the child's difficulties are seen as reflective of how the family functions, family therapy might be used. The focus might be behavioral, helping the parents to regain control and teaching the children that they can be safe if not in control. The focus might be on family communication or family interactions. With family therapy, the goal is to help all family members find a way to make the family a happier, safer, more positive place to be.

## Psychopharmacology

The use of medications to treat behavioral or emotional disorders may be essential. The medication may be to address anxiety or depression. It may be used to treat ADHD or one of the modulating disorders. If a child has several disorders—for example, ADHD, obsessive compulsive disorder, and a tic disorder—several medications may be needed.

You may find that your son's or daughter's family doctor or pediatrician can treat the ADHD. For the psychiatric disorders, it is best, if possible, to work with the most skilled person in psychopharmacology. This professional is usually a child and adolescent psychiatrist.

Medication should not be used in isolation. Education, counseling, and/or other interventions are needed as well.

## General Comments

There are many approaches to therapy and several types of therapy within each approach. It is important that the mental health professional or professionals doing the evaluation select the most appropriate intervention for your son or daughter. At times several approaches will be needed. As progress is made, changes in the approach might be appropriate.

Some mental health professionals believe that the type of therapy being done requires minimal or no contact with the parents. "Therapy is between your child and me, and it will interfere with our therapeutic relationship if he or she knows I am talking with you." I must respectfully state that I have difficulty with this approach. Parents are lost and hurting. They need help in helping their daughter or son. They must be given guidance along with any individual therapy for their child.

## In Summary

A multimodal treatment plan is necessary to treat ADHD and any related neurologically based disorders or secondary emotional, social, or family problems. It is important for parents to understand that being told your child has ADHD and being handed a prescription is not enough. If that's all your family physician can do, you will have to seek out others to complete the assessment.

Ideally, your child's or adolescent's primary physician will be the person who coordinates the necessary assessments, integrates the multiple findings, and coordinates the treatment plan. Or, he or she might feel comfortable handling the medication part and referring you to others to address the other problems.

The questions you need to have answered are:

1. Does my son or daughter have ADHD?
2. If yes, what medication and nonmedication treatments are needed? Who will provide each treatment need?
3. How can I and my family be helped? Who will provide what is needed?
4. What must I communicate to my school professionals? How?

Remember, the use of medication alone is not the treatment for ADHD. There are necessary nonmedication interventions needed for the child or adolescent, parents, and the family. These interventions involve the individual, the family, and the school. The following chapters will expand on each aspect of this multimodal treatment model.

# 12

## Individual and Family Education

Many of your son's or daughter's behavioral and school problems are confusing. These problems might reflect ADHD plus any or several of the associated disorders. Classroom teachers might focus on the behaviors without recognizing the underlying problems. They describe your child's inability to sit still, stay on task, or complete a task, or impulsive behaviors such as interrupting or fighting. As a parent, you might repeat the concerns of the teachers to your family physician and add your own observations and frustrations. You might remind this clinician that you have been expressing the same concerns for several years, only to be told that you are an "overworried parent" or that your child "will outgrow it." But neither statement turned out to be true. The problems have persisted and possibly become worse.

Moreover, the school professionals might displace their own feelings of frustration and helplessness onto you, the parent. Parents only infrequently get a call from a teacher saying "Your child had a great day. I want to compliment you on being such a good parent." Instead, the call is more likely to communicate that your child has been disruptive or is not paying attention or completing class work. The nonverbal message to the parent is clear: "Do something about it. Make your child behave and learn."

Children and adolescents with ADHD will also be frustrated. Their disabilities are not obvious. They don't understand why they can't be like their classmates. All they know is that they want to be good, they want to be successful in school, and they try as hard as the others, yet they do not succeed and they seem to get into trouble. They are accused of being bad, being lazy, or not trying. They are called troublemakers. They do not always understand what they have done. Eventually, they might begin to believe that what they are told is true. They begin to feel that they are not as bright as their classmates or that they are bad.

The critical first step in any multimodal approach to treatment, therefore, must be to educate the parents and then their child or adolescent. This educational process may be needed for other significant individuals such as brothers, sisters, grandparents, and child care workers. Each must understand these invisible handicaps. Each must understand that, although invisible, these disabilities are just as debilitating as any other chronic handicapping condition. Each must also understand that having these problems does not mean that the child or adolescent is bad or dumb. Finally, each must understand the treatment plan.

Over the past thirty years of working with individuals who have ADHD and often also have learning disabilities, I have followed many of them through their childhood and adolescence and into their young adult life. Often I ask them to tell me which interventions were the most helpful for them and which were not. The most consistently helpful information they told me they got was, "When you first explained who I was and what my problems were." Before this time, they saw themselves as inadequate, not smart, or bad. After this time, they began to understand their disabilities, and with this new knowledge of themselves, they were able to rethink who they were and to begin to change their self-image.

As with any chronic problem, these children and adolescents must understand their disability and how it affects them during each stage of life. They also must understand the plans for treatment, what each intervention is to accomplish, and their critical role in what happens to them. By understanding and playing an active role in what happens to them, they are more accepting of and compliant with the treatment programs.

## The Educational Process

This educational process starts with the interpretive or wrap-up session when the professional or group of professionals reviews with you what are believed to be the problems and what is needed to address these problems. In my session, I explain each disorder or problem and my proposed treatment. I present a model for understanding ADHD so that the parents will understand what the disability is and why specific treatments are recommended. This model for understanding ADHD will be reviewed later in this chapter. If the child or adolescent also has a learning disability, I explain this disability using the input-integration-memory-output model explained in Chapter 6. During this session, I try to integrate the results of all previous evaluations into my findings.

If I believe there are emotional, social, and/or family problems, I discuss each and explain whether I see these difficulties as primary and a cause of the academic difficulties or as secondary and a consequence of the ADHD and possible other problems. At the end of this interpretive session, I summarize the necessary multimodal treatment plans, who will do each part of the plan, and my specific role as part of the treatment team or as coordinator of this team.

My second session in this educational process is with the child or adolescent. I review the same materials I did with the parents. If I feel the parents can explain this information to the child or adolescent, I let them decide if they will provide this education or if they would like me to do so. To me, the only difference between explaining ADHD to a five-year-old, a ten-year-old, or a fifteen-year-old is the vocabulary used and my style of communicating. To help her or him understand, I try to use material from my diagnostic sessions. For example, I might say, "Do you remember that you told me that when you tried to do homework, it had to be quiet or you could not pay attention? Well, the problem is that it is hard for you to block out unimportant sounds. This is called auditory distractibility." I try to use similar examples to explain hyperactivity or impulsivity.

At the end of this session I emphasize again these children's strengths. They are not dumb or bad. I stress that now that we know why they are having difficulties in school and with their family and peers, we can do many things to make their life better and more successful. This last theme is critical. It is not acceptable to tell someone—a child or an adolescent or a parent—what the problems are without following with what will be done to address and help these problems.

If needed or requested, my third meeting might be with the full family. In addition to the brothers and sisters, I encourage other significant adults to attend. If a grandparent believes that there is nothing wrong with the grandchild and that the only problem is that mother is not strict enough, this grandparent needs to be educated. If a caregiver is part of the family, she or he might need to learn. At this session, I review again my findings and treatment recommendations. This time, though, I try to get the child or adolescent to help me. "Mary, I am not sure that I am doing a good job of explaining the problem to your brother. Can you think of an example that might help?" My intent is to educate each member of the family and to begin to change the role this child or adolescent has had in the family. He or she is not lazy, dumb, or bad. There are reasons for his or her behaviors and difficulties, and something can be done to help. It is important, also, to support parents and siblings. Some of the behaviors that they have had to put up with should not be permitted to continue. They, too, have rights in the family. During this session, it is often possible to clarify what family issues might need to be worked on.

This individual, parent, and family education process is critical to implementing the treatment efforts. Everyone needs to understand the diagnosis and treatment plan and be given a chance to ask questions. I believe that the knowledge base built in this session will be valuable throughout the treatment process. Since ADHD may be a chronic disorder, this initial knowledge base can be built on over the years as new developmental challenges are faced.

## Educating the Teacher and
## School Professionals

It is important that the child's or adolescent's teacher understand and accept the clinical findings. The classroom teacher will need to understand ADHD and what accommodations might be needed. If the student needs medication, this teacher will need to know what behaviors might change as well as what side effects to look for. If a learning disability is suspected, the appropriate school professionals will be needed to do the necessary psycho-educational testing to clarify if this clinical impression is correct. If it is, appropriate services and accommodations will be needed.

In Chapter 19 I will provide you with information on education laws and your rights within these laws. I will also review relevant civil laws of importance. The specific procedures to use in seeking and obtaining the necessary services for your son or daughter will also be discussed.

## Understanding the Use of Medication

The medications discussed in this book should not be used unless the diagnosis is ADHD. It is important to understand that ADHD is not a school-based disorder but a pervasive disorder that affects not only time in school but also time with the family and peers, and during sports and other activities. The clinician must understand this. Parents must understand this. This concept of helping the total child or adolescent during all of his or her life is essential. Let me emphasize this point:

1. *Remember: ADHD is not just a school disability; it is a life disability.* The brain does not know the difference between 9:00 A.M. and 6:00 P.M., nor the difference between Monday and Saturday, November and August, school days and holidays or vacations. If the clinician only treats the child's ADHD from 8:00 A.M. until 3:00 P.M. on school days, this child may do better at school; however, he or she may continue to have difficulty within the family, doing homework, interacting with peers, or participating in sports. This clini-

cian and parents must understand the need for medication during all hours of each day and use medication for each period of time when the hyperactivity, distractibility, and/or impulsivity might interfere with the individual's possibility of success.

2. *ADHD may persist beyond puberty, even into adulthood.* About 50 percent of children with ADHD will improve by puberty; however, 50 percent will continue to have ADHD as adults. There is nothing magical about puberty. If the individual continues to have ADHD, he or she will continue to need treatment.

It is important that parents understand the neurological bases for ADHD and the need for medication. It is equally important for the child or adolescent to understand. I know that parents will be concerned or fearful of medication. Some worry that they will be "drugging," "sedating," or "tranquilizing" their child. It is important to understand that the medications used do not drug, sedate, or tranquilize the individual. These medications correct an underlying neurochemical deficiency and allow the individual to function "normally."

The professional literature on ADHD has been in reasonable agreement on ADHD, its cause and treatment. Parent concerns and fears are often based on information found in popular magazines, on television talk shows, or on the Internet. A recent study by the Council on Scientific Affairs of the American Medical Association on the diagnosis and treatment of ADHD notes this contrast. Debate within the research and medical communities on ADHD has been mild and primarily focused on subtle nuances in the diagnostic and treatment approaches. By contrast, highly inflammatory public relations campaigns and pitched legal battles have been waged in the print and electronic media.

I try to remind parents of the source of their concerns. Did they read or hear it on the radio or television? Did they find it on a personal web page on the Internet? Did they read it in a newspaper article citing a nonprofessional? Or did they read it in a professional, edited, and monitored reference? Do not let misinformation interfere with your son or daughter receiving appropriate help.

## A Model for Understanding ADHD and the
## Rationale for the Need for Medication

Let me describe how I explain ADHD and the role of medication
to parents and to their child or adolescent. The descriptions I use
are based on research findings. I do simplify some of the concepts
to illustrate what could be a complex issue in a way that can be
understood by nonprofessionals. Yet, I believe that I am providing the best current information on ADHD and its treatment.
The model used may seem simple; yet it is complex, and it is an
accurate reflection of what is known.

In this model, I review what research strongly supports about
our understanding of ADHD. I find it best to present this model
as if I were sitting in an office with you, describing your son or
daughter. I start by explaining that your child or adolescent is hyperactive, inattentive, distractible, and/or impulsive (depending
on the specific clinical problems present.) Let me continue as if I
were talking to you.

First, let's discuss hyperactivity. As you know, we are referring
to the fidgety, restless behavior. What causes this hyperactivity?
There is an area in the brain that stimulates muscle activity. It is
in the thinking part of the brain, or the cortex. I call this area the
"accelerator." There are other areas in the lower parts of the
brain that decide how much of these messages will get through to
the muscles. I call these areas the "brakes." Normally, there is a
balance between the accelerator and the brakes, with the brakes
appearing to be the controlling factor. Children and adolescents
with hyperactivity due to ADHD have a brake that is not working effectively. Thus, the accelerator is not as controlled, and the
individual has an increased amount of muscle (motor) behavior. I
will come back to the brake and why it is not working effectively.

Then there is distractibility. This distractibility makes it difficult for the individual to filter out unimportant stimuli in the environment and/or to filter out his or her own thoughts so that
only one thing can be focused on. The result is difficulty sustaining attention and a resulting short attention span. Our brain has
a series of "filter systems" that screen out unimportant stimuli or
thoughts, allowing the person to focus on what is important. In

this way, the cortex is not cluttered with too many stimuli and can maintain focus on what is important. In ADHD, the filter systems are not working effectively. Depending on which systems are ineffective, the individual will experience auditory distractibility, visual distractibility, and/or internal distractibility. I will explain why the filter systems are not working effectively in a moment.

Finally, there is impulsivity, the inability to stop and think before talking or acting. We know less about this behavior. It appears that our brain operates somewhat like a computer. Information is entered through a "keyboard," then relayed to many areas of the brain for a rapid assessment of options. Then, the appropriate decision is relayed through the keyboard leading to actions. For some, this keyboard is not working effectively. Thus, thoughts and ideas come in and decisions go back out without the brief fraction of a second of reflection needed. The result is impulsive behavior.

If I may continue to use these symbols, the braking system, filter system, and keyboard appear to be in a similar area of the brain. What they have in common is that each uses the same chemical to transmit messages from one nerve ending to another—the same neurotransmitter. We believe this neurotransmitter to be norepinephrine, although it might be one of its precursors, either dopa or dopamine. Individuals with ADHD appear not to produce enough of this neurotransmitter in these areas of the brain. Thus, the systems that use this neurotransmitter cannot work effectively. If the brake is not working effectively, one is hyperactive. If the filter systems are not able to screen appropriately, one is distractible. If the keyboard is not operating as it should, one is impulsive. Thus, depending on which areas of the brain are involved, the individual will be hyperactive and/or distractible and/or impulsive.

What was first learned in 1937 is better understood now. Certain medications can affect these areas of the brain and increase the amount of this neurotransmitter. Once the level is raised to the normal level, the brakes begin to operate effectively and the individual becomes less hyperactive and calmer, the filter systems begin to operate effectively and the individual becomes less distractible with an increased attention span, and the keyboard begins to operate effectively and the individual becomes less impulsive and more reflective. It is clear, therefore, that these medications do not drug, sedate, or tranquilize individuals. These medications simply correct an underlying neurochemical deficiency, allowing the individual to function "normally." The effect is analogous to diabetes. When a diabetic is given insulin, a chemical deficiency is corrected and he or she can function normally. This medication does not cure the diabetes; when it is metabolized, the person returns to difficulty regulating sugar. When the medications used to treat ADHD are metabolized, the person returns to being hyperactive, distractible, and/or impulsive.

The way I describe the research findings that help us understand ADHD may appear to be too symbolic to be correct. I am using poetic license with anatomy and physiology. But most parents have not gone through medical school, and these symbols and descriptions help them to understand their son or daughter. Once these terms have been introduced, they can be used during the treatment phase. For example, "He is still more fidgety than he should be. We may need more medication to get the brakes working better." This information also helps parents understand that the use of medication is not to drug their son or daughter so that others can live with him or her. The medications help this child or adolescent function normally so that she or he can be successful within the family, at school, and with friends. Parents have no reason to feel guilty because they placed their child on medication.

Now that you understand that ADHD is a neurochemical disorder, you can appreciate that it exists all of the time. To have your child or adolescent on medication only during school hours and school days may make no sense. Yes, the school is delighted with the change, but you and your family and the kids in the neighborhood have to live with the ADHD behaviors and the unfinished homework.

## In Summary

Education of the child or adolescent, the parents, and the family is a critical part of addressing the treatment of ADHD. Often, this educational process is all that is needed to help the child or adolescent and her or his family move ahead with the multi-modal treatment approaches. Sometimes, more is needed. Either the individual, a parent, the couple, or the family is in need of counseling or other forms of intervention. The next chapter discusses these more intensive approaches for helping.

# 13

## Individual, Parent, Couple, and Family Therapy

The educational efforts described in Chapter 12 often result in emotional and behavioral changes for everyone and an improvement in the behavior of the child or adolescent with ADHD. Parents begin to be assertive advocates for their son or daughter, resulting in more appropriate programs within the school system. They begin to understand their child or adolescent and begin to modify their parenting behaviors to better meet the needs of this family member.

If, after these educational efforts, you and your clinician decide that you, your child or adolescent, or your family needs further help, specific therapeutic interventions may be necessary. Behavioral management techniques might help address specific problems. One parent or both parents might need help with their emotional difficulties in working through their resistance or struggles with the reality of ADHD. Both parents might feel the need for help in developing more effective parenting approaches or in agreeing to a consistent behavioral management program. The child or adolescent might need help in addressing his or her emotional or behavioral difficulties or with the denial or noncompliance with the different therapeutic approaches used.

It might be necessary for parents to enter couples therapy, for the child or adolescent to enter a form of therapy, or for the family to start in family therapy. It is important to delay such decisions until this point in the process so that you and your clinician can assess if the problems have been improved or resolved through the educational process or the initial counseling efforts, along with the use of appropriate medications.

Whichever form of clinical intervention is started, it is essential that the professional providing this help be aware of the impact that ADHD and any associated disorders might have on the child or adolescent with this disorder as well as on other family members. It is equally important to understand how ADHD might affect the treatment process.

## Helping the Child or Adolescent

Often the ADHD is not picked up until age eight or ten, sometimes not until early adolescence. The years of frustration, poor school performance, negative interactions, and behavioral difficulties experienced before diagnosis and treatment contribute to a child's poor self-image, low self-esteem, lack of peer acceptance and success, conflicts with family, and possibly academic failure. Until the reason or reasons for these problems were understood, the child or adolescent might have been told he or she was not sitting still, not paying attention, calling out in class, not completing work or disrupting the class because he or she wanted to be this way. All it took was a willingness to change. All was under his or her control.

Once the ADHD is diagnosed and treated, most individuals blossom. Their behaviors improve. Their school performance improves. They seem happy. Yet, for others, the damage done prior to the diagnosis remains. All of the emotional and behavioral problems persist. Psychological help is needed to undo what has been done.

If this individual has learning disabilities, they must be addressed. Progress may not be noticed until the child or adolescent benefits from remedial interventions or develops strategies to compensate for their disabilities. This takes time. Then the student needs to learn what he or she missed over the years before these disabilities were recognized. The student with ADHD might not have learning disabilities. However, he or she may not have been available for learning for years prior to the diagnosis of ADHD. This student will need special educational interventions to help fill in the gaps of knowledge.

The treatment approaches are similar to those used with children or adolescents with emotional or behavioral problems. However, the constant focus is on educating the child or adolescent about ADHD and the impact these behaviors have had. This individual must develop both understanding and compensatory strategies for handling his or her hyperactivity, distractibility, and/or impulsivity. He or she must rethink his or her self-image and build confidence and self-esteem.

It is important to think through with the clinician working with your son or daughter the type of help needed. Individual psychotherapy might be helpful for the children or adolescents ready to understand and learn about themselves. For the student who externalizes the emotional stress and pain, starting with the parents or family might be more helpful. Once this student is ready to accept ownership for his or her problems, individual efforts might be added.

If the child or adolescent with ADHD has poor social skills and limited success with peers, social skills training might be helpful. Social skills needed for social competence include physical factors (such as eye contact and posture), social responsivity (such as sharing), and interactional skills (such as initiating and maintaining conversation). In addition, as described in Chapter 9, some children and adolescents with ADHD do not appear to be able to read social cues such as the look on the face, the tone of voice, or body language. Before a child or adolescent starts in a social skills group, it is important to identify the individual's areas of social incompetence and the specific skills that appear to be missing.

There are many programs described in the literature for doing social skills groups. As I've said, they generally focus on a series of steps. The first step involves helping the child or adolescent develop a sensitivity for his or her social problems. This step is critical. Because of their impulsivity and inattention, some children with ADHD have only limited awareness of their socialization difficulties and may deny having them or project the source of their problems onto others. It is always someone else's fault. Or they might not be aware that they are missing visual or auditory clues that their behaviors are bothering others. Some interrupt or say the wrong things because they don't stop to think before they talk. Some speak too loudly or misjudge space and get too close to others. They need to become aware of their behavior and how others react to it. Some group exercises focus on teaching the types of social skills most seem to develop naturally. Through pictures or role playing, participants learn body language signals or what voice changes mean. They learn the concept of distance and personal space.

The second step involves having the child or adolescent generate alternative solutions for the identified problems. Here, the group therapist and the other group members can help. How else might you handle a situation? What else could you do? Have you thought about . . . ?

The third step involves helping the child or adolescent step by step through the process of learning the newly identified solution to the problem. Role playing and practice are important ways of learning these new solutions: "Let's practice asking a friend to a movie." The individual learns and practices in the group until both awareness of the problem and the ability to try different solutions become more routine.

The final step is to help the child or adolescent link the new knowledge to past events and difficulties as well as to future events. He or she is encouraged to try out the new social skills and techniques in situations outside of the group and to report on the outcome. What worked? What didn't? What can you learn from what didn't work? What might you try next?

## Helping Parents

The problems of children and adolescents with ADHD go beyond hyperactivity, distractibility, and impulsivity. These family members might be aggressive, oppositional, negative, or disruptive within the family. They might be anxious or depressed. They might be doing poorly in school or have no or limited peer relationships. They might be unsuccessful in any sport efforts. For many, medication will minimize or control these behaviors. It isn't difficult to see why a parent might feel overwhelmed and helpless. It also isn't difficult to see how such chronic stress can affect the couple's ability to agree on how to parent and how to manage these behaviors. This constant stress, year after year, can strain or overwhelm the marital relationship as well.

An individual parent might need help with his or her own feelings of inadequacy and failure as a parent. He or she might be depressed or might be made to feel so helpless that anger becomes the only response. The two parents might feel overwhelmed as a parenting team. They might disagree on behavioral strategies, and the child or adolescent with ADHD may succeed in splitting them or causing fighting between them. One parent might relinquish his or her role by becoming passive or by minimizing time spent at home. The other parent, already overwhelmed, now has all of the parenting responsibilities. Often, the parent who elects not to parent starts to blame all problems on the way the other parent handles situations.

If there had not been stress in the marriage, it might develop. If there had already been marital stress, parenting this child or adolescent might lead to a major crisis. The rate of separation and divorce in families with ADHD is high.

Add to all of this the possibility that the mother or father has ADHD as well. His or her hyperactivity, distractibility, and/or impulsivity create stress in the family as well. This parent might be relieved to learn of the problem and seek help. Or he or she might minimize the problems and refuse help. Or he or she might get angry at the child or adolescent with ADHD because he or she doesn't like the same behaviors in himself or herself.

Depending on the types of difficulties found with each parent, individual therapy for one, couples therapy relating to behavioral management approaches, or couples therapy relating to marital stress might be needed. Sometimes, all of the above are necessary.

## Helping the Family

Sometimes the family is under so much stress and is so dysfunctional that family therapy is needed before any educational or other therapeutic efforts can be considered. The early phases of this therapy might focus on giving the parents back the controls and on helping the child or adolescent with ADHD feel safe not being in control. Specific behavioral management approaches, such as those discussed in Chapter 15, must be started. Later, when the family is functioning better, other clinical interventions can be considered as the needs become clarified.

Family therapy can help change family members' perceptions and expectations of the child or adolescent with ADHD. Sibling conflicts can be addressed. The focus is often on changing unacceptable behaviors and on strengthening the positive relationships between family members. As siblings learn why the child with ADHD is the way he or she is and as they see positive changes within the family, they can become advocates for their brother or sister with ADHD at school, in the neighborhood, and with sports and activities. They can help with problems of peer teasing or rejection.

## In Summary

After the impact of individual and parent education and the use of appropriate medications are assessed, individual, parent, or family therapy may be necessary. It is essential to work closely with the school at each step of the interventions.

The specific approach used will depend on the need. It is important that one professional coordinate all efforts to be sure that each identified problem is addressed. Whatever form of individual, couples, family, or other therapy is used, it is important that the clinician understand the impact that ADHD and any of the associated disorders might have on the problems being addressed as well as on the model of therapy being used.

# 14

# Working with the School

Once the diagnosis of ADHD is established, it is important to work with your son's or daughter's classroom teacher(s) as well as with the school system. Your goal is to create the best classroom environment as well as to clarify what services or accommodations your child might need. I will start by discussing the classroom environment. Later, I will discuss broader issues relating to the school system.

## The Classroom and Classroom Teacher

Hopefully, the use of appropriate medication will minimize or stop your child's hyperactivity, distractibility, and/or impulsivity. If so, the classroom teacher needs to understand the medications, their schedule, how they work, what side effects might occur, how to observe the student's behaviors, and how to communicate with the clinician managing the medications. If the use of medication is less than successful, the classroom teacher will need to provide special efforts to help the student in the classroom.

The teacher and school nurse must be sensitive to the child's or adolescent's feelings. They must be taught not to call out in class, "Billy, it's time to take your pill," or, when Billy misbehaves, to scold, "Billy, did you take your pill this morning?" The school nurse must know not to use the school's loudspeaker system to page, "Will Billy please come to the Health Room to get his medication?" These examples might sound so insensitive that no educator or nurse would do them. However, I mention them because I have heard such examples more than many times.

I'll review general suggestions for the regular classroom teacher first. Then I'll review specific suggestions for specific problems.

## General Guidelines

There are four aspects of the regular classroom that should be addressed: establishing the best learning environment, giving instructions and assignments, modifying unacceptable behaviors, and enhancing self-esteem.

### Establishing the Best Learning Environment
The classroom should be modified to address the child's or adolescent's ADHD behaviors. Specific approaches will be discussed later in this chapter. In addition, the student should be surrounded with good role models, preferably students who will not get pulled into inappropriate behavior. The classroom should be as calm, quiet, and organized as is possible for the grade. The student will need additional structure and supervision during out-of-the-classroom time—in the hall, at lockers, at lunch, on field trips. All teachers should be informed of the child's special needs, including the art, music, and physical education teachers.

### Giving Instructions and Assignments
When giving instructions and assignments, the teacher should be sure to have the student's attention and to make the information clear and concise. There should be consistency with daily instructions and expectations. The teacher should be sure that the student understood the directions before beginning the task. If necessary, the teacher should repeat the instructions. The student should be made to feel comfortable when seeking help. A daily assignment notebook might be helpful.

### Modifying Unacceptable Behaviors
Rules of the classroom should be clear and understood. If the student breaks a rule, the teacher should remain calm, state the

infraction, and avoid debating or arguing with the student. It is helpful to have preestablished responses or consequences for inappropriate behaviors. The consequences should be presented quickly and consistently. It is important that the teacher avoid ridicule and criticism.

### Enhancing Self-esteem

Building or rebuilding self-esteem is important. The teacher should reward the student more than punish. Any and all good behavior and performances should be praised immediately, and emphasis should be on encouraging the student. If the child or adolescent has difficulty, it is important that the teacher find a way of reestablishing contact and trust so that new solutions can be found and tried.

## Specific Guidelines

If the student remains hyperactive, distractible, and/or impulsive, each of these behaviors must be addressed. It is important to plan individually for each student and for his or her specific problem areas. The classroom teacher should try these accommodations. If these approaches do not work, it may be necessary to reconsider if the student can be best handled in a regular classroom setting.

### Hyperactivity

The goal is to channel the student's excessive energy into acceptable activities. If possible, this student might be permitted to stand up or walk around the room as he or she works. More breaks might be useful. These breaks might be blended into specific tasks such as taking messages to the office, delivering something to another classroom, or getting something for the teacher. If the child or adolescent sits and fidgets by tapping a pencil or fingers or by playing with paper clips or other objects, the teacher might try to work out a hand signal. For example, he or she might place a hand on the student's desk to get the student's attention, then use one hand to tap the other. The student knows this signal means that he or she is fidgeting and should stop. No one else in the class needs to know of the interaction.

### Distractibility

Tasks might be shortened by breaking one task into smaller parts to be completed at different times. Fewer assignments might be given. Homework assignments might be briefer also. The teacher might have the student work with other students and try to increase the interest and novelty of the tasks.

If the student is distracted by sounds, he or she might sit in the quietest area of the class, away from windows, doors, or air conditioners. It might be best to have this student sit next to the teacher's desk. The teacher might work out a hand signal to point out that he or she has been distracted. Perhaps the teacher could place a hand on the desk to get the student's attention, then touch an ear. The student knows what this means and refocuses.

If the student is distracted by visual stimuli, it would be best to decrease such stimuli. He or she might sit in the front row. (For the student who is distracted by sounds, sitting in the front row might be a problem in that most sounds are now behind him or her.) Working in a corner or inside a cubicle might help. The other students would have to understand that being told to work in a corner, facing the wall, is not for punishment. The idea of hand signals might work. Here, the signal might be a hand on the desk and then touching an eye.

For the student who is distracted by his or her own thoughts, the best approach may be to have the desk next to the teacher. The teacher might assist in bringing the student back to task by getting his or her attention and then either whispering or using a hand signal (maybe touching the top of the head) to alert the student to get back on task.

### Impulsivity

Impulsivity is a difficult behavior to manage in the classroom. Efforts might be tried to help the student learn to wait. He or she might be given a piece of paper on the desk to write down what needs to be said or to doodle on until the teacher is free. The teacher might ask the student to hand him or her a note instead of interrupting, or wait on line for help. A reminder, such as a picture on the desk of a child with a finger over his or her lips, might help.

Sometimes the teacher can intervene after the student calls out or interrupts. If the student is receptive, a hand signal might be enough to remind the student that he or she just acted impulsively. The student might see the teacher turn toward him or her and place a finger over the his or her lips. The student might be able to say "I'm sorry" and wait.

## In Summary

Ideally, the student should be on the appropriate medication at the right dose so that she or he is not hyperactive, distractible, or impulsive. If this approach is not possible, the above classroom adaptations often will help. If, even with these efforts, the student is unavailable for learning or disruptive in the classroom, it is best if the classroom teacher and parents request a meeting with the other school professionals either to rethink the classroom placement or to consider what additional services might be provided the classroom teacher to help. Examples of such services would be a psychologist who could work out a behavioral management program or a counselor who might try group therapy.

## The School System

Ideally, the child or adolescent is on medication and the medication is working well. If the medication isn't helping, you might want to discuss this with your physician or seek consultation. If you do not have your son or daughter on medication, it will be necessary for the school to design a program to handle the child's hyperactivity, distractibility, and/or impulsivity.

The school system must address the following concerns:

1. If the student is on medication, the classroom teacher will need to understand the medication and its effects, any side effects, and what observations need to be communicated to the parents and to the physician.
2. If the student is not on medication or the medication is not effective in reducing the behaviors, the classroom teacher

and other professionals will need to develop strategies for handling these behaviors.

3. If the student also has learning disabilities, the school professionals will need to provide appropriate special education services and accommodations.

4. If the student does not have learning disabilities but has "gaps" in specific skill or knowledge areas because she or he was less available for learning prior to the diagnosis and treatment, remedial interventions might be needed to "fill in the gaps."

## School Guidelines and Procedures

The federal guidelines issued by the U.S. Department of Education for school systems to use when working with students who have ADHD reflect the tasks listed above. These guidelines state that there are two primary "decision factors" to use in planning the school program: (1) Is the child or adolescent successfully on medication or not? and (2) does the child or adolescent also have a learning disability?

Schools use two different sets of legal guidelines when addressing these federal guidelines. There are education laws and civil laws. The education law is the Individuals with Disabilities Education Act, or IDEA. The civil law refers to the Rehabilitation Act of 1973, especially to Section 504 of this act and to the more current Americans with Disabilities Act. Each of these important pieces of legislation will be discussed in detail in Chapter 19.

The regulations for IDEA clarify the criteria to be used to classify (or code) a student as having a disability. If a student is coded, appropriate services and accommodations must be provided in the least restrictive environment. The so-called Section 504 guidelines also clarify what criteria are used to identify an individual as having a disability. However, if so identified, only accommodations are necessary. If your son or daughter is coded under IDEA, he or she will get special education services and accommodations. If he or she is identified under Section 504 guidelines, only accommodations are provided. Thus, it is critical when possible to use the education law and have your son or daughter identified under IDEA rather than Section 504. Let me elaborate.

Under the guidelines of IDEA, there is no category for ADHD. Under federal regulations, there are three options for students who have ADHD:

1. If the student also has a learning disability, he or she can be coded as having a learning disability (and thus be eligible for both services and accommodations).
2. If the student has significant emotional problems that make him or her unavailable for learning or that so disrupt the classroom that others can not learn, he or she can be coded as being seriously emotionally disturbed (and thus be eligible for both services and accommodations).
3. If the student does not qualify as having a learning disability or is not seriously emotionally disturbed, he or she may be coded as "Other Health Impaired" (and thus be eligible for both services and accommodations).

If the school professionals do not feel that the student with ADHD meets one of these categories under IDEA, they can use Section 504 guidelines. Here the student will get only accommodations. He or she might get extended time while taking tests or other helpful adaptations. But there will be no specific interventions. The difficulty is often with the student who has ADHD and learning disabilities, but where the degree of discrepancy is not great enough to code the student as having a learning disability. She or he still needs services, but will not get them under Section 504.

## In Summary

It is important that parents work closely with the classroom teacher and with the school professionals who must develop the most appropriate school environment and program for the student with ADHD. To be informed and assertive advocates, you must understand both the needs of your son or daughter and his or her right to specific services or accommodations.

If you are not as successful with your child's or adolescent's teacher or with the school system, seek help from a parent advocate or from a parent support group. Information on support groups is listed in the appendix.

# 15

## How to Handle Unacceptable Family Behavior

I will teach you a model for assessing your child's behaviors within your family and for setting up your own behavioral program to change unacceptable behaviors. It should work. If it doesn't, you may need to seek help from a professional. Let me describe the types of problems, the models for clarifying what needs to be changed, the basic model for demanding change, and additional models that might be used along with the basic models.

These ideas are to be actively applied. If you read this section and say, "This is what I need," try it. Go step by step. If it doesn't work, rethink your strategy and try again. This approach will work with most children and adolescents. But, it takes time, effort, and commitment—from *both* parents.

Sometimes a parent calls me and describes a son or daughter who sounds like a tyrant. This child must have his or her way or all hell breaks loose with screaming, throwing things, hitting his or her sister or brother, messing up his or her room, etc. Later, I meet this "tyrant"—a four-foot seventy-pound little boy with a sweet smile who could be picked up and carried under one arm. Where is the monster?

Then I begin to work with the family, and I soon find out. This child's behavior does dominate the family. Too often the parents avoid confrontations because they don't want to face the consequences. They "look the other way" until pushed so far that they have to react. By that time, feeling helpless, the only possible reaction often is anger. They yell or hit. Or they give out a punishment like "no television for one week" and then have to back down because they have no way to enforce it or because enforcing it leads to more confrontations and fights.

As my evaluation progresses, I gain clues or clarify the dynamics within the child or within the family that explain the behaviors. More often, I cannot clarify the underlying issues but can see that something has to be done, and quickly. One has to "put out the fire" before an in-depth assessment can be considered. What is clear is that the child is in control and the parents are not in control or are equally out of control. What may also be clear is that parents disagree and, rather than supporting each other, they are split and fighting with each other. This situation in the family is anxiety-producing for the child and not compatible with healthy psychosocial development. It's also dysfunctional for the parents and for the other members of the family as well.

Perhaps I will find patterns. Without meaning to do so, the parents may be reinforcing the very behaviors they do not want. The child acts badly and gets a lot of attention—negative attention. The parents get upset and this proves to the child that she or he can control one part of the world—the family. This, along with getting what the child wants, is the reward for bad behavior. The other children see the parents forced to give in. They become angry. Soon, they may learn that the only way to get attention or to get what they want in this family is to be bad.

Whatever the dynamics or initial cause, the family dysfunction must be addressed first. Parents must regain control. The child or adolescent must feel that he or she can be controlled. These changes are essential for the parents, for the child or adolescent, and for the family. Such negative control of parents is unhealthy and unproductive for children. They must learn different behavioral patterns before they can apply them to the school, to peers, or to the community.

Once the behaviors are under better control, the child or adolescent can begin to learn new and better techniques for functioning within the family and coping with stress. Parents and children or adolescents can rework styles of interacting and roles within the family. First come the behavioral changes, then come awareness and insight.

Related to this goal is an important concern when the child or adolescent who has ADHD is impulsive. Behavioral programs do not work well with individuals who are impulsive. The goal of the program is to help this individual think before he or she acts. "If you do this behavior, you will have to spend time in your room." A person who is impulsive acts and then thinks. The consequences are remembered only after the act, so awareness of a consequence can't help the individual rethink a planned behavior. Children and adolescents with ADHD who are impulsive must be properly medicated before a behavioral program will be successful.

It is not uncommon to find that the same child or adolescent who is out of control at home is functioning very well in school, at friends' houses, or when playing with friends away from the house. Sunday school teachers, activity leaders, sports coaches, and other parents might think the child is great and a perfect lady or gentleman when around them. In this case, one might assume that the behavioral difficulties are not neurologically driven or they would occur in every setting. If the behaviors are only expressed at home, it is possible that they reflect family dynamics or conflict. It is also possible that the child or adolescent holds in all of his or her frustration and anger all day so as not to get into trouble. He or she comes home where it is safe to let out these feelings, and any little frustration leads to an explosion. As one child told me, "I can't act this way at school. The principal will suspend me. But my parents love me and will never get rid of me. So, I can get away with acting this way at home." Another possibility is that the child has ADHD and is on the appropriate medication and dose during the time he or she is out of the house. Thus, there are no behavioral problems. However, if the medication covers only school hours, this child is off medication when at home and the hyperactivity, distractibility, and/or impulsivity cause behavioral difficulties. Adding medication for evenings and weekends might lead to a significant improvement in the child's behaviors at home.

If the unacceptable behaviors occur only at home, a behavioral management program will be needed for the home and family. If these behaviors expand into the school, a similar program might be needed at school. If these behaviors also expand into after-school activities or settings, a behavioral program may be needed throughout the day.

## Basic Concepts of Behavioral Management

Any behavioral plan, to be successful, must be based on two basic concepts:

1. One is more likely to succeed in changing behavior by rewarding what is seen as desired behavior than by punishing what is seen as undesirable behavior.
2. For a plan to work, the responses to acceptable and to unacceptable behaviors must be consistent and must occur each time. Inconsistent response patterns may reinforce the negative behaviors.

As parents, you must learn that there is no right or wrong way to raise children. You must collaborate in developing a plan with which you both can be comfortable and can agree. Once decided upon, the plan must be practiced in a consistent and persistent way. No more splitting. No more parents disagreeing in front of the family about how best to handle misbehavior. The child or adolescent must get the same responses from both parents. This concept is harder to accomplish but must be the goal in divorced families when the children share two households.

Initially, it is important that you be omnipotent. No more reasoning, bargaining, bribing, threatening, or trying to provoke guilt or shame. Parents make the rules; parents enforce the rules; parents' decisions are final. "Life may not seem to be fair as you see it; but, this is what I expect." As parents, you must learn that if you "step into the arena" and agree to debate or argue with your child, you will lose. If a parent says it is time to go to sleep and the child says "But can I stay up fifteen minutes more?" the answer must be "I did not ask you what time you wanted to go to sleep. I said it is bedtime." Argue about the fifteen minutes and it will become twenty minutes, then thirty minutes. Soon, your frustration and anger will result in fighting. Later in the plan you can be flexible, but not initially.

## Developing the Initial Intervention Strategy

Initially, parents are usually overwhelmed. They have exhausted their choices of action, and none have worked. They may feel helpless and that they are failures as parents. If there are two parents in the family, there may be stress between the two, disagreeing on how to handle the behaviors or blaming the other for the problems. One, often the father, may feel so frustrated and unsuccessful that he finds ways of working later and later, coming home after the kids are in bed. Try to develop and follow the plan I suggest. If you are too worn out or overwhelmed or if the stress between parents is too great, seek professional help.

The first step is to collect data on your observations of the behaviors. Each parent should collect data separately. The differences between the two will be very useful. Don't be embarrassed by what you do. Record what really happens without worrying what someone will think. We already know that things aren't working well. Just record what you live so that you can begin to change things.

You will need a structure to collect this data. The easiest model to use is called an ABC chart. You record three things: A, the *antecedent* to the behavior (what happened right before it), B, the *behavior* observed, and C, the *consequences* of the behavior. The chart will look like this:

| Date/Time | Antecedent | Behavior | Consequence |
|-----------|------------|----------|-------------|

An example of an ABC chart might read like "Billy's Chart," shown here.

### BILLY'S CHART

| Date/Time | Antecedent | Behavior | Consequence |
|-----------|------------|----------|-------------|
| Monday 4:30 P.M. | Don't know; not there. | He hit sister; she hit back. | Told both to go to room. |

| 6:00 P.M. | Talking to sister. | He teased her; she cried. | Yelled at Billy. |
| 9:00 P.M. | Told him to get ready for bed. | Refused to take bath, get in PJs; yelled at me when told. | Took 30 min. of reminding finally hit him and he went to take his bath. |

Each parent may have different lists. In part this reflects when each is home and with the child or adolescent. One may be the firm disciplinarian and the other the easygoing, "give them another chance" type. Each parent will see and list different things. Each has different experiences and expectations. Possibly the father comes home at 6:30 P.M. looking forward to being with the children and playing with them. Frustrated and short of temper, the mother may have had it by then and wants the kids to be quiet and to get their homework and other chores done so that they can go to bed.

Neither parent is right or wrong. The important goal is that both parents agree on their expectations and be consistent in asking that they be met. Consistency is the key. Inconsistency reinforces the bad behavior; consistency lessens or stops the bad behavior.

Certain patterns should become clear for each column and for overall behaviors. Certain antecedents lead to certain behaviors. The consequences that follow the same behaviors are inconsistent. Or one parent gets mad and yells at everything or other family members seem to get punished as much as the child who caused the problems. A common theme may be that when a child or adolescent does not get what he or she wants or is asked to do something he or she does not want to do, this child or adolescent misbehaves.

Once the data is collected, analyze it. Look for patterns. The first task is to clearly define the unacceptable behaviors that need to be changed. Often, parents start with a long list of behaviors. Once the data is studied, the behaviors can be clustered into two or three major areas. By doing this, you will not be as overwhelmed. You are not dealing with an impossible list of problems, but can focus on a few major areas.

Frequently, the unacceptable behaviors fall into one of three basic groups. Try to see if items in your list can be placed into one of these groups.

*Physical abuse:*  This includes hitting, threatening to hit, breaking something, or threatening to break something. Thus, hurting a pet or damaging property would be physical abuse.

*Verbal abuse:*  This includes any words, tone of voice, or sounds you wish to identify as verbal abuse. Yelling, cursing, teasing, taunting could be included. At any time a parent can include something as verbal abuse by saying, "The next time you do that behavior I will call it verbal abuse."

*Noncompliance:*  This includes not completing a required or requested chore, not listening to what is said, or refusing to do what a parent requests. Often, three warnings are given. Following the third, action is taken. "If I have to ask you to hang up your coat again, it will be for the third time and the consequence for noncompliance will be given."

Once the bad behaviors are identified, it is useful to study the relationship between the antecedents and the behaviors. Look for themes. Often, the behaviors are more likely to occur if the child is tired, hungry, or about to be sick. Perhaps they're more likely to occur during the first hour after coming home from school, or during times of transition, whether leaving the house or returning to the house. Typically, these behaviors are more likely to occur if routines are disrupted or planned activities have to be changed, or when he or she is off medication or the medication is wearing off, or if he or she does not get what is demanded or is asked to do something he or she does not want to do. You might find that the behaviors relate to your child's learning disabilities or sensory integration disorder. Maybe you gave too many instructions at once. Maybe the chore is too difficult. Maybe he or she is frustrated with homework or wants to avoid doing homework because he or she doesn't understand it or it's too hard.

These themes might lead to possible interventions. These

themes also will make parents more sensitive to the times or situations when problems are most likely to occur. Try to identify these themes and think of how this information can be helpful in both understanding and addressing the problem behaviors.

Finally, study the pattern of consequences. Are you consistent? Do you use consequences and later give in and not carry them out? Do you use consequences you cannot enforce; thus, you have to back down?

## Setting Up the Initial Program

Once you have a clearer idea of the behaviors that need to be changed, you can develop a plan. Define the behaviors as clearly as possible, and work out a consequence that can be consistently imposed and that is compatible with your family's philosophy and values. Work out the plan in great detail; then introduce it to the family. The plan should be for all siblings. Even if the other children or adolescents do not cause problems, it will not affect them negatively to be part of the program. It might benefit them by rewarding them for their good behavior. It might have been that the "bad" child took so much attention that the "good" child was ignored or not thanked for being good. This plan will help you remember to reward each child for being good. If a sibling is provoking or encouraging the negative behavior, it will become clear if he or she also is on the plan.

As parents, you need to understand that there are several basic principles to reverse the pattern of punishing bad behavior and ignoring or inconsistently rewarding good or positive behavior. This plan will reward positive behaviors and withhold rewards for negative behaviors. Furthermore, you will have preplanned responses that can be used every time. Your child or adolescent cannot catch you off guard, making you feel helpless and therefore angry. Each time a behavior occurs, there will be the same response from either parent.

Let me illustrate this point about consistency. Suppose a boy hits his sister five times in a week. On one occasion the mother was in such a rush she yelled at him but did nothing about the hitting. On another occasion she was tired and didn't want to deal with him so she pretended she didn't see what happened. On the other three occasions, she did punish him by making him go to his room. If this child gives up hitting his sister because his mother tells him to, he has to give up hitting her 100 percent of the time. If he continues to hit her, he has a 40 percent chance of getting away with it. He is only punished three out of five times. He would be a fool to give up this behavior! If a parent is consistent, the behaviors will decrease, then stop. If the parent is anything less than consistent, the behavior might persist or get worse.

## Step One

Divide the day into parts. For example, on a typical school day there will be three parts: (1) from the time the child or adolescent gets up until he or she leaves for school, (2) from the time he or she returns from school until the end of the evening meal, and (3) from the end of this meal until bedtime. Weekend, holiday, or summer days can be divided into four parts by using meals as the dividers: (1) from the time he or she wakes up until the end of breakfast, (2) from the end of breakfast to the end of lunch, (3) from the end of lunch to the end of dinner, and (4) from the end of dinner until bedtime.

## Step Two

Make a list of the child's or adolescent's unacceptable behaviors. This list should be brief and limited to the major problems. If the basic three noted earlier are used, a list might read:

1. No physical abuse (define in detail for the child; for example, no hitting brother, pulling cat's tail, kicking mother, breaking toys).
2. No verbal abuse (define in detail for the child; for example, no cursing, calling someone stupid, teasing).
3. No noncompliance (define in detail for the child; for example, refusing to do what you are told to do). For younger children, the term *not listening* might be used. Make it clear that you will request several times. Then you will say, "If I

have to ask you again, I will call it noncompliance." Any behavior that continues after this warning is considered noncompliance. In this way, the child or adolescent can never say "But you never told me I had to do this."

## Step Three

The purpose of the plan is to reward positive behaviors. Negative behaviors are not mentioned as such. The child or adolescent can earn one point for each behavior he or she *does not do* during a unit of time. Later in the chapter we will discuss "time out." With time out, too, the focus is on the positive and not the negative. The wording is important. The parent says, "What you did is so unacceptable in this family that you must go to your room and think about the need to change what you do." The parent does not say "Go to your room!" with the connotation that doing so is punishment.

The child can earn points by not doing the unacceptable behaviors. He or she can earn one point for not doing each negative behavior during a unit of time. For example, suppose a boy gets up in the morning, does all of his chores, and gets to breakfast on time. He does not hit anyone, but he does call his sister "stupid." As he leaves for school the parent would say "I am pleased that you earned two points this morning. You followed all rules, and you didn't hit anyone. I wish I could have given you the third point; but you did call your sister a name, and that is verbal abuse." This parent might say to the sister "I am happy that you earned all three of your points. Thank you for not calling your brother a name when he called you one." Remember, behavior is changed by rewarding what you want and not by punishing what you do not want.

Record the points given in a book or chart. If the child is too young to understand points, use a calendar or chart and paste stars on it. For some, a more concrete approach would be to have a jar and fill it with marbles to represent each point earned.

Handle each part of the day in the same way. In the model designed above with three units of time on school days and four units of time on the weekend, the maximum number of points that can be earned on a school day is 9 and the maximum each weekend day is 12. The maximum total for a week will be 69 points. These points can be used in three ways:

A daily reward
A weekly reward
A special reward

Count the points daily, then weekly or accumulatively. The child or adolescent should participate in developing the rewards for meeting predetermined point totals. Parents make the final decisions, but suggestions are welcome. If the child or adolescent says "This is stupid. I won't participate," the parent replies "The plan starts tomorrow. Either you suggest what you might like to work toward, or I will make the decisions for you."

Each reward must be individualized for each member of the family and must be compatible with the family's style of child-rearing and philosophy. I would encourage rewards that involve interpersonal experiences rather than material reward. The daily reward could be an additional half hour of television time with a parent or being able to stay up thirty minutes later to read a book or play a game with a parent, or thirty minutes of special time with one parent. For example, let's say that a child is expected to be in his or her room by 8:30 P.M. with lights out by 9:00 P.M. Normally, the half hour in the room is spent with quiet activities like talking or reading together. If this child earns the daily reward, he or she could stay up until 9:30 P.M. and have an extra half hour with a parent. However, if he or she did not earn the daily reward, this child must be in the room by 8:00 P.M. and lights out is 8:30 P.M. He or she loses a half hour of time with the family.

Again, we are trying to reverse the pattern of rewarding unacceptable behavior by having to spend time with the child or adolescent when this occurs at a cost to other members of the family. Often less time or no time is spent when he or she acts appropriately. Now, if he or she acts appropriately there is special time together. If he or she acts inappropriately, there is less time with the family.

The weekly reward might be going to a movie or out to eat with the family, or having a friend sleep over, or any other special activity. If possible, decide on the activity earlier in the week. "On

Sunday, the family is going to the park to play and then have a picnic." Points are counted from Saturday morning to Friday night; thus, you know if the child or adolescent has enough points before the weekend starts. In this way, if your child doesn't accumulate enough points, a sitter can be lined up or other arrangements can be made before any family activity begins. In the past, your son or daughter might have been impossible all week, yet he or she would still get to go out with the family on the weekend. His or her behavior might even spoil the fun of this weekend activity. Now, this child or adolescent stays home and misses time with the family while those members of the family who earned their points get to spend positive time with the family.

A special reward might be something important that must be worked toward. A new bicycle, a special toy, or a special trip should be planned so that at least a month or more will be needed to accumulate enough points for this reward.

For the daily and weekly rewards, set a goal initially of earning 80 percent of the maximum number of points possible. After several months of success, this goal might be increased to 90 percent. It is best not to set the goal at 100 percent. No one can be perfect all of the time. Any negative behavior early in the day or week could destroy all hope of a reward, and the child or adolescent might give up.

For the plan described earlier, the child or adolescent would need 7 points each weekday evening to get the reward (80 percent of 9 points). He or she would need 55 points by Friday night for the weekend reward (80 percent of 69 points).

## Time Out

Before starting the plan, define which behaviors will be considered so unacceptable to the family that they will result in the child's not only not earning a point but also being removed from the family for a period of time so that he or she can think about the need to change this behavior. I always include physical abuse as "so unacceptable that you must spend time in your room thinking about the need to change." You could consider using time out only for these behaviors.

You might start by saying that this time can be spent in a different part of the house than the rest of the family is in as long as the child is quiet and stays isolated. If you feel a need to do so, you can pick a guest room or the laundry room. If he or she cannot handle this location, the child might have to be in his or her room. If he or she cannot stay in his or her room with the door open, the door will be shut. You might be concerned that your child's room is full of fun distractions and that he or she will not sit quietly and think. That is okay. The main theme is that your child loses precious time with the family. While he or she is in his or her room, the rest of the family is interacting.

This time out should be spent quietly thinking about what happened and why he or she needs to change the misbehavior. Quiet time means quiet time. Set a timer for the predetermined length of the time out. If he or she calls out or yells, reset the timer. If he or she comes out, send the child back and reset the timer. (Later I will discuss what to do if you cannot get your child or adolescent to go into the room or to stay in the room.)

It is important that this time to think not be too short. Except for young children, a few minutes have little meaning. For children over eight, I often suggest thirty minutes. For adolescents, I suggest one hour. If they will not be quiet or stay in the room, the initial thirty minutes might turn into hours.

Time out can be used out of the home as well. Try to plan ahead. "We are going to Aunt Sara's house. I spoke to her, and she told me that if you need a time-out room to think about your behavior while we are at her house, you can use the guest room." If you're out at a restaurant, ask that he or she sit in the waiting area at the front of the restaurant. If you're at a shopping mall, place the child or adolescent on a bench and say you will return at a certain time, keeping him or her within sight. There will be times when you cannot use time out immediately, for example, in the car. As soon as you return home, the child or adolescent is expected to go to the time-out site for the time assigned.

For the plan to work, it must be exact as to expectations, behaviors that are rewarded, and consequences. Once initiated, I can promise you that your son or daughter will find loopholes in the plan. That's okay. You and your spouse should put your heads together and find a way to close the loophole. You are in control, not the child.

## Dealing with Resistance

It is important to solve issues that prevent this plan from being implemented prior to starting it The most common problem is having a son or daughter who will not go to his or her room for time out or will not stay in the room. You don't want to have to chase this son or daughter around the house or table. You don't want to have to drag this person to the room, often fighting all of the way. You don't want to have to hold the door shut as he or she bangs and tries to open the door. You must find a solution to this problem and be prepared to implement it. If you find that there really is no way that you can control your son or daughter, you will need professional help.

My plan for addressing this situation only requires the cooperation of one person, the parent. This plan has two parts to it. Discuss the plan before you implement the full program and use it whenever the child or adolescent refuses to go to his or her room or stay there.

First, announce how much time is acceptable for the child or adolescent to get to his or her room. "I will give you three minutes to get to your room so that you can begin to think about the need to change." The son or daughter is informed that every minute it takes to get to his or her room after this announced time will be doubled and added to the original time. If the original time is thirty minutes and it takes the child thirty minutes to give in and go to the room, he or she now must spend ninety minutes in the room.

The second part of the plan may sound difficult, but it is not. The parent announces that he or she will always love this son or daughter. Love is unconditional. However, during the time that this child or adolescent chooses to abuse the parent by not listening to the parent, he or she chooses not to parent the child. The parent does not take away love but takes away being a parent. The message is clear. If you abuse me as a parent, I do not choose to parent you. What does this mean? You don't talk to your child or interact in any way. When mealtime comes, set a place for everyone in the family but this person. If he or she wants to eat, he or she can make his or her own meal and sit somewhere else.

If you were supposed to car pool to a meeting or sports practice or game, it will not be done. The child or adolescent will have to face the consequences of not attending. You will not write an excuse. If the behavior persists until bedtime, do not respond to your child nor put him or her to bed. When it is time for you to go to sleep, turn out the lights and go to your bedroom. Your child will be left in the dark and alone. Once your son or daughter goes to his or her room to spend the quiet time, parenting starts again.

Suppose your son or daughter would run outside if told to go to his or her room. Then the plan must include informing this child or adolescent that if he or she runs outside, you will not follow. The time it takes to come in and go to the room will be counted, doubled, and added to the original amount. If it gets dark, you will call the police and report a missing child. It is no fun hiding behind a bush as it gets dark and cold if no one is going to chase you.

Some parents find that the "I love you but if you abuse me as a parent I do not choose to parent you" approach too painful to consider. I remind this parent that allowing the unacceptable behaviors and teaching the child or adolescent that he or she is in control is more painful and potentially more harmful to the child in the long run than the model suggested.

If the child or adolescent will not stay in his or her room, you have a problem. It may be possible to put a lock on the door. (Buy a bathroom door set and put it in in reverse so that the lock is outside.) Should you need to lock the door, be sure to remain in the hall to listen in case it becomes necessary to come in. Your son or daughter may put up a real battle not to let you win. If locked in the bedroom, he or she might trash the room. The next day, while he or she is in school, take everything out but the mattress on the floor and place it in another room. Let your son or daughter earn back the furniture one piece at a time.

### Dealing with Loopholes

I have been teaching this model in various forms for thirty years. Thus, I can tell you that there are other frequent loopholes. With physical abuse, the child or adolescent does not earn a point and must go to his or her room for a given length of time. For any further such behaviors during the same time period, he or she will have to return to his or her room. But, what about verbal abuse? The first time it happens, he or she will not earn a point. What does the parent do for the remainder of the time in this time period if the child or adolescent is verbally abusive again? I suggest that for the second occurrence and for every other occurrence during the time period, he or she must have a time out. I usually use half of the time assigned for physical abuse. If the child is verbally abusive all the way to the room, by the time he or she reaches the room the time to be spent there might be four or five times longer than when you started the process.

What about noncompliance? You ask the child to do a chore, and he refuses. He doesn't earn the point for that time period. What then? He already didn't get the reward, so why should he listen to you? Do you now have to do the chore? Later in this chapter I will suggest strategies to use for noncompliance.

This reward-point system along with the time-out plan almost always works. The key is to be consistent. You must develop a plan that is feasible and then implement the plan. Your child or adolescent will test and test. But stick to it. No child or adolescent wants to give up being the boss of the family. It will take time, but the plan will almost always work. Once the external controls work and your son or daughter begins to have internal controls, everyone will be happier and less frustrated. Continue the plan even when you notice improvement. If you stop too soon, the bad behaviors will return. If the plan doesn't work or the child or adolescent sabotages every effort, seek professional help.

## Setting Up the Second Phase of the Plan

The first phase of intervention provided external controls. The goal of the second phase of intervention is to help the child or adolescent internalize the controls. Now, the effort shifts to helping build these controls into the behavioral patterns of this child or adolescent. The first phase continues; however, you now use a more interactive rather than omnipotent approach.

Once the unacceptable behaviors are under better control, introduce *reflective talking*. Initially, these discussions are held after the fact. The best time might be at night when the two of you are sitting on the bed and talking. A child or adolescent has been in a fight or a yelling match with you. He or she has spent time in his or her room. Later in the evening, you sit with your child in private and discuss what happened. For example, "You know, all day long at work I just could not wait to come home so that I could spend time with you. I feel so disappointed that your behavior resulted in your being in your room so that I could not spend that time with you. What else could you have done?" Or "I'm sorry you had so much trouble this afternoon. I love you, and I don't like being angry with your behavior or having to ask you to remove yourself from the family. What do you think we can do to stop such things from happening?"

Let your son or daughter talk. At first he or she may only make angry accusations of unfairness or of others causing the trouble and getting away with it. You might respond, "I don't know if your brother was teasing you before you hit him or not. I wasn't there. But, let's suppose that he did. What else could you have done? By hitting him, you got into trouble and he didn't. There must be a better way. Maybe you could have told me what you thought he was doing." Such conversations may have to occur many times as you try to get your son or daughter to accept responsibility for his or her behaviors and to think about the need to change. It is always important not only to point out the behavior but to offer alternative solutions.

Gradually, you will be able to point out themes, then suggestions. "You know, Mary, I notice that you are most likely to get into difficulty right after you come home from school. Do you suppose that you hold in all of your problems with the schoolwork or the kids until you get home so that you won't get into trouble at school? Then you let it out the first time you are upset at home. If so, maybe you and I can do something to help. Maybe as soon as you come in the house we can sit in the kitchen and have a snack. We can talk about your day, and you can tell me about the problems you've had. You may feel better and then won't have to let your unhappy feelings out at the family."

Soon you will be able to do the reflective thinking before the fact. "John, you and I both have learned that if you keep playing with your brother once the teasing starts, there will be a fight. Do you remember what we talked about? What else could you do? Isn't this a good time to try out that new idea?" Or "Juanita, you are forcing me to be a police officer and to yell at you or punish you. I do not like doing that. I'd rather enjoy being with you than yelling at you or punishing you. Why do you think you force me to be a police officer? Remember what we talked about the other night? Do you want to try some of the ideas we talked about? For example, why don't we both take a five-minute break to calm down and then try to talk about the problem." Gradually, the child or adolescent will begin to try the new behaviors.

He or she can learn from hearing parents openly discuss feelings and thoughts. Let the child understand how you feel—angry, sad, afraid, worried. You can model how to handle these feelings. "I am so angry with what you did that I cannot talk to you now. I am going into the other room to calm down. Later, we can talk." Not only will you feel more in control later, but you have demonstrated a way to handle angry feelings.

It is important for parents to begin to explain or model acceptable ways for their son or daughter to handle feelings. Many families are quick to tell their children how they may not act out in anger, sadness, or disappointment, but they do not teach them acceptable ways of showing these feelings. Anger is a normal feeling, and children and adolescents must learn how to handle it in an acceptable way in the family. Can they yell as long as they do not curse? Can they stamp their feet or slam the door shut as long as they do not break anything? Watch out for confusing messages. One parent in the family yells or throws things when angry. The other parent pouts or goes to a room alone when angry. But when the child gets angry and starts to yell, he or she is told "You may not yell at me." If he or she walks off pouting, the parent says "You come back here. I am talking to you." It is acceptable for families to have different rules for the adults than for the children. However, parents must then teach their children or adolescents the acceptable ways to express feelings within the family.

# Handling Noncompliance

The points reward system may not work if the child or adolescent has caught on that once the point is not earned there is no reason to comply. "You put away the toys! I lost my point, so why should I do it now?" Let me suggest a few strategies to try. You might come up with approaches of your own.

## Handling Chores

To avoid any confusion about chores or other duties expected by the family, you must make a detailed list of expectations. For example, individual chores might include putting dirty clothes in the hamper, making one's bed, and picking things up off the floor. Family chores might include setting the table, loading or emptying the dishwasher, and vacuuming. Place the list in an obvious place. Clarify if these chores are to be rewarded by money or if they are expected as part of family responsibility. If the family chores are to be shared on different days, make a list that is clear as to what each child is to do each day. For example, Francine clears the table on even-numbered days and Charlie clears the table on odd-numbered days.

If the expected chores are not done, what will be the consistent consequence? What can you do if the child "forgets" or does not do an expected chore? Should you continue to nag, then shout? Several models are suggested below. Each gives the parents the controls. If a task is not done, there is a clear consequence. The choice is for the child or adolescent. If he or she does the chore there is the expected reward. If he or she does not do the chore, there is the expected consequence.

### Maid Service
Establish that not all parent services are supplied free of charge. If chores are not done by a preset time, a parent will do the chores, but not for free. Make a list of the chores expected and the exact time expected; for example, the bed must be made before leaving for school; the dinner table must be set by 6:00 P.M.;

the bike must be in the garage by the time it gets dark. Set a reasonable fee next to each chore if a parent must do it. Be realistic for the age and financial resources of the child or adolescent. For example, 50 cents to make the bed, 25 cents for picking up things from the floor of their room, 50 cents for putting a bike in the garage. Then, stop arguing, reminding, or nagging your son or daughter. If the chore is done by the preset time, fine. He or she earns a point and a thank-you. If it is not done, do the chore without comment. At the end of each day or week, submit a bill for the service. If your child gets an allowance (which I recommend), you might present a bill at the end of the week; for example:

| | |
|---|---|
| Allowance | $5.00 |
| Maid service | -3.75 |
| Balance due | $1.25 |

He or she might get upset and ask how he or she is supposed to buy lunch snacks or drinks. You reply calmly, "Think about that next week when you decide not to do a chore." If the child or adolescent doesn't get an allowance, you might be able to use birthday or savings money. If there is no such money or if the child or adolescent owes much more than the allowance, he or she is given specific work details to earn the money owed. "I will pay you $3 an hour to clean the garage. You owe me $3; so, I expect you to work one hour this weekend."

If you can't use money, explore ways of using the equivalent as barter. Consider television time or time playing computer games. Set a number. "You are entitled to play five hours of computer games a week." Then, instead of money, list units of time next to each chore. At the end of the week, the bill for maid service might read:

| | |
|---|---|
| Computer time allowed | 5 hours |
| Maid service | −3 hours 15 minutes |
| Time remaining to use | 1 hour 45 minutes |

Your child will get upset. But the computer game is locked up and given out for only the amount of time earned that week.

No more getting angry. No more reminding. No more fights. Your child has two choices: Do the chores and get the rewards or not do the chores and pay someone (you) to do them.

### The Sunday Box

Set up a box in a secure place. A closet or room that can be locked or the trunk of a car will do. Make it clear that any items left where they should not be after a predetermined time of the day (toys, bike, books, coat, shoes) will be placed in this box. (For bicycles, put the front wheel in the box.) The box is emptied every Sunday morning. This means that if a favorite game or bike or piece of sports equipment is left out or not put away on time, it is lost until Sunday. If the objects are clothes or shoes and cannot be done without, the child or adolescent must pay a fee to retrieve them early.

This plan has worked so well in some families that one mother placed the father on the plan as well. His clothes, work papers, and other objects that had been left lying around disappeared into the Sunday Box.

### Handling Property Damage

The initial response from parents regarding property damage will be based on the plan in place. If this behavior is called physical abuse, your child will not earn a point and must spend time in a quiet room thinking about the behavior and the need to change. The time out might be much longer. The child or adolescent could be made to pay to repair or replace the item. The money could come out of an allowance. If the amount is large, the money might come out in installments until paid off. If this model for payment isn't possible because your child doesn't have an allowance or birthday money, give him or her a way to earn the money. Assign other than expected tasks and pay by the hour—cutting the grass, washing clothes, washing the kitchen floor, cleaning the garage, helping a neighbor, or doing community service. The first time a child or adolescent gets angry and kicks over a lamp, breaking it, and then learns that it will cost $50 to replace the lamp and that he or she will have to work for twenty hours to pay for the damage, may be the first time that he or she starts to think before acting. This is the goal: getting the child or adolescent to stop before acting and to think about the consequences of his or her behavior.

### Handling Dawdling

Many parents reinforce dawdling by reminding, nagging, yelling, screaming, and then, in anger, doing the task with or for the child. All this behavior does is teach the child that he or she can get away with inappropriate behavior, force the parents to help, or succeed in getting a parent upset. Instead, define the limits for a behavior, then establish clear consequences.

Let's say your child doesn't get dressed on time. He or she is not openly oppositional, but is so busy playing or looking out the window that the task just never gets done. As the time for the school bus gets closer, he or she hasn't dressed or eaten yet because he or she is dawdling and playing. You probably go into the bedroom, yell at the child, and quickly dress him or her so that there will be time to eat and then catch the bus. Your child has succeeded in getting you upset and angry and in getting you to help. It is important in this situation to consider whether the difficulty getting dressed might relate to a learning disability (for example, sequencing, organization, or fine motor problems) or is caused by ADHD behaviors present because the child is not on medication prior to leaving for school.

For this type of behavior, you might first establish the rules. For example, the kitchen is open until 7:30 A.M. You must be dressed to enter. If you come in before 7:15, you may have a hot breakfast. If you come in after 7:15, there is only time for cold cereal. No food is served after 7:30. You will have to go to school hungry and wait for lunch. You must be ready to leave for the bus by 7:40.

What do you do if it is 7:40 and your child still isn't dressed? An older child or adolescent should be told that if he or she misses the bus or car pool, you will not be able to take him or her to school at all or not until later when you were planning to go out anyway. He or she can use public transportation or make arrangements with friends or neighbors. And you will not write a note if he or she is late or absent; thus, there might be detention. Remind your child, "The problem is yours, not mine. Maybe tomorrow you will get dressed on time." Another plan to consider, if family location and circumstance allow, is using a taxi. If you must leave early as well, arrange for a contract with a reliable taxi service. This means that your son or daughter can call a cab when ready to go to school and only has to sign a voucher to pay the driver. This child or adolescent is expected to pay you back or work off the cost of the cab. And, no written excuses for being late. The child must accept the consequences.

If the child or adolescent decides to stay home, he or she must be in his or her room with no television or interaction with parents during school hours. No written excuse will be provided to explain the absence.

If the child is young and the school personnel are willing to cooperate, another plan can be developed with the help of the bus driver, the classroom teacher, and the principal. The child is told the plan in advance. When it is time to leave for the bus, quietly take all of the clothes that have not yet been put on and place them in a bag. Wrap the child in a robe or coat and walk him or her to the bus, pajamas and all. The bus driver, having been briefed, smiles and says hello and makes no other comment. The child gets on the bus with the bag of clothes. The parent then calls to alert the principal. If the child finishes dressing on the bus, fine. If he or she arrives at school in pajamas, the teacher quietly says, "Would you like to go to the bathroom and get dressed?" The child will not starve without breakfast on this day. He or she will not have succeeded in defeating you. This child will learn that dawdling no longer works. Only he or she is affected by the misbehavior.

This approach might work in other situations. At bedtime, whether in pajamas or still in street clothes, put the child in bed and turn out the lights. When the family is ready to leave for a movie, a visit, or a shopping trip and the child isn't ready by the requested time, you should leave with the rest of the family. If the child cannot be left alone, have a sitter on call for the early phase of this approach so that you can follow through with the plan. Once the sitter is called, it is too late to change plans. Even if he or she quickly dresses, the child still stays home. After a time or two, this individual will get the message. "Finish your tasks on time or accept the consequences. You lose, not the rest of us."

# In Summary

When you use a consistent behavioral plan, your child's unacceptable behaviors will begin to change to more acceptable behaviors. Both parents regain control and confidence in their ability to parent. Children and adolescents learn that they can be controlled and that they will not be overwhelmed by not being in control. They are usually happier. Now, all of the positive experiences within the family reinforce the behaviors as well.

If this plan does not work or does not work as well as desired because the child's learning disabilities and/or ADHD are not fully managed, these issues must be addressed. If the plan doesn't work because the parents or one parent doesn't follow the plan or defeats the plan or because the child or adolescent has such emotional problems that he or she cannot give up being in control or the need to be bad or be punished, more intensive help will be needed.

# 16

## Treatment with Medications

The material covered in this chapter is not meant to substitute for the decisions made by the family physician or other specialist working with your child or adolescent. This information is meant only to inform you about the issue of medication. For detailed information on each medication discussed, you will need to read the literature provided by the pharmaceutical manufacturer and talk with the prescribing doctor.

It is important that the necessary differential diagnostic process be considered before establishing the diagnosis of ADHD. If the clinician establishes this diagnosis, it is presumed that your child's behaviors are not due to anxiety or depression but are neurologically based. Therefore, ADHD is both chronic and pervasive. As discussed in Chapter 12, children's ADHD behaviors are present not only during school hours but all of the time, every day. There are physicians who insist that children and adolescents take medication only during school hours. They are off evenings, weekends, holidays, and summers. These kids often have behavioral, social, and family problems during these times off medication and have difficulty doing homework. During the summer they might do poorly at camp or in other activities. Let me use this problem to illustrate the difficulty with keeping all physicians current.

One study done in the 1970s on a small number of children suggested that Ritalin might inhibit the production of human growth hormone and thus stunt growth. "Vacations" from Ritalin were suggested so that the body could catch up with this deficiency. Many physicians heard of this concern and began the practice of insisting on vacations off medication. Since this small initial study, there have been several major studies that show that Ritalin does not decrease the production of human growth hormone. Any decrease in height is considered negligible (less than one inch), and even this finding is questioned. The general understanding is that Ritalin does not affect growth and that the medication can be used whenever it is needed. But not all physicians are up to date on these other studies or on the current consensus.

Another example of information not getting out to every practitioner relates to the use of medication following puberty. We used to teach that everyone "outgrew" what is now called ADHD by puberty. Thus, teenagers would no longer need medications. It became clear in the 1980s that about 50 percent of children continue to have ADHD into adulthood. This is why a parent so often reports that he or she, too, has ADHD. It does not always go away. Some practitioners, not knowing this, take all children off medication when they reach puberty. Not too surprisingly, about 50 percent begin to do very poorly. Adults respond to the medications for ADHD in the same way as do children. Everything I discuss for treating children and adolescents applies equally to adults.

There is one more problem that occurs from time to time in the professional literature. A specific finding is observed and reported. Until this problem is understood, cautious guidelines are appropriately suggested. Gradually, the initial findings are better understood and these guidelines are softened or dropped. Several examples will be given where an initial alarm was followed over time with a decrease in concern. It can be difficult to keep up with these changes.

The use of medication to treat what is now called ADHD was first described in 1937. During that year there was an epidemic of viral encephalitis. Some of the children as they recovered from this disease were observed to be hyperactive and distractible. A pediatrician, Dr. Charles Bradley, tried a stimulant medication (Benzedrine) and found that the children became less active and distractible. Stimulants have been used to treat these behaviors

since that time. It is important for you to understand that the
stimulant medications have been used for more than sixty years.
ADHD may be more popular and known about by the public in
the 1990s. But it is not a new disorder.

About 80 percent of children and adolescents with ADHD
show improvement on the appropriate medication, used properly. These medications decrease or stop the hyperactivity, distractibility, and/or impulsivity. They do not treat learning
disabilities if those are also present. For some individuals with
ADHD, medication may result in improved motor control and
possibly in improved handwriting. Although not understood,
some children and adolescents with a language disability show
improved speech and language when on stimulant medications.
However, the underlying processing problems seen with learning
disabilities do not improve.

One other thought before I become specific about medication
management of ADHD: Some or much of what I present might
differ from the views or practices of the physician working with
your son or daughter. I believe that I am presenting the most current information. It is possible that your family physician is not
as up to date. How could this happen? Most physicians work
very hard to keep up with their field. They read their journals
and newsletters, discuss new medications with pharmaceutical
representatives, and attend conferences. They know of the
newest concepts and treatments for infectious diseases, metabolic
diseases, and other commonly seen problems. However, most of
the research and clinical literature on ADHD appears in the child
and adolescent psychiatry and general psychiatry literature as
well as in some of the psychology journals. Most family practitioners and pediatricians do not receive these publications. Thus,
they find it difficult to keep up with the ever-expanding literature
on ADHD.

There is no established protocol for treating ADHD with medication. I present an approach I find helpful. The protocol discussed should be seen as one possible model for thinking through
each step of the clinical treatment process. Each clinician might
use a variation of this model.

# A Clinical Protocol

In the absence of an established protocol, I will discuss the one I use as a possible way to approach treatment. I try the stimulant medications first. Thus, I call them the Group One medications. If these medications do not help or if the side effects create problems that cannot be clinically resolved, I try a second group of medications, mostly what are called tricyclic antidepressants. I call these the Group Two medications. If these medications do not help or only help control some of the behaviors, I might try a combination of Group One and Group Two medications. Usually, up to 85 percent of correctly diagnosed children, adolescents, and adults with ADHD will respond to one or the other group or to a combination of the groups. I will discuss so-called non-responders later.

Recall that ADHD is caused by a deficiency of a specific neurotransmitter, norepinephrine. The goal of medication use is to increase the level of this neurotransmitter at the nerve interfaces in the areas of the brain involved. At this time, there are two different mechanisms for accomplishing this increase. I like to think of the analogy of a lake without enough water in it. There are two ways one can increase the level of water in the lake. First, more water could be poured into the lake. The second way would be to build a dam. No more water is flowing into the lake than before; but the water flows out more slowly. Thus, the level of water will go up.

One mechanism for increasing the level of this neurotransmitter is to produce more of it. The stimulants (Group One medications) appear to work by stimulating the nerve endings to produce more norepinephrine. The other mechanism, like the dam, decreases the breakdown or metabolism of the neurotransmitter, thus causing what is produced to stay around longer. The relative amount of the neurotransmitter then goes up. The tricyclic antidepressants and other medications in the Group Two medications appear to inhibit the uptake of norepinephrine, resulting in an increase in the amount at the nerve interface.

Each medication has a generic or chemical name and a trade name. The medications used to treat ADHD are listed below with the generic name first and the trade name in parentheses.

## MEDICATIONS USED TO TREAT ADHD

### GROUP ONE MEDICATIONS
Methylphenidate (Ritalin)
Dextroamphetamine (Dexedrine, Dextro-Stat)
Pemoline (Cylert)
Dextroamphetamine and levoamphetamine mixture
(Adderall)

### GROUP TWO MEDICATIONS
Imipramine (Tofranil)
Desipramine (Norpramine)
Nortriptyline (Pamelar)
Bupropion (Wellbutrin)
Clonidine (Catapres)
Guanfacine (Tenex)

I'll discuss each of the medications in these two groups in detail in this chapter. But first let me discuss the non-responder group. The most frequent reason for a child or adolescent not to respond to one of the above medications is that the medication is not being used correctly. Either the dosage or the coverage is not correct. The second reason for not responding is that the role the medication plays is misunderstood. A parent might call me and say her child has been on every medication and has not improved. When I ask for more information, I learn that he or she is calmer and more focused but still cannot read well or spell. I need to explain that these medications treat ADHD but not learning disabilities. Or a parent might say that the child is better focused but still oppositional and defiant. I need to explain that these medications treat ADHD but not oppositional defiant disorder. A different clinical intervention is needed for this disorder. A third reason noted is that the diagnosis is not correct. The hyperactivity, distractibility, and or impulsivity is a reflection of anxiety, depression, or learning disabilities but not of ADHD.

There is a small group of true non-responders. These children and adolescents often have several or all of the previously discussed continuum of neurological disorders. They might have ADHD, but they might also have a learning, language, or motor disability, one or more of the modulating disorders, and/or a tic disorder. These medications might be helping the ADHD but other medications are needed to address the other disorders.

I will discuss treatment with the Group One medications, then with the Group Two medications. Then I'll discuss indications for combining medications from each group. Later I will discuss the medication treatment for the child or adolescent who has ADHD and other disorders within the continuum. The proper protocol is to use generic names only. However, parents are more likely to be familiar with trade names. Therefore, I will use the trade names in my discussions. Refer to the list opposite to find the generic name.

I firmly believe that parents must know as much about the medications their son or daughter is taking as the physician. Thus, I will discuss each medication in detail, including how the dose is selected and adjusted, what the side effects might be, and how to address these side effects.

## Group One Medications: The Stimulants

It is difficult to predict whether a child or adolescent with ADHD will respond better to one stimulant medication versus another. Some will respond poorly to one and have a positive response to another. Some will have side effects with one and not with another. Clinicians must use their own judgment as to which one to try first.

Each of these medications has shared characteristics, effects, and side effects. Ritalin and Dexedrine come in a short-acting and a long-acting form. Cylert is only long-acting. Adderall lasts for six hours.

Caffeine is also a stimulant. However, it has not proven to be a useful medication for ADHD.

Prior to starting one of the stimulant medications, your child needs a general medical evaluation. This medical workup should include measurements of height, weight, pulse rate, and blood pressure. A family history of a tic disorder or a history of a tic disorder with the child or adolescent should be obtained. Medical follow-up visits should include observing for tics and involuntary movements and recording of pulse rate, blood pressure, weight, and height. If Cylert is used, blood studies of liver function should be done every six months. (I'll explain why later in this chapter.)

Stimulant medications may aggravate symptoms of anxiety, tension, and agitation; thus, they should be used with caution in these situations. These medications might also exacerbate a tic disorder, and this possibility must be considered. Cylert should not be used with individuals with known impairment of liver function.

Ritalin is available in 5-, 10-, and 20-mg tablets and in the long-acting Ritalin-SR 20 tablet. Ritalin-SR 20 is designed to release 10 mg initially and 10 mg four hours later (for a total of 20 mg). The short-acting Ritalin tablet lasts an average of four hours; however, for some it may last less time or more time. Although there are references to the amount of Ritalin needed based on body weight, the amount needed by each individual does not seem to relate to body weight. This concept will be elaborated on later. The recommended upper limit is 20 mg four times a day.

Dexedrine is available in 5-mg tablets and in long-acting Dexedrine Spansules of 5-, 10-, and 15-mg strength. Each tablet lasts an average of four hours. The Spansule lasts eight hours. Dexedrine is approved for use starting at age three. The upper limit of dosage is the same as with Ritalin, 20 mg four times a day. Dextroamphetamine is also available as Dextro-Stat. It is the same medication manufactured by a different company. Dextro-Stat comes in 5- and 10-mg tablets, each lasting an average of four hours. A new medication in this same group is Adderall. This medication is a mixture of several different salts of amphetamine. Research is not yet available to clarify if this mixture of amphetamine salts offers benefits over the single-salt dextroamphetamine. Adderall comes in 5-, 10-, and 20-mg tablets and is designed to last six hours.

Cylert is available in 18.75-, 37.5-, and 75-mg tablets and in a 37.5-mg chewable tablet. It is administered as a single oral dose each morning and lasts for twenty-four hours. The recommended starting dose is 37.5 mg per day. The dose is gradually increased by 18.75 mg each week, with the maximum recommended daily dose being 112.5 mg. Cylert is approved for use starting at age six. During early 1997, several cases were reported of children on Cylert developing acute liver function problems. An alert went out from the manufacturer of this concern. For this reason, many professionals are hesitant to use Cylert at this time. It may be that like other sudden alerts, the problem will be of less concern over time.

Since Ritalin is the most frequently used of the Group One medications, I will use it as a prototype of this group of medications. Its use and management will be discussed in detail. Most of what is presented is true for all of the medications in this group. When there are exceptions, it will be noted.

## Ritalin

The short-acting Ritalin tablet begins to work in thirty to forty-five minutes and lasts about four hours. It does not accumulate; thus, at the end of four hours it is no longer found in the blood. If a child takes 10 mg three times a day, one does not say that he or she is taking 30 mg a day. One says that at any moment during the day he or she has 10 mg in the blood. Studies show that there is little difference between taking Ritalin on an empty versus a full stomach. Food does not impair absorption; thus, it can be given before a meal, with a meal, or after a meal. As noted earlier, the dose is not based on body weight but on how rapidly the medication is metabolized by the individual. It appears that once the therapeutic benefits are noted, the blood level is the same for the individual who needs 5, 10, 15, or 20 mg per dose.

When Ritalin is used there are three clinical questions that must be addressed. These same questions are relevant for the other stimulants.

1. How much medication is needed per dose?
2. At what time interval is the medication taken?
3. During what time periods should the medication be taken?

Each of these issues is important to understand.

*How much medication is needed per dose?* It appears that the dose needed to reach clinical benefit is not related to body weight but to how rapidly each individual metabolizes the medication. I have two-hundred-pound adults taking 5 mg and thirty-pound children taking 20 mg. Each person seems to need a specific amount to reach the full benefit. There are no readily available tests to measure the blood level of Ritalin. Thus, clinical observations are used to establish the dose. I start the individual on 5 mg per dose. With very young children, I might start at 2.5 mg per dose. At five-day intervals I get feedback from parents and teachers. If no benefits are noted, the dose is increased by 5 mg every five days until a decrease in hyperactivity, distractibility, and/or impulsivity is reported. There are two side effects that would suggest that the dose of Ritalin or any of the other stimulants is too high for that individual. These are being emotionally labile (swinging back and forth between emotional extremes) and demonstrating hyperfocused/spacy behaviors. Unless one of these side effects is noted, the dose is raised every five days. If I reach 20 mg per dose with no noted benefits, I rethink the diagnosis or the use of the medication. Usually, each increase in dose is done for every dose. At times I might want to assess the impact of an increase in dose. Thus, I might increase the morning dose but leave the noon and afternoon doses the same. Then, I will ask parents and teachers if they notice a difference between the morning and afternoon parts of the school day. If I find that the child or adolescent is doing much better in the morning than the afternoon, I increase the noon and afternoon doses.

Feedback from parents and teachers is critical in adjusting the dose. One efficient way for the physician to do this is to ask a parent to discuss the child's or adolescent's improvement with the teacher at the end of the school day and then to call the physician. In this way, feedback from school and home can be obtained with one phone call. Rating scales can be used if a more formal feedback model is desired.

I find it best to start with a short-acting form of Ritalin until the appropriate dose and time of dose is established. Then, if needed, a longer-acting form might be considered. With Ritalin, the long-acting Ritalin-SR can only be used if two consecutive doses are 10 mg. For other doses, Dexedrine Spansules or Adderall might be needed.

*At what time interval is the medication taken?* The average length of action for a short-acting tablet is four hours. However, for some individuals, the medication may last two or three hours and for others it might last up to five hours. Thus, the dose interval must be established for each individual. There is nothing absolute about using Ritalin every four hours.

The dose interval is determined clinically, using feedback from parents, the individual, and teachers. As an example, a child is placed on Ritalin, 5 mg at 8:00 A.M., noon, and 4:00 P.M. daily. If the feedback throughout the day is good, the dose interval in place may be best. If the teacher says, "You know, John is great in the morning. But, about 11:00 or 11:30 he begins to wiggle in his seat and cannot stay on task. He is much better after the noon medication is given." Perhaps the dose interval for John is three hours. He may need his medication at 8:00 A.M., 11:00 A.M., and 2:00 P.M., with a 5:00 P.M. dose added if needed.

If the teacher reports, "Alicia is great in the morning. Only between 12:30 and 1:00 she gets so upset. If I look at her the wrong way, she cries," or "Between 12:30 and 1:00 she appears so spacy that she seems out of it." By 1:00 or 1:30 P.M. she is fine again. How do we explain this? There are two behaviors that suggest that the dose of Ritalin (or Dexedrine) is too high for that individual. One is being emotionally fragile. The child or adolescent is more irritable or tearful than usual. The other is that the child or adolescent is now so overfocused that she or he appears to be spacy. It is possible that for Alicia each dose lasts five hours. She gets the next dose in four hours, and for about an hour she is on the remains of the first dose plus the second dose. For her, the combined dose is too high and thus the side effects. For her, the doses should be five hours apart.

*During which time periods should the medication be taken?* ADHD is a neurologically based disorder having to do with how the brain functions. Thus, the behaviors—the hyperactivity, distractibility, and/or impulsivity—will be present throughout the person's day, every day. Thus, the rule to use for deciding a medication schedule is: Medication is used whenever the hyperactivity, distractibility, and/or impulsivity interferes with that individual's success in life. Medication shouldn't be used to make parents or teachers happy. Medication should be used to help the child or adolescent succeed in the family, in school, with friends, in activities, in sports—everyplace. For some, medication will be needed only during school and homework hours. For most, medication will be needed all day, each day.

As noted earlier, it was the misinformation that Ritalin inhibited growth hormone and, thus, stunted growth that led to the concept of vacations from medication on afternoons, weekends, holidays, and summers. For too many children and adolescents, the family physician does not know that concern about growth is no longer an issue, and medication is only used at 8:00 A.M. and noon Monday through Friday, September through June. This individual struggles with homework and has difficulty getting along at home, with friends, and everyplace he or she goes.

My preference is to place the child or adolescent on medication all day, every day, and ask parents to observe. If they find that the medication is only helpful related to school, I will set up a plan to cover school and homework time only. I'll teach parents how to use a single dose for special occasions like going on a long car ride. More frequently, parents report that the medication helps their son or daughter function better at home and with all out-of-the-home activities. Some note, "He actually sat through a whole meal and talked with us." "She can now entertain herself." "He plays better with his friends." "I asked her to do something, and she actually did it." Unless parents can observe their child or adolescent in all situations, it is difficult to assess when medication is needed.

The key is to think of the behaviors—hyperactivity, distractibility, and/or impulsivity. When do these behaviors interfere with your child's success with life? Let me give a few examples. A parent reports that the medication works well. Their son gets his doses at 8:00 A.M. as he leaves for school, at noon, and at 4:00 P.M. But between the time he gets up and the time he leaves for school is impossible. He plays with his toys rather than getting dressed, runs around the house, jumps on his sister's bed, talks loudly, and gets everyone angry with him. Finally, at 8:00 A.M. mother gives him his medication, hands him a piece of bread and butter, and shoves him out of the door. Not good for mother, sister, or the child with ADHD. The problem is clear. The first dose is given at 8:00 A.M. From the time he gets up until about 8:45 A.M., he is "very ADHD." The solution is also clear. I asked the mother what time her son gets up on school mornings. She said 7:00 A.M. I asked her to wake him up at 6:15 A.M., give him his medication, and let him go back to sleep. He wakes up at 7:00 A.M. pleasant and cooperative. He gets dressed, comes to the kitchen, has a good breakfast, and leaves for school with hugs and kisses. Then, he will get his other doses at 10:45 A.M., 2:45 P.M., and if necessary at 6:45 P.M.

Suppose a child gets her medication at 8:00 A.M. as she leaves for school and the second dose at noon. She is about to be suspended from the school bus because on the morning trip she runs up and down the aisles and won't stay in her seat. The problem is that the medication doesn't start to work until she is already in school. The noon dose lasts till 4:00 P.M. and covers the trip home. She needs the first dose at 7:15 A.M. so that it is working before she gets on the bus.

For some children and adolescents who take their medication at 8:00 A.M., noon, and 4:00 P.M., the difficult time is from 8:00 P.M. until bedtime. An additional dose at 8:00 P.M. may be needed. With each of the examples used, the key is that medication is used whenever medication is needed to help the individual be successful in life.

The need for medication might vary depending on the age, grade, school demand, and family style. For example, a first or second grader might have little or no homework. Thus, if he or she is primarily distractible, medication will be needed during school hours but not for after-school hours. However, this same child, when older and in a higher grade, might have homework and need medication during after-school hours. A hyperactive child might need medication during school hours. However, if he or she is young and spends most of the after-school hours playing outside and if the family does not mind the fidgetiness, medication may not be needed at home. This same child might need medication for these hours when older and homework or family demands increase.

Each situation should be thought through based on the guideline noted. Suppose a family plans to drive to the grandparents' house, a four-hour car trip. Once there, their child will run around and play with cousins all weekend. Then there is the four-hour ride home. This child might need medication for the car ride there and back. While there, he might not need medication or might need it only for the quieter family dinner times.

### Side Effects and Their Management

Let me review the possible side effects of Ritalin and how they are managed. If there are any unique side effects found with the other Group One medications, I will note them.

The two most frequent side effects found with Ritalin are loss of appetite and difficulty falling asleep at night. Much less frequently, some individuals will complain of a stomachache or headache after most doses. Rarely, some individuals develop tics (these will be described later). As discussed earlier, there are two side effects that suggest that the dose of the medication is too high—being emotionally labile and/or overfocused or cloudy.

#### LOSS OF APPETITE

This side effect may lessen over the first several weeks and cease to be a problem. If it persists, something should be done. The first thing you should do is to observe your child's eating patterns. The medication may take the edge off his or her appetite; thus, the child or adolescent might not finish his or her meals but may eat candy, cake, and other more desirable sweets. If you see this happening, you'll need to limit such sweets until the meal is eaten. Some children on three doses a day eat breakfast (because the first dose has not started to work), show no appetite for lunch or dinner, and then come into the kitchen at 8:00 P.M. starved and eat everything they can find. Try to observe your son's or daughter's eating patterns.

One effort to overcome this problem with appetite is to try to create "windows of opportunity." Try to get your child to eat a good breakfast before the first dose starts to work. Accept that lunch will be a loser. Maybe he or she will eat part of a jelly sandwich but often nothing at all. Try to hold off the 4:00 P.M. dose until 5:30 or 6:00 P.M. During this time provide more structure and supervision and don't expect the child to do his or her homework. Hopefully, your child's appetite will return in time for dinner. Then give the third dose.

If nothing works and your child is losing weight or not gaining weight, Ritalin will have to be stopped. For reasons we do not understand, some children will have less appetite suppression on one of the stimulant medications than another. Thus, some physicians might try one of these other medications before moving on to the Group Two medications.

### SLEEP DIFFICULTIES
Some children and adolescents on Ritalin have difficulty going to sleep at night. This problem often lessens or goes away over several weeks. If it does not, an intervention is needed. The issue is this: For some, it is the medication that keeps them awake, and for others, it is the lack of medication that keeps them awake. Both possibilities must be explored. Each reason leads to a different management approach.

It is not possible to predict which of these situations is the reason for an individual's sleep problem. The only way to clarify this is to find out by trial and error. I pick an evening when a sleep problem might not be a disaster since the child can sleep later the next day, maybe a Friday or Saturday night. I ask the parents to give the child another dose of Ritalin at 8:00 P.M. If he or she goes right to sleep, I know it was the lack of medication that caused the difficulty. If he or she is even more wired and unable to sleep, I know it is the medication that is causing the difficulty. (On such a night I don't want the child to be up all night. Thus, I will have the parents give the child Benadryl to get through that night. This medication will be discussed below.)

If the medication only occasionally makes it difficult for your child to fall asleep at night, your physician might recommend the use of Benadryl to help him or her get to sleep. A dose of 25 to 50 mg, depending on weight, might be needed. However, it is important for your child to know that Benadryl is not a sleeping pill. He or she can't read or play until he or she gets sleepy. However, if the child waits about forty-five minutes and then lies quietly in the dark and tries to sleep, the medication might help. It is all right to use this medication as your doctor recommends. Don't use it every night or the effect might be lost.

If the sleep problem persists, try decreasing or stopping the 4:00 P.M. dose. If this decrease creates behavioral problems in the afternoon and evening or with doing homework, a change to a Group Two medication may be needed.

Suppose it is the lack of medication that causes the sleep problem. If the child or adolescent takes three doses a day, he or she is functioning "normally" from about 8:00 A.M. until about 8:00 P.M. Then, the medication wears off and the child becomes hyperactive, distractible, and/or impulsive. In bed, he or she cannot lie still, hears every sound in the house, and cannot turn his or her mind off. For this child, a fourth dose at 8:00 P.M. may allow for ease of going to sleep.

If every medication in Group One and Group Two has been tried and it is concluded that Ritalin or one of the other stimulant medications works the very best but that this medication causes significant sleep problems, there is a possible approach to use. Catapres, a medication in Group Two to be discussed later, can be added one hour before bedtime. I will explain how Catapres works in this situation when I discuss it later in this chapter.

### STOMACHACHE
The reason for this side effect of Ritalin is not understood. If your child takes a dose on an empty stomach, try feeding him or her before giving the medication. Usually, if a child's stomachaches persist, it is necessary to change to a Group Two medication.

### HEADACHE
The reason for this side effect is not known either. If headaches persist, it is necessary to move to a Group Two medication.

### TICS
Tics and tic disorders were described in Chapter 7. Motor tics are sudden, involuntary movements of specific muscle groups. The most frequently seen involve blinking or moving of the eyes or twitching of the face, mouth, neck, or shoulder muscles. If the muscles in the back of the throat are involved, the child or adolescent might make sniffing, snorting, or coughing sounds. Sometimes the tics begin immediately or soon after the medication is started. Occasionally, they start later. At times the tics are noted only after the dose has been increased.

If tics occur, it is best to stop the medication and try one of the Group Two medications. For most, the tics will stop immediately. For others, the tics might last for several months before going away.

If there is a family history of a tic disorder, the child or adolescent might be genetically loaded to develop a tic disorder. In this case, the medication will trigger this tic disorder earlier than it might have started on its own. Stopping the medication will not stop the tics. Here, the medication did not cause the tics but hastened the genetically programmed appearance of the disorder. For most individuals who are going to develop a tic disorder, the tics start between the ages of eight and twelve. Thus, the closer the child is to adolescence without evidence of tics, the less likely that Ritalin or one of the other stimulants will set off a tic disorder that was probably genetically determined. Thus, if there is a family history of a tic disorder, the physician might start your child with one of the Group Two medications as a precaution. When a child is adopted and no family history is available, you'll have to discuss this possibility of tics and weigh the use of a Group One medication.

If all of the possible medications have been tried and only one of the stimulant medications works but it causes tics, you've got to make a decision with the help of the physician. Should the stimulant be used and another medication be added to treat the tic disorder? In some cases, the result of not treating the ADHD is so harmful to the child or adolescent that the decision to continue the medication and to treat the tic disorder is necessary.

## BEING EMOTIONALLY LABILE OR SPACY

As mentioned earlier, these side effects suggest that the dose is too high and should be reduced. Being emotionally labile means that, based on that individual's normal behavior, he or she is more tearful or irritable. Spacy behavior means that the child or adolescent is so overfocused that he or she seems to be in a cloud or "zombie-like." Sometimes this problem is noted as a "blunting" of the personality. A parent notes that the spark is missing from the child's personality; he or she seems "flat."

Neither of these behaviors should be accepted. The dose needs to be lowered. If lowering the dose results in a loss of effective-

ness, another medication should be tried. As with the other side
effects, it is possible that one of the other stimulant medications
might not cause the same side effects and should be tried. Usually, however, if one does the others will.

OTHER SIDE EFFECTS

Some children and adolescents show a "rebound effect" about
twenty to thirty minutes after the last dose wears off. For those
on three doses a day, this occurs about 8:30 to 9:00 P.M. For a
half-hour or more they may become very hyperactive and talk
constantly or may be excitable or impulsive. If this side effect becomes a concern, reduce the last dose to see if it makes a difference. Another approach, if the medication does not cause sleep
problems, is to give a fourth dose at 8:00 P.M. so that the medication does not wear off until the child is asleep.

There are other very uncommon side effects. Some children on
Ritalin or one of the other stimulant medications become explosive, with limited ability to control their anger. Some may become depressed or very anxious. Others might become very
obsessive (with intrusive thoughts) or compulsive (needing to do
certain behaviors or patterns of behavior). With each of these
side effects, the child will return to normal either immediately or
within a few days after the medication is stopped.

### The Use of Long-acting Stimulants

Ritalin comes in one long-acting form. It is called Ritalin-SR
20, meaning Ritalin, Sustained Release for a total of 20 mg. It releases 10 mg immediately and 10 mg in four hours. Experience
shows that this SR form does not always work as it should. For
some individuals, the total effect is only about five hours. For
others, each release lasts three hours. Thus, the child does well
from, say, 8:00 to 11:00 A.M., then has difficulty until about
12:30 or 1:00 P.M. He or she then does well for another three
hours. We now understand that if the surface of the Ritalin-SR
20 tablet is broken (chewed, cut in half), the whole dose is released at once. The child or adolescent gets 20 mg immediately
and nothing four hours later. For some, the sustained-release
dosage causes emotionally labile or spacy behavior during the
first four hours and hyperactivity, distractibility, and/or impulsivity during the second four hours.

Dexedrine comes in a capsule form, called a Spansule. There are 5-mg, 10-mg, and 15-mg Spansules. Each dose lasts eight hours and releases the medication reasonably evenly. The capsule can be opened and sprinkled over food if necessary without any effect on the absorption pattern and length of action. Another form of dextroamphetamine called Dextro-Stat comes in both 5-mg and 10-mg tablets. This is not a long-acting form of the medication. Each dose still lasts four hours. The advantage is that an individual might have to take fewer pills per dose. Adderall, a mixture of three salts of amphetamine, lasts six hours and can be used as a longer-acting medication than the basic Dexedrine.

## Special Issues

At what age can a child be started on the Group One medications? Dexedrine is approved at age three. The other stimulants are approved at age six. However, it is not unusual for all of the stimulant medications except Cylert to be used starting at age three.

Clinical observations to date do not show that children and adolescents on Ritalin or one of the other stimulant medications develop tolerance, requiring a gradual increase in dose. Many individuals can take the same dose for many years. Since the amount needed is not based on body weight, it is not necessary to raise the dose with growth. For some, the dose may have to be increased slightly over time.

Cylert is long-acting; thus, it is always in the bloodstream. For this reason, it is necessary to monitor the child's liver function. This blood test is usually done about every six months. More information on the need to monitor liver function with long-acting medication will be discussed later in this chapter.

Earlier literature raised the question of what is called "state-dependent" learning. That is, if a child learns something while on a medication, will he or she retain this information when off the medication? All studies show no such problems with any of the Group One medications.

Do children become addicted to Ritalin? Can they abuse it? At the doses used, addiction has not been reported to be an issue. Recent articles in newspapers report the increased use of Ritalin by students to get a "high." Most reports note that the individual ground up the Ritalin and sniffed it. Thus, the entire dose was absorbed into the bloodstream all at once rather than being slowly absorbed over time. These students report feeling high and stimulated. They don't report such feelings if they take the medication properly by mouth. If I might try to summarize my understanding of the literature relating to the stimulants and addiction, it is this: If the individual has ADHD and is properly managed on medication as well as with appropriate nonmedication help, the likelihood of substance abuse is no greater than expected for that individual's peer group. If the individual has ADHD and is not on medication or not managed properly on medication or the necessary nonmedication interventions are not in place, the likelihood of substance abuse may be higher than what would be expected for that individual's peer group. The conclusion I reach is that using medication to treat ADHD does not increase the possibility of substance abuse. The lack of proper or comprehensive treatment with the resulting frustrations and failures might result in an increase in substance abuse. It is not the disorder or the medication that is the issue. It is the lack of recognition of the disorder or the absence of or incomplete treatment that might result in substance abuse.

Earlier literature also noted concern with the use of a stimulant medication for individuals with a seizure disorder. The current guidelines suggest that this issue need not be a concern. The use of a stimulant medication with a child or adolescent who has ADHD and a seizure disorder should be decided by the physician on an individual basis.

Parents might be concerned with the long-term use of Ritalin or the other stimulants. How safe are they? We have long-term follow-up studies of children who took Ritalin in the 1960s but stopped by adolescence. They had no long-term side effects. However, these days we might start a child on a stimulant medication and he or she might continue to use the medication into adulthood. We do not yet have long-term follow-up reports for this length of use. The best evidence to date suggests that there will be no long-term side effects. Parents must understand that hard data are not in at this time on using these medications continuously over many years.

## The Group Two Medications

The Group Two medications are used if the Group One medications do not work or if they produce side effects that cannot be clinically managed. They might also be used to obtain a smoother, more even effect from the medication. If the Group One medication lasts only two to three hours, a long-acting Group Two medication might be added to get a more even coverage by filling in the "valleys" when the stimulant is not working.

Most of the Group Two medications are in a family of medications called tricyclic antidepressants; thus some people refer to the whole group by this name. However, there are several medications in this group that are not tricyclic antidepressants. The common theme for this group is that the mechanism of action results in a decrease in the breakdown or absorption of the identified neurotransmitter at the nerve endings, resulting in an increase in this neurotransmitter.

There are several reasons why the medications in this group are our second choice when treating individuals with ADHD. The first is that they do not always address each of the three behaviors seen with ADHD. With the Group One medications, there is a decrease in hyperactivity, distractibility, and/or impulsivity. For reasons we do not yet understand, the medications in Group Two do not cover all of these behaviors. The tricyclic antidepressants (Tofranil, Norpramine, Pamelar) and Wellbutrin seem to help with the hyperactivity and distractibility; however, often they do not address the impulsivity; thus, a second medication might need to be added. Catapres and Tenex seem to help with impulsivity but often will not address the hyperactivity or distractibility. Thus, again, a second medication might have to be added.

The second reason that these medications are our second choice is that we have to manage long-acting medications differently from short-acting medications. When a medication is in the bloodstream all of the time (unlike, say, Ritalin, which even if used three times a day is out of the bloodstream half of each day), it is necessary to monitor liver function. This step is a precaution since the liver metabolizes most medications. This need is not unique to these medications for ADHD; it's also true for medications for asthma or arthritis or other medical disorders. The child will need to get a blood test about every six months to monitor liver function. The possibility of a negative effect on liver function is rare, and this time interval is believed to allow for early enough recognition of such a problem to stop the medication. On rare occasions, the tricyclic antidepressants might result in a decrease in a particular white blood cell (neutrophil); thus, along with the liver function test, a complete blood count (CBC) is done.

Tofranil (imipramine) is the most frequent medication used in Group Two. Thus, I will use it as the prototype for this group. Later, I will discuss the unique features of other medications in this group.

## Dosage and Use

Tofranil is available in 10-, 25-, and 50-mg tablets. Since it is long-acting, the medication is often taken in the morning and in the evening, avoiding the need to take medication at school. The suggested guideline is that it be used in individuals age six and older. As with the stimulant medication, there appears to be no relationship between the dose needed to treat ADHD and body weight. Thus, the dose should be determined by clinical observation. Often with children, 10 to 20 mg twice a day is enough. Sometimes the dose may go up to 100 to 150 mg, given in divided doses.

Tofranil and the other tricyclic antidepressants are also used with adolescents and adults to treat depression. However, the dose needed to treat depression is often 200 to 300 mg a day. Thus, one cannot use the blood level of Tofranil to determine the dose needed. The range used is based on these higher doses to treat adult depression. Also, the side effects noted in the material provided by the pharmacist are not accurate for our population. Again, these side effects are seen at the higher doses used to treat depression and not at the lower doses used to treat ADHD.

Tofranil may take a week or two to begin to work or for it to be possible to observe the effects of an increase in dose. Thus, the dose is usually increased every week to two weeks until the desired effects are noted. If the two doses a day cause fatigue or if the child seems to do less well in the late afternoon, the total dose can be divided into three doses a day. For convenience, this can be in the morning, when the child returns from school, and in the evening.

## Side Effects

The most frequent side effect is being tired or sleepy. Often this side effect decreases over time as the individual gets used to the medication. If this doesn't happen, the dose can be decreased or divided into three smaller doses each day. If these shifts don't help, the child may not be able to take Tofranil. As with the stimulant medications, sometimes a different tricyclic antidepressant might work without this side effect and should be considered.

Less common side effects seen are constipation, dry mouth, or blurred vision. If these occur, another medication should be considered. A very uncommon side effect is morning insomnia. The child wakes up at 4:00 or 4:30 in the morning wide awake and wants to play. Often this problem can be minimized by giving more of the imipramine in the morning. If not, a different medication may be needed.

Tofranil and other tricyclic antidepressants might affect brain wave activity. Thus, if the child or adolescent has a seizure disorder, there is the possibility that the medication may potentiate a seizure. Your physician should be able to make the proper decision on using Tofranil in this situation.

If a tricyclic antidepressant is stopped, it must be tapered off slowly. If stopped abruptly, the child or adolescent might develop flu-like symptoms.

### The Tricyclic Antidepressants and Heart Function

These medications might cause a slight shift in the electrical conduction pattern of the heart. Most studies show that this shift is minimal and does not cause symptoms. A very small percentage of children and adolescents have what is called a subclinically abnormal electrical conduction pattern of the heart. That is, there are no clinical symptoms of the abnormal pattern. If a tricyclic antidepressant is given to this child, it is possible that the effect of the medication added to the underlying shift might combine to cause a rapid heart beat (tachycardia). The individual complains of a pounding heart or racing in the chest and the neck "feeling full." This side effect is uncommon. Some literature on this medication recommends that an electrocardiogram (EKG) be done prior to starting the medication and again after the dose is stabilized. Other reports suggest that the possibility of tachycardia is minimal and the impact is not life-threatening; thus, getting an EKG is not considered essential. Clearly, if a child or adolescent has a known history of a conduction problem, these medications should not be used. You will have to discuss this concern with your family doctor and find out her or his orientation.

### The Other Group Two Medications

Wellbutrin is not related to the tricyclic antidepressants. It works in a similar way as Tofranil and the other tricyclics. Wellbutrin is recommended starting at age eighteen. The side effects are the same. It comes in a 75-mg and 100-mg tablet.

Catapres and Tenex are two medications that are used with adults who have high blood pressure and result in a decrease in blood pressure. At lower doses, these two medications increase the amount of norepinephrine at the nerve ending. The exact mechanism is different than with the other Group Two medications, but the result is the same. Whereas the other Group Two medications decrease hyperactivity and distractibility but not the impulsivity, these two medications seem to have minimal benefit with the hyperactivity and distractibility but do decrease impulsivity. Thus, they are used along with the other Group Two medications when impulsivity is an issue. Catapres comes in a 0.1-, 0.2-, and 0.3-mg tablet. Tenex comes in a 1.0- and 2.0-mg tablet.

The main side effect is sedation. With Tofranil, the child might be tired in class. With Catapres, he or she could fall asleep in class. Thus, minimal doses are given. With Catapres, each dose will last about six hours. Often, a 0.1-mg tablet will be used, giving one-half or one-fourth of a tablet in the morning and a similar amount about 3:00 P.M. Even this low dose can be sedating for some children, in which case even lower doses must be tried. With Tenex, often one half of a 1-mg tablet will be used in the morning and in the afternoon.

If either Catapres or Tenex is stopped, it should be tapered off slowly. If stopped abruptly, some children or adolescents complain of headaches or dizziness.

As mentioned earlier, if a child or adolescent has been tried on many medications and one of the short-acting stimulants seems to be the only one to help but this medication causes problems going to sleep, Catapres can be used at bedtime. Here, the Catapres may help with the impulsivity. We take advantage of the sedating effect and use a slightly higher dose than would be used during the day. This dose is given one hour before planned bedtime and frequently helps the child or adolescent go to sleep. (There was a brief concern about using Ritalin and Catapres in this way because of one reported case of death. A more detailed study of this case and of the use of these medications concluded that this mixture is safe.)

Catapres also comes in a slow-absorption patch, called a TTS (transdermal therapeutic system) patch. The medication is in a small gauze square similar to the center of a Band-Aid. There is a waterproof cover that can be used. Each patch releases the medication slowly over seven days. These patches come in various doses and can be selected to provide steady coverage over a week with a decreased likelihood of sedation. There are two problems with the patch. Some children do not like them and keep pulling them off. Also, the patch can sometimes cause an itchy skin rash. If Catapres is helpful and sedation is a problem, the doctor can consider the possibility of using small amounts over a long period of time.

## Other Medications for ADHD

Only the medications discussed above have been found to be effective with ADHD. If this child or adolescent has other problems in addition to the ADHD, other medications might be tried. In the first chapter, I reviewed other neurologically based disorders that might be seen with (are comorbid with) ADHD. These include disorders reflecting problems with modulation of anxiety, anger, or mood and obsessive compulsive disorder and tic disorders. Each of these problems may need to be treated.

If a child or adolescent has several related disorders, it is important to work with a physician who is familiar with the appropriate medications to use and the interactions of these medications. Often, the child and adolescent psychiatrist is most knowledgeable on these issues.

## In Summary

Medication to treat ADHD must be seen as part of a multimodal approach that includes education, counseling, behavioral management and family therapy along with the medication. If any of the associated disorders are present, they must be addressed as well.

If your son or daughter has ADHD and needs medication, work with your physician. The information provided in this chapter is meant to help you be informed so that you know what is being done and why. If you find that you now know more than your family doctor, lend him or her a copy of this chapter. If your physician does not believe in medication or seems not to be current on the use of the medications, try to find another physician.

# 17

## The Controversial Therapies

Our knowledge of ADHD and learning disabilities is not complete. I've discussed here the approaches to treatment that are based on research and are considered accepted practices. I would now like to discuss the less acceptable or more controversial approaches to treatment. The controversy might be based on the theory behind the treatment, on the way the treatment is done, or on the lack of research data to support the findings reported by the people using the treatment approach.

Controversial therapies have been with us throughout history. Perhaps you have heard claims for curing cancer or other diseases that are challenged by the medical profession. Remember ground up apricot pits to cure cancer? Professionals who study controversial therapies comment on specific themes that exist for most, whether for cancer or learning disabilities:

1. The individual who publicizes and pushes for the treatment claims to have research to prove what is being stated; yet no research is provided from respected journals.
2. The individual stresses that practitioners of "traditional medicine" are too conservative and refuse to accept what does not fit what they already know.
3. Claims for cure or improvement are made with literature provided by that individual to prove these claims. One is left to wonder why, if what is claimed is accurate,

the treatment is not used by most professionals in the field.

4. The person seems to be saying "I'm a genius" or "I'm a quack," and it is up to the public and the establishment to prove which is true.

Often parents turn to their family physician for guidance only to learn that she or he does not know any more than they do. The difficulty is that there are many professionals and nonprofessionals proposing approaches for helping. If research has been done to support a particular approach, it will be published in professional journals that are carefully reviewed to assure that the results reported are accurate. Usually, others try to replicate the findings found by the first researcher. If others support the treatment findings, the approach is accepted by the professional groups. When information is communicated through popular books, newspapers, popular magazines, or television shows, it is difficult to evaluate the claims. Thus, professionals only know what they read or hear through these sources or from parents who tell them about the treatment.

I will discuss controversial approaches to treatment that have been proposed and are still being used. I will not review controversial research that focuses on causes but that has not resulted in proposed treatment approaches. Where there is research to show that the proposed treatment does not work, I will present this. When all of the facts are not yet in or agreed upon, I will review the information known from both perspectives and let you decide for yourself.

The treatment for ADHD only works during the hours the child or adolescent is on medication. Let the medication wear off, and he or she is "ADHD" again. Thus, I can understand why parents would want to try almost any approach that might work better and faster for their son or daughter. I can especially understand a parent wanting a cure rather than an intervention. But parents must be informed and intelligent consumers. Before committing yourself and especially your daughter or son to any new or different approach, ask questions. Remember this general rule-of-thumb: If the treatment approach you are about to try is so successful, why isn't everyone in the country using it? No professional, regardless of discipline, would avoid using a treatment that has been shown to work.

I find it helpful to group these controversial therapies by the proposed mechanism of action—physiological changes or chemical changes. A few proposed treatments do not fit this model and will be listed separately. *Physiological changes* refers to the concept that by stimulating specific sensory inputs or exercising specific motor patterns one can retrain, recircuit, or in some way improve the functioning of a part of the nervous system. *Chemical changes* refers to the concept of orthomolecular medicine, introduced by Dr. Linus Pauling. This involves the treatment of mental disorders and other disorders by the provision of the optimum concentrations of substances normally present in the human body.

## THE CONTROVERSIAL THERAPIES FOR ADHD

Physiological:
Patterning
Biofeedback
Vestibular dysfunction

Chemical:
Megavitamins
Trace elements
Food additives
Refined sugars
Herbs

Other approaches:
Allergies

## Patterning

This theory and technique were initially developed by Dr. Glenn Doman and Dr. Carl Delacato. The underlying concept follows the principle that failures to pass properly through a certain sequence of developmental stages in mobility, language, and competence in the manual, visual, auditory, and tactile areas reflect poor "neurological organization" and may indicate "brain damage." The proposed treatments involve repetitive activities using specific muscle patterns in the order in which the child should have learned them if development had been normal; for example, rolling over, then crawling, then standing, then walking, and so forth. The method is described in their literature as reaching "all of the stimuli normally provided by this environment but with such intensity and frequency as to draw, ultimately, a response from the corresponding motor systems."

Reports from the American Academy of Pediatrics and other professional organizations, based on a review of all the literature, deny any evidence of success. These reports from the American Academy of Pediatrics conclude "that the patterning treatment offers no special merit, that the claims of its advocates are unproven, and that the demands on families are so great that in some cases there may be harm in its use."

This approach remains popular in the United States and around the world. Parents must know that patterning will not improve their son's or daughter's ADHD or learning disabilities.

## Vestibular Dysfunction

Several investigators have suggested that the vestibular system is important in learning. The vestibular system consists of a sensory organ in each inner ear that monitors head position and the impact of gravity and relays this information to the brain, primarily to the cerebellum. These investigators claim that there is a clear relationship between vestibular disorders and poor academic performance involving children with learning disabilities.

The first to stress this view was Dr. Jean Ayres. She proposed a theory of sensory integration needed to allow for the development of higher learning and intellectual functioning. Her theories propose the interrelationship between the visual, vestibular, tactile, and proprioceptive senses. Much of her research and that of others explores these interrelationships. There is controversy about aspects of her theory of sensory integration. These will not be discussed, since the focus of this chapter is not on theory but on treatments. The treatment model that evolved from her theories is

Sensory Integration Therapy. There are individuals who question the usefulness of this therapy approach for children and adults with learning disabilites who have visual perception, motor planning, vestibular, and tactile difficulties. However, the majority view of the field is positive about sensory integration therapy.

Dr. Harold Levinson has written several books describing his views on the causative role of the vestibular system and the vestibular-cerebellar systems with dyslexia and ADHD. He proposes the treatment of dyslexia with anti–motion sickness medication to correct the vestibular dysfunction. His books do present his own research, not published in scientific journals. There is little evidence to support his theory or the effectiveness of his treatment. In one of his recent books he proposes multiple other interventions along with the anti–motion sickness medication, including many other medications and special education.

Much research has been done on the vestibular system. The consistent finding is that there is no significant difference either in the intensity of vestibular responsivity or in the prevalence of vestibular dysfunction between children who are normal learners and those with learning disabilities. Furthermore, these researchers point out that the technique used by Dr. Levinson to diagnose vestibular dysfunction (i.e., a rotating cylinder with a picture on it with the child reporting when the picture is no longer clear) is a measure of "blurring speed" and, thus, a measure of visual stimulation and not of vestibular stimulation.

Dr. Levinson continues to write and publish. Much of the publicity for his approach is through these books and appearances on television talk shows. Other professionals have not started to practice what he proposes. Yet he remains busy, with a long waiting list.

## Auditory Processing Training

Several treatment approaches for improving auditory processing have been developed in the United States within recent years. Organizations offer auditory processing training as a treatment for ADHD and learning disabilities. As one reads these flyers and other advertisements, no research is offered and none is known to have been published. Yet, like other promised treatments, many parents read the flyers and started their child or adolescent in treatment at a not-inexpensive fee.

One treatment is called "Auditory Integration Training" and is based on the theory of Guy Bernard, a physician in France. The second is the "Listening Training Program" and is based on the theory of Alfred A. Tomatis, also a physician in France. The first approach uses amplifed sound and the second method focuses on proposed overly sensitive hearing.

The only literature available for study were the advertising flyers and instruction booklets supplied by the providers of the service. Two reviews of these approaches were published by the Edmonton Canada Public School System and the Manitoba Canada Speech and Hearing Association. Each of these reviews expressed caution about the treatment approaches and concern about the lack of research data. I will describe the methods and the concern with the lack of research.

Bernard's Auditory Integration Training is based on the theory that some individuals have auditory perception defects such that they hear distortions of sound, have unusually sensitive hearing, or have uneven patterns of auditory sensitivity that are within the range of normal hearing yet are uncomfortable. Auditory testing is done with a device called an Audiokinetron to determine at what frequencies a person has hyperacute or hypoacute hearing. Based on this audiogram, various compact disks are selected containing music determined to be the best for the person receiving the training. This music is played through the Audiokinetron, which has been set based on the individual's audiogram to amplify some frequencies and to filter out other frequencies of the sound spectrum. During twenty half-hour sessions (two per day), the frequencies that are hyperacute and painful are filtered out. This approach is described as similar to immobilizing painful joints or muscles until they heal. They report that after the treatment, the audiometric curve tends to flatten, and hearing is normalized. It is proposed that this treatment allows the auditory cortex to reorganize. In addition, the exercise strengthens the muscles that control the three bones of the middle ear, preventing sensory overload.

The Tomatis method is based on the theory that some children lose or turn off their ability to listen to certain parts of the normal sound spectrum. They do not, therefore, effectively absorb, comprehend, and interpret what they hear. Thus, these children's normal language development and, therefore, their relationship to the world beyond themselves can be affected. The intervention is done through a controlled process of auditory stimulation using sophisticated electronic equipment and special control interviews with the child and the parents. Treatment typically involves a three-week treatment session followed by a six-week rest period and then another three-week session. During the sessions, the child listens to filtered music and other sounds to "help the ear focus on the sounds he hears." In the later phases of treatment, the child is to repeat what is heard through earphones in order "to strengthen the now sensitized ear."

The ads and flyers are full of claims of success. Parents are almost made to feel guilty if they do not avail their child of this treatment. No research supports the theory or claims. It may be too early to report whether these approaches help students with learning disabilities. These treatments are controversial because they are being used before any research has shown validity for the theory or benefit from the treatment.

## Megavitamins

Using massive doses of vitamins to treat emotional or cognitive disorders was first proposed in the 1940s for the treatment of schizophrenia. It was argued that this disorder was the result of a biochemical problem and that this problem could be avoided by the use of massive amounts of vitamins, especially the B vitamins. No research supported the theory or the treatment and few professionals consider this approach today.

In the early 1970s, Dr. Allen Cott proposed that learning disabilities could be successfully treated with megavitamins. As with other professionals mentioned in this chapter, he presented his concepts in his own book, citing no outside research to support his thesis. The American Academy of Pediatrics issued a report specifically focusing on megavitamin therapy to treat learning disabilities. The conclusion: "There is no validity to the concept or treatment."

Within the past several years the concept of megavitamins to treat ADHD has surfaced again. These approaches will be discussed later in the section on Herbs.

## Trace Elements

Trace elements are chemicals found in the body in minute amounts that are essential to normal functioning. They include copper, zinc, magnesium, manganese, and chromium along with the more common chemicals calcium, sodium, and iron. In recent years iodine, aluminum, and cadmium have been discussed.

Individuals are evaluated for the level of these trace elements in their body. Hair or nail clippings are used for this analysis. If deficiencies are found, replacement therapy is given. No data has been published to support the theory that deficiencies in one or more of these elements are a cause of learning disabilities. No formal studies by professionals other than those offering the diagnosis and treatment have validated the proposed successes.

This concept remains popular in this country. Centers are available to diagnose deficiencies and to treat learning disabilities with trace elements.

## Allergies

Professionals who work with children have reported for many years that they see a higher percentage of children and adolescents in their practice with allergies who also have learning disabilities and/or ADHD. Most studies have been done on the possible relationships between allergies and learning disabilities.

There does appear to be a relationship between allergies and brain functioning. No specific cause and effect has yet been clarified. Two clinicians have written about specific issues relating allergies to learning disabilities and ADHD. Each has proposed a treatment plan. As with other approaches, the theory and treatment concepts are presented in books written by these clinicians. Little, if any, research is presented. The established profession of pediatric allergy does not accept these treatments. Since you might learn of these clinicians or of their approaches, I would like to review their views.

Dr. Doris Rapp believes that there is a relationship between food or other sensitivities and learning as well as with hyperactivity. She proposes a diet that eliminates the identified foods or the avoidance of other suspected allergens as a treatment. She believes that the traditional allergy skin testing for foods does not always detect the foods that cause problems. Her critics say that her challenge test, with a solution placed under the tongue, is not a valid measure of allergies.

Dr. Rapp identifies certain foods or food groups that children might be allergic to: milk, chocolate, eggs, wheat, corn, peanuts, pork, and sugar. She suggests that parents try a specific elimination diet described in her books. This diet consists of eliminating all of the possible allergy-producing foods and then adding one back each week to see if there is a change in behaviors.

She studies other possible allergens by using a food extract solution placed under the tongue in her tests. If the child is found to be sensitive to certain foods or chemicals in the environment (for example, paste, glue, paint, mold, chemicals found in new carpets), these items are eliminated or avoided. She reports an improvement in the behaviors of the child. Most specifically, she reports less aggressive or oppositional behavior and less hyperactivity. Other professionals have not been able to duplicate her findings or claimed successes.

Dr. William Crook has written extensively on the relationship between allergies and general health, learning disabilities, and ADHD. He writes of the "allergic-tension-fatigue syndrome." He also reports that specific allergies can result in hyperactivity and distractibility.

Many of his more recent publications and presentations focus on a possible allergic reaction to a specific yeast and the development of specific behaviors following a yeast infection. He reports that treatment of the yeast infection improves or corrects the problem. No clinical or research studies have confirmed his theories or proposed treatment program.

## Food Additives

In 1975, Dr. Benjamin Feingold published a book, *Why Your Child Is Hyperactive*. He proposed that synthetic flavors and colors in the diet were related to hyperactivity. He reported that the elimination of all foods containing artifical colors and flavors as well as salicylates and certain other additives stopped the hyperactivity. Neither in this book nor in any of his other publications did Dr. Feingold present research data to support this theory. All findings in the book were based on his clinical experience. He and his book received wide publicity. Parent groups advocating for the Feingold diet formed all over the country. It was left to others to document whether he was correct or incorrect.

The federal government sponsored several major research projects to study this theory and the treatment. In 1982, the National Institutes of Health held what is called a consensus conference on this issue. A panel of experts reviewed the results of these major research studies, read all available literature, held hearings to allow anyone who wished to present to do so, and questioned experts. The panel members then spent time synthesizing what was known and finally wrote a consensus on the topic.

They concluded that there does appear to be a subset of children with behavioral disturbances who respond to some aspects of Feingold's diet. However, this group is very small, possibly 1 percent of the children studied. The experts also commented that with notable exceptions, the specific elimination of synthetic food colors from the diet does not appear to be a major factor in the reported responses of a majority of these children. They concluded that the defined diets should not be used universally in the treatment of childhood hyperactivity.

Two studies done after this consensus conference reached the same conclusions. The Feingold diet is not effective in treating hyperactivity in children. There may be a small group, perhaps 1 percent, who appear to respond positively to the diet for reasons that are not clear.

There is no way for physicians to identify in advance which patients might be part of this small percent group. Sometimes a parent will report that if their child eats foods with specific food colors (for example, Kool-Aid, Hawaiian Punch, certain cereals) or takes a medication with specific food colors (for example, penicillin with red or yellow food dye), he or she will become more hyperactive. Perhaps this is the child with ADHD who might respond to a diet that eliminates that specific food color. The basic ADHD would still be present and need treatment.

## Refined Sugars

Clinical observations and parent reports suggest that refined sugar promotes adverse behavioral reactions in children. Hyperactive behavior is most commonly reported.

Several formal studies have been done to clarify and/or verify these parent claims. Each used what is called a challenge study. Children who were reported by parents to become more hyperactive when they ate refined sugar were given either refined sugar (glucose), natural sugar (fructose), or a placebo. The results failed to support the parent observations.

Another study explored whether the reported increase in activity level with children who ate a high-sugar snack or meal might be related to the amount of refined sugar eaten and not to the exposure to the sugar. In this study, children were given a breakfast high in either fat, carbohydrates, or protein. They were then given the challenge test with either refined sugar, natural sugar, or a placebo. Researchers found that some children appeared to be more active after a high-carbohydrate breakfast and exposure to refined sugars. Possibly, then, some children with ADHD will become more hyperactive if they eat high levels of refined sugar in foods and snacks throughout a period of time (sugared cereal for breakfast, cookies for snack, jelly sandwich and candy for lunch, cake for after-school snack, and so on).

## Herbs

The use of alternative medicines is popular around the world. Herbs, spices, and other ingredients have been known to be therapeutic in certain situations. The idea of using these items as a treatment for ADHD and possibly for learning disabilities has become very widespread within the past several years. As with most of the controversial treatments discussed in this chapter, most of what is known is found in flyers and advertisements distributed by the individuals selling the product. No research is presented. Claims are made about the effectiveness of the treatment.

In preparation for this update of my book, I wrote for more information on each of these products I either saw advertised or found exhibited at a meeting. I was struck by the absence of anything more than advertisements. I was also struck by the fact that three of the products to which I wrote "for more information" included an offer for me to be the exclusive salesperson for the product in my area. I was told how much good I would do for children by making them aware of this treatment.

I list those products I know of now. The uniform theme is that there is no research provided to defend the claims made. Testimonials were common. Large technical words were used. The advertising was designed to make me feel that if I didn't use the product, I was preventing my child from making progress. This list is meant to inform parents of the most common products available at the time this book was finalized. It is not a complete list. I'm sure there are others.

God's Recipe: This is a mixture of colloidal minerals, antioxidant with ginkgo biloba, and multienzymes.

Pedi-Active ADD: This is phosphatidyl/serine and is stated to contain the "most advanced neuronutrients available" including a diversified combination of other ingredients.

Kids Plex Jr: The ingredients are multivitamins, amino acids, a mixture of "Ergogens and Krebs Cycle Intermediates and Lipotropics."

Calms Kids: This is a mixture of vitamins, minerals, and amino acids.

Pycnogenol: This is described as a "water processed extract from the bark of the French Maritine Pine Tree . . . [the most] potent nutritional antioxidant discovered by science."

*New Vision:* This is a mixture of sixteen juices and eighteen fruit blends made into a capsule.

*Super Blue Green Algae:* This product comes in many forms and its benefits are stated to be based on the fact that algae is the "very basis of the entire food chain—it is largely responsible for creating and renewing all life on earth."

None of the producers of these products give many details. For example, what vitamins or amino acids? Many of the terms used were not defined and make little sense. No evidence to support the claims is given. I encourage parents to think carefully before buying these products.

## Biofeedback

A professional in California proposed that ADHD is a result of an altered pattern of brain waves and that this pattern can be identified on an electroencephalogram (EEG). This approach is presented as a diagnostic instrument. It is proposed that by using a biofeedback technique, it is possible to teach individuals to change their brain wave pattern. Once the pattern is corrected, the ADHD is improved or treated.

There is controversy about the theory relating to diagnosis and to treatment. There is greater controversy relating to EEG biofeedback as a treatment for ADHD. Yet the equipment is sold, and many professionals throughout the United States do this form of treatment.

Recently the Professional Advisory Board of the organization Children and Adults with Attention Deficit Disorder (CHADD) published a position statement. These professionals reviewed all of the literature on these concepts. In their statement, the use of EEG biofeedback for ADHD was challenged and parents were advised not to use this treatment approach.

## In Summary

There is a relationship between brain function and nutrition as well as between brain function and allergic reactions. These relationships appear to be true for ADHD, learning disabilities, and other neurological disorders. However, at this time we do not understand these relationships and there are no known treatments based on these relationships that are clinically successful.

When you learn of a new treatment or technique, you have good reason for showing interest. We all want a better and faster way to help these children and adolescents. Please take the time to become as informed as possible. Ask yourself why this amazing approach is not used by everyone. If the person proposing the treatment tells you that "most professionals are biased and do not believe my findings because they are different from the usual treatments," ask to see the data supporting the concept and treatment. Don't accept popular books published by the person proposing the theory or treatment as validated facts. Discuss the approach with your family physician, with the school professionals, and with other parents.

Don't put your son or daughter through something unproven and unlikely to help. Please spend as much time researching these treatments as you would considering a medication for yourself.

# PART SIX

## Special Topics

# 18
## The Adult with Attention Deficit Hyperactivity Disorder

The exact percentage of children and adolescents who continue to have ADHD as adults is not known. It is estimated that about 50 percent of adolescents with ADHD will continue to have this disability as adults. If the current estimate is correct, 3 to 6 percent of youth have ADHD, so we might expect 1.5 to 3 percent of adults to have ADHD.

The reality that adults have ADHD is relatively recent. Thus, many physicians who treat adults are not familiar with this possibility. Mental health professionals who work only with adults might not know to consider this possibility. With the increase in books and other literature on adult ADHD and the frequent coverage of this topic in the media, more and more adults have questioned if they have this disorder. Yet they might have difficulty finding a professional to evaluate them or find that through their reading, they know more about ADHD than the professional they are seeing.

The process for establishing the diagnosis is the same—the presence of a chronic and pervasive history of hyperactivity, impulsivity, and/or inattention/distractibility. The medications used for children and adolescents work exactly the same way with adults. The impact of ADHD on the individual might be the same as it is for children and adolescents but be reflected in a postsecondary educational setting or on the job and might be experienced with the adult's friends and family. This impact can be different because of the different life demands and expectations.

This chapter will focus on many issues relating to adults, but may not be in as much depth as an adult with ADHD might want. There are many excellent books available on adult ADHD. You can find them in most bookstores or obtain a list from CHADD, the national organization for individuals with ADHD. (See the appendix for information on CHADD.)

## ADHD in Adults

The same three behaviors are noted with adults who have ADHD as with children: hyperactivity, inattention, impulsivity.

### Hyperactivity

Adults with ADHD often find careers and lifestyles that are most compatible with being more active. They might seek jobs that require or permit moving about rather than sitting at a desk. They seem to find other adults who accept their activity level. Yet the ADHD behavior is there. They might sit, but their knees are moving up or down or their leg is swinging or their fingers are tapping. They have a difficult time sitting through long meals or movies.

I have met many adults with ADHD who find that the only way they can relax is to exercise to the point of exhaustion. If they go to the gym and work out or if they jog long distances, they can relax more for the hours that follow this activity. Others find that they need to keep an active pace all day and make sure that their work demands allow this.

For some adults, the hyperactivity does not become an issue until they become so successful on the job that they get promoted to middle management. Now, they have to sit at a desk and orga- nize the work of others, and they can't. For others, the stress be- gins when marriage and children create the need to be more calm, to sit for longer periods of time, and to "be still."

## Distractibility

As discussed earlier in this book, adults with ADHD might have the same problem with external distractibility as children. They might show greater problems with internal distractibility. Their mind jumps from thought to thought, or they find themselves trying to pay attention but drifting off. As with hyperactivity, these problems escalate with career success and promotion to more demanding levels of performance. Marriage and the demands of children only add to their difficulties.

## Impulsivity

Adults with ADHD might speak or act before they think. Many adults become very aware of this problem and concentrate on controlling themselves. As they go into a meeting, they might say to themselves "Keep your mouth shut." However, they still interrupt people or say things before thinking, hurting the feelings of others or sounding foolish. Others will act impulsively. They might buy things before they think whether they have the money or start to do something without thinking if they have enough time to complete what they started.

Some adults have difficulty with stealing, gambling, lying, or other impulse-control problems. Some do poorly when driving. They speed, change lanes without looking and reflecting, take risks, and have more accidents or traffic tickets.

## Organization

What about organization? Every article or book on ADHD discusses the problems of the "organizationally impaired." Adults with ADHD, like children and adolescents with ADHD, can have major problems with organization.

Adults with ADHD have trouble organizing materials at work or home as well as difficulty organizing schedules and time. Their life can be one big disorganized problem at work, with per-

sonal time, and with family. Is organization one of the characteristic problems of ADHD? We do not yet know the answer. I
would like to offer my views on this issue.

I believe that organization is a significant problem for many
children, adolescents, and adults with ADHD. I also believe that
there are several different causes that result in the outcome of
disorganization. For some, it is a consequence of the inattention
and distractibility; thus, it is seen with individuals who have
ADHD. For some, it is a consequence of a learning disability or
an executive function problem. Thus, disorganization is seen
with adults who have these problems. Since a high percentage of
individuals with these problems also have ADHD, this behavior
might be seen with adults who have ADHD.

*Disorganization secondary to distractibility is real.* For example, a woman goes into the kitchen to start dinner. She notes
some papers on the kitchen table. Because her attention shifts,
she sits down and begins to read over the papers. At one point
she looks up and notices a yellow Post-it note on the telephone
and remembers she has to make a telephone call. So she gets up
and uses the phone. While talking on the phone, she glances
across the kitchen and sees a magazine on a counter. She hangs
up and goes to look at the magazine. Now, twenty minutes after
she entered the kitchen, her children come in asking about dinner. Suddenly, she remembers why she had gone into the kitchen.
Her life is full of such examples of visual distractibility, resulting
in a life of disorganization. Clearly, the disorganization is a consequence of her ADHD.

Another adult might describe starting to do a home task (laundry, cleaning house, paying the bills). Suddenly, his mind jumps
to something else, and he starts to do this other activity. Then,
his mind jumps again, and off he goes. His day is full of incomplete piles of tasks, and his life is disorganized. Here, the internal
distractibility of the ADHD results in the disorganization.

I believe that many adults who have problems with organization and completing tasks have this disorganization as a secondary consequence of their external or internal distractibility.
Thus, I can see why many books on adults with ADHD focus on
the problems with organization.

*Disorganization secondary to learning disabilities is also real.*

Recall that one of the processing tasks of integration is organization. With the processing model, organization means the ability to synthesize pieces of information together into a concept and the ability to break a concept into its parts. Organization also refers to the ability to structure one's thoughts, materials, and time. Characteristic of the children, adolescents, or adults with an organizational disability as part of their pattern of learning disabilities is that their notebook and papers and materials are a mess, with items misfiled or sticking out. They lose things and forget things. They complete work and misplace it before it is turned in. They can't organize their space or room, and they get overwhelmed when their environment is disorganized. They have difficulty organizing time. Clearly, we see adults who have the same problems on the job (or in college) and within the family. Sorting, folding, and distributing laundry can be as overwhelming for the adult as keeping notebooks and homework organized was for the child.

Adults with an organizational disability as part of their learning disabilities might have difficulty deciding how to subdivide or put together materials. Their office or home is cluttered with piles of papers or other materials. Their desk is cluttered. They sort of know which pile to look through to get what they want, but others think they are disorganized and messy. Partners do not like living with such clutter. This adult will tell you that she or he does not know how to subdivide material into categories so it can be filed. If he or she files the material, he or she would never know where to look to find it again. Thus, it is better to keep everything in visible piles. At least then he or she knows what pile to look for.

Adults with organizational problems secondary to learning disabilities might have major difficulty with time planning. They just can't get themselves organized or plan their day to get everything done. They make schedules but somehow can't follow them. They misjudge how long a task or errand will take and seem to be constantly late.

Another example of learning disabilities leading to disorganization is that of adults with short-term memory problems. They never remember what to do or where to be. They make lists to help themselves but lose the lists or forget to look at them. They forget to do things or forget to show up. Their lives are disorganized.

*Executive function disorder problems may result in disorganization.* Recall that the term *executive function* refers to the ability to define and assess a task, plan a strategy for carrying out the task, begin this process, make any adjustments needed along the way, and complete the task. Some adults with ADHD describe an inability to take on tasks. They have difficulty deciding how to solve the problem, or they start but get lost or stuck. Again, their life is disorganized. Here, though, psychoeducational testing might clarify that the reason is not ADHD but the processing problems characteristic of executive function disorder.

## Recognition and Diagnosis

Since, at this time, few physicians and mental health professionals who see adults are familiar with ADHD, this diagnosis is often missed. It is not uncommon for the individual seeking help to know more about this disability than the professional seen.

For some, the diagnosis becomes clear when their son or daughter is diagnosed with ADHD. "That's me. I have had the same problems all of my life." Or one parent might point to the other and say, "He [she] is just like our child." For others, articles in the newspaper or a magazine or book or specials on television might make them aware that there might be a reason for the problems they have had most of their life. Let me start with an example, Fran.

Fran was diagnosed as having learning disabilities when she was in the third grade. Although she attended special classes all through high school, she had increasing difficulty doing her schoolwork. Fran's teachers and her parents complained that she would not stay on task or make an effort to complete her work. During her senior year of high school, she began psychotherapy for her "lack of seriousness about school." Her psychiatrist thought she was depressed and placed her on an antidepressant medication with no benefit.

She went to a college that offered resource help and accommodations for her learning disabilities. Yet she found the work difficult. She couldn't concentrate when she studied in the dormatory and began to worry that she might not make it. On the advice of her former psychotherapist, she went to the college mental health service. The psychologist who saw her questioned if she might have ADHD and referred her to me.

Fran gave a classic history of hyperactivity, distractibility, and impulsivity throughout her life. She was fidgety and had been so "forever." Her friends, even the new ones in college, teased her about her constant need to move some part of her body. Any sound would distract her. She could recall examples from elementary school of listening to what was going on in the hall rather than in class. Fran cried as she described her impulsivity. She constantly hurt her friends' feelings by saying something before thinking, and her teachers often yelled at her for answering out of turn.

With Fran's permission, her mother was invited to a session. We asked her to bring all of Fran's old report cards and the psychoeducational evaluations done in the past. The hyperactivity, distractibility, and impulsivity were described year after year, starting in kindergarten. Her teachers and parents assumed these problems to be part of her learning disabilities.

I started Fran on Ritalin. At a dose of 10 mg three times a day, she showed significant improvement: "It's a miracle. I feel so relaxed. I can concentrate so much better, even in the dorm. I am getting my work done so much quicker and better. My friends have commented that I seem so different. I pay attention when they are talking to me; and, I don't interrupt them when they are talking. . . ." She then added, "Why was I not given this medication when I was a child?"

This last question opened up her feelings of anger and sadness that she had had to struggle for so long. She also felt the pain of years of being told it was all her fault and that she could do better if she tried. We continued to work together to help with these concerns and feelings.

Howard's father is another example.

During my interpretive session with Howard's parents, I explained why I felt Howard had ADHD and how I wanted to approach helping him. Both parents agreed with the diagnosis, the need for medication, and the need for further educational efforts. The next day

Howard's mother called me. She mentioned that she was never comfortable talking about her husband during our meetings but she was worried about him.

Her husband was described as explosive at home. He would yell, throw things, and "explode." On several occasions, he made a hole in the wall with his fists. She also commented that he dropped out of college and that he had difficulty keeping jobs because of complaints about his not getting the work done. She thought he had ADHD. We agreed that I would try to explore this theme during our follow-up meeting.

When I met with Howard's parents to discuss behavioral management issues within the family, I mentioned that in about 50 percent of children with ADHD, one of the parents had the same problems. I then reviewed how these problems might look with an adult. I asked each parent if any of what I was describing "sounded familiar." After a brief silence, Howard's father commented that he had been thinking about himself since our last meeting. The more he opened up and described himself as a child, adolescent, college student, and adult, the more he showed evidence of hyperactivity, distractibility, and impulsivity. He agreed to see me on his own.

The further history obtained confirmed the diagnosis. Howard's father agreed to start medication and showed significant improvement in all areas. He felt that his work performance improved. His wife reported that he was so much more relaxed and into being part of the family. He was not losing his temper.

I arranged for him to work with a coach (described later in this chapter) to focus on his work-related difficulties. He also decided to disclose his problem to his supervisor at work. We had to think this approach through to clarify what he wanted to say and what he wanted to have as accommodations on the job.

As these examples show, the diagnosis of ADHD with adults starts with establishing clinical evidence of one or more of the three behaviors. Then, the presence of these behaviors must be shown to be pervasive—to affect two or more areas of the adult's life. Finally, these behaviors must be documented to have existed since at least age six. Often, this chronic theme is based only on the memory of the adult. Sometimes the adult will remember that he or she used to take medication in grade school so that he or she could sit still or pay attention. Preferably, previous records or information from parents or siblings should be obtained to validate this history.

## Treatment with Medication

The use of appropriate medications is just as essential with adults as with children. Since the dose of these medications is not based on body weight, the amount used might be the same with adults as with children. The amount needed has to be evaluated for each individual.

John, a thirty-five-year-old attorney, came to see me after reading an article in the paper. He told me that from age nine to sixteen he had been on medication because of overactivity and trouble concentrating. He remembered that two of his sisters took the same medicine. At my request, he contacted his mother who contacted the family doctor. We learned that he had been on dextroamphetamine (Dexedrine).

During college and law school, John occasionally was able to get Dexedrine from his friends. When he took it, he studied better and more efficiently. Now, he was working for a law firm and having great difficulty staying on task and getting his work done. He said he was frustrated with his performance. He knew he could do the work, but he had great difficulty staying organized and keeping track of his "billable hours." He also found that it was difficult to get any work done during the day because of the talking and noise in the office. He worked best late at night or when he took the work home to do.

I placed John on dextroamphetamine. At a dose of 5 mg every four hours, he reported a dramatic improvement. He was able to concentrate and stay on task. He was able to work despite the activity around him. His thoughts were more organized, and he became effective and efficient at work. Even his direct supervisor noted the changes.

If an adult responds to medication, the concept of using medication whenever it is needed is just as important as with children and adolescents. They might need coverage during evenings and weekends in order to function better within their family.

I have had some adults agree that the medication helped them be more calm and less impulsive. Yet they liked the way they were. They were used to "living with" their level of activity and liked the level of excitement they experienced. Knowing how the medication worked, they elected not to be on medication. I supported this decision.

## Nonmedication Treatments

As with children, ADHD interferes with all aspects of life. For adults, these areas of life include postsecondary education, on-the-job relationships and performance abilities, interactions with friends and more casual relationships, ability to participate in recreational activities, and success with more intimate relationships with a significant other. For many adults, the major area of difficulty is work. For many others, this major area of difficulty is the family.

For some adults, the emotional consequences of ADHD throughout life might need to be addressed. The resulting anxiety or depression or difficulty with anger control or with relationships is as important to treat as the basic ADHD. For others, it is clear that they have ADHD plus one or more of the related disorders discussed throughout this book. These problems must be identified and addressed as well.

ADHD might have significantly affected academic success in high school and in postsecondary programs. Once diagnosed, it might be necessary to assess for educational, vocational, or career themes. This is especially true for the adult who has had limited success in the world of work or who did not complete his or her education.

Thus, once the diagnosis is made it becomes important to do several things. First, what secondary emotional, social, or family problems might need to be addressed? Second, are any of the related disorders present? The most frequently found is a learning disability. What job or career-related difficulties exist and how might they be approached? I find that the selection of a medication and the adjustment of dose and timing is often the easiest part of the treatment program. Addressing these other areas requires time, networking, and effort.

Some adults find that once their ADHD behaviors are under better control and their learning disabilities, if present, are understood, they can rethink many aspects of their life and move forward. Others might need vocational testing, vocational guidance, or accommodations in their current job. Some might want to return to college or continue in college and need appropriate accommodations. In a later chapter I will review the legal issues of importance when helping an adult with ADHD.

*Coaching* is a new and exciting approach to help some adults with ADHD. Some professionals who were special education tutors for children and adolescents with learning disabilities have retrained to help adults with ADHD. They call themselves coaches rather than tutors. Coaches work closely with the individual adult, identifying the areas of difficulty. The coach then works with this adult, analyzing the reasons for the problem. Together they develop and try compensatory strategies.

These strategies are modified until they work and then practiced until they are used routinely. Or the conclusion might be that the problem is so complex that it would be best to have others help when doing the task or to find someone else to do the task.

The task might be financing and balancing a checkbook, or organizing one's life or day, or getting rid of those piles of things and learning how to compartmentalize and file materials. Tasks might be work-related (helping an attorney to handle the task of monitoring billable hours or a plant supervisor to keep an inventory list). Whether the adult with ADHD is a disorganized parent who can't manage the home and kids or someone who can't handle the demands of a job, a creative coach can help develop strategies for greater success.

## In Summary

ADHD is a reality for many adults. The clues for recognizing the possibility that an adult has ADHD and the process for diagnosing are the same as for children and adolescents. The treatment approaches are also the same except for the need to address the special issues faced by an adult. This chapter on adults identifies areas of difficulty but does not go into the models for helping in enough depth for the adult with ADHD. I encourage you to read some of the excellent books available for adults.

# 19

## Legal Issues of Importance to Parents

Fortunately for your son or daughter and for you, today laws require school systems to provide services for children and adolescents with disabilities. This was not always the case. Before 1975, about half of the children with disabilities in this country could not get an appropriate education. About one million were excluded entirely from the public school system. The situation with children and adolescents who have ADHD is still not ideal. As will be explained later in this chapter, this disorder is not formally recognized in the education law but only in the civil laws.

These laws, however, do not automatically assure that your child or adolescent will receive the appropriate programs and services he or she needs. This reality is even more true now because of the decrease in federal and state funding for education. You must be fully informed on ADHD and on your rights, and you must learn to be an assertive advocate for your daughter or son. You must know the laws and know your rights, and then you must work actively with the school professionals to get what your child needs, insisting on these rights. The school personnel care about the education of *all* students. You care especially about the education of *your* student.

What are these laws? What do they mean for your son or daughter? What must you know and do to assure the best help you can possibly get? What can you do if you are not pleased with your school professional's effort? Let me try to answer these questions.

## Parent Power

The major force behind today's legislation was a consumer movement led by organizations of parents of children with disabilities. Later, the people with disabilities themselves joined in this effort. They focused on the lack of an appropriate public education and on the exclusion of children and adolescents from programs provided by the public education system.

In the 1960s, various groups of parents whose children had different disabilities used publicity, mass mailings, public meetings, and other well-organized, opinion-molding techniques to put pressure on state legislatures. They wanted laws making educational opportunities for persons with disabilities not simply available but mandatory. Most states responded with legislation, some more than others.

A few states did nothing. Most of the more progressive state governments passed the laws but provided no enabling funds for facilities or trained professionals to carry out their intent. The focus of these pressure groups then shifted toward enactment of a federal law that could have an impact on all states.

In 1971, the Pennsylvania Association for Retarded Citizens filed a suit in that state that directly involved the federal government in these issues for the first time. Citing constitutional guarantees of due process and equal protection under the law, the group argued that the access of children with mental retardation to public education should be equal to that afforded other children. The court agreed. A year later the federal court in the District of Columbia made a similar ruling involving not only persons with mental retardation, but those with a wide range of disabilities. This 1972 decision established two major precedents critical to future progress: (1) Children with disabilities have the right to a "suitable publicly supported education, regardless of the degree of the child's mental, physical, or emotional disability or impairment" and (2) concerning financing, "if sufficient funds are not available to finance all of the services and programs that are needed and desirable . . . the available funds must be expended equitably in such a manner that no child is entirely excluded from a publicly supported education." More than forty such cases were won throughout the United States following these two landmark decisions.

These court actions also had a profound influence on federal legislation. The Rehabilitation Act of 1973, referred to as "The Civil Rights Act for the Handicapped," prohibits discrimination on the basis of physical or mental handicaps in every federally assisted program in the country. Public education, of course, accepts federal assistance. Section 504 of this law focuses on the rights of the individual people in these programs, and it has been the keystone of parents' demands and of numerous successful court actions. The most critical issues in Section 504 are:

1. As disabled job applicants or employees, handicapped people have the same rights and must be guaranteed the same benefits as nonhandicapped applicants and employees.
2. They are entitled to all of the medical services and medically related instruction that is available to the general public.
3. They are entitled to participate in vocational rehabilitation, day care, or any other social service program receiving federal assistance on an equal basis with the nonhandicapped.
4. They have the equal rights to go to college or to enroll in job training or adult post-high school basic education programs. Selection must be based on academic or other school records, and the disability cannot be a factor. (If a person has learning disabilities, the standard entrance testing procedures, the Scholastic Aptitude Test, for example, can be modified, and admission standards can be based on potential as well as on past performance.)
5. State and local school districts must provide an appropriate elementary and secondary education for all handicapped students.

In 1990, this law was expanded to all programs, not just to federally funded programs. The Americans with Disabilities Act ended discrimination against individuals with disabilities in the area of employment, education, public accommodations, and licensing of professional and other activities. It extends the coverage of basic civil rights legislation to a wide range of public and private entities. I will discuss this act in detail later in this chapter.

Section 504, especially the fifth point noted, became the basis for Public Law 94–142, the "Education for All Handicapped Children Act." It was passed overwhelmingly by the House and Senate and enacted in November of 1976. It was a final victory for the parents who fought so hard for their children. This law is unique in several ways. There is no expiration date. It is regarded as permanent law. It does more than just express a concern with children with disabilities; it requires a specific commitment. The law sets forth as national policy the proposition that education must be extended to persons with disabilities *as a fundamental right.*

Thanks to these parents, the right of the person with learning disabilities to a good education is now guaranteed by education law. This assurance, as will be discussed later, is not yet as clear for persons with ADHD. The challenge for today's parents is to insist on the transformation of this promise into reality.

Your need as a parent to educate yourself and to be appropriately assertive is more critical now than ever. With federal, state, and county budget cuts, services to persons with disabilities have been significantly cut. Because of these budget cuts and loss of personnel, some school systems lead parents to believe that their child is not entitled to services or that the minimal services offered are adequate. This crisis in services is compounded by another problem. The initial law, Public Law 94–142, provided services for parent education. There was an understood need to inform parents of their rights under the law. This knowledge helped parents enter the system and function within the system. These parents have sons and daughters who have graduated from high school. After this initial funding for parent education ended, most school systems stopped providing such an education. None of the parents of the current public school students benefitted from this initial educational process. As I lecture around the country, I am distressed by the frequency with which I meet parents who do not know of their rights or how to fight for the services their son or daughter needs.

# Public Law 94–142: The Education for All Handicapped Children Act

Because Public Law 94–142 is so important to you, let me review first what the original law included and then explain the many amendments enacted since. I will suggest how you can work within this law to be an advocate for your child or adolescent. This law is the only hope for fighting for services. You must know and understand it.

The initial law listed eleven categories of children with disabilities: mentally retarded, hard-of-hearing, deaf, deaf-blind, speech-impaired, visually handicapped, seriously emotionally disturbed, orthopedically impaired, other health-impaired, *specific learning disabilities,* and multihandicapped. In a 1986 amendment (to be discussed later), two new categories were added: autism and traumatic brain injury. Despite the efforts of parent groups, ADHD was not added to this list when the revisions were made.

Learning disabilities are included, defined in the law as applying to those children "who have a disorder in one or more of the basic psychological processes involved in understanding or in using language, spoken or written, which disorder may manifest itself in imperfect ability to listen, think, speak, read, write, spell, or do mathematical calculations. Such disorders include such conditions as perceptual handicaps, brain injury, minimal brain dysfunction, dyslexia, and developmental aphasia. Such terms do not include children who have learning problems which are primarily the result of visual, hearing, or motor handicaps, or mental retardation, emotional disturbance, or of environmental, cultural, or economic disadvantage."

This law entitles children and adolescents with a handicapping condition to the following:

1. A *free public education* is guaranteed to all between the ages of three and twenty-one. (The term *free and appropriate public education,* or *FAPE,* is often referred to in school procedures.)
2. Each handicapped person is guaranteed an *individualized education program,* or *IEP.* This IEP must be in the form

of a written statement, jointly developed by the school officials, the child's teacher, the parent or guardian, and if possible by the child her- or himself. It must include an analysis of the child's present achievement level, a list of both short-range and annual goals, an identification of the specific services that will be provided toward meeting these goals, and an indication of the extent to which the child will be able to participate in regular school programs. The IEP must also be clear about when these services will be provided and how long they will last, and it provides a schedule for checking on the process achieved under the plan and for making any revisions in it that may be needed.

3. Handicapped and nonhandicapped children must be *educated together* to the fullest extent that is appropriate. The child can be placed in special classes or separate schools only when the nature and severity of his or her handicap prevents satisfactory achievement in a regular education program. This concept of placement is referred to as being *in the least restrictive environment* possible.

4. Tests and other *evaluation materials* used in placing handicapped children must be prepared and administered in such a way as not to be racially or culturally discriminatory. They must also be presented in the child's native tongue.

5. An intensive and ongoing effort must be made to *locate* and *identify* children with handicaps, to evaluate their educational needs; and to determine whether these needs are being met.

6. In all efforts, *priority* must be given to those who are not receiving an education and to those severely handicapped people who are receiving an inadequate education.

7. In all decisions, a *prior consultation with the child's parents or guardians* must be held. No policies, programs, or procedures affecting the education of handicapped children may be adopted without a public notice.

8. These rights and guarantees apply to handicapped children in *private as well as public schools.* Any special education provided to any child shall be provided *at no cost to the*

*parents* if state or local education agency officials placed the child in such schools or referred the child to them.

9. States and localities must develop comprehensive *personnel development programs,* including in-service training for regular as well as special education teachers and support personnel.

10. In implementing the law, special effort shall be made to employ qualified handicapped persons.

11. All architectural barriers must be removed.

12. The state education agency has jurisdiction over all educational programs for handicapped children offered within a given state, including those administered by noneducational agencies.

13. An *advisory panel* must exist to advise the state's education agency of unmet needs. Membership must include handicapped people and parents or guardians of those people.

This law guarantees *procedural safeguards.* Parents or guardians have an opportunity to examine any records that bear on the identification of a child as being disabled, on the defined nature and severity of his or her disability, and on the kind of educational setting in which he or she is placed. Schools must provide written notice prior to changing a child's placement. If a parent or guardian objects to a school's decision, there must be a process in place through which complaints can be registered. This process must include an opportunity for an impartial hearing that offers parents rights similar to those involved in a court case—the right to be advised by counsel (and by special education experts if they wish), to present evidence, to cross-examine witnesses, to compel the presence of any witnesses who do not voluntarily appear, to be provided a verbatim report of the proceedings, and to receive the decision and findings in written form.

The rights and safeguards of Public Law 94-142 are critical. Take the time to reread the above paragraph. Each school system is required to provide you with a written guideline explaining your rights of appeal. If they have not, ask for it.

## Revisions to Public Law 94-142

In September 1986, Congress passed Public Law 99-457. This law, entitled "Education of the Handicapped Act Amendments of 1986," included provisions for children with disabilities of all ages. The upper age was kept at twenty-one. The original starting age of three, however, was lowered to include "handicapped and 'at risk' children between the ages of birth and age six and their families." There are two major components to this law.

A new mandate for state education agencies to serve all three-, four-, and five-year-old children with disabilities by 1991 was created. All of the rights to an education in the original law for ages six to twenty-one are now required *down* to age three. As with the initial law, services for these children in the three-to-six age group are not encouraged but mandated. If a state does not comply, it can lose many areas of federal funds.

The second landmark in this early intervention program established by these amendments is the Handicapped Infants and Toddlers Program. This section of the law creates a brand-new federal program for children with disabilities and who are at risk, from birth to age three years, and for their families. While the infant and toddler program is voluntary for states, that is, they may elect not to participate, if a state does choose to participate or to apply for funding under this law, it must meet the requirements of the law and assure that services are available for all eligible children.

Public Law 99-457 stresses the importance of a coordinated and multiagency approach to the planning and dialogue that is necessary to implement the new early childhood initiatives. A wide variety of local providers, public and private, must work together to provide the services.

In 1988, the 101st Congress approved a change in the name of Public Law 94-142 from *Education for All Handicapped Children* to *Individuals with Disabilities Education Act,* or *IDEA.* This change was in keeping with the increased concept of political correctness. One does not speak of disabled children but of children with disabilities.

Changes never cease. IDEA was considered for revision during the 1997 session of Congress. Many of the proposed changes would have significantly weakened the law. Through constant efforts by parent volunteers, the law was saved in a strong form. In April of 1997, the latest amendments were passed by Congress and signed by the president. These amendments provide the following changes:

1. Schools must obtain informed consent from parents prior to their child's initial evaluation to determine the presence of a disability and any re-evaluation.
2. Parents are now members of their child's eligibility, IEP, and placement teams.
3. The three-year, or triennial, re-evaluation no longer automatically requires extensive or prescribed testing. The IEP team (including parents and other professionals) will determine what re-evaluation information and testing is necessary based upon the needs of the individual child.
4. Children with disabilities must be included in all general and districtwide assessment programs. Appropriate accommodations will be provided when necessary.
5. Alternative assessments must be developed by July 1, 2000, for those children who cannot participate in state or districtwide assessment programs.
6. To resolve disputes about a child's special education, all states and local education agencies must make available a mediation process. Participation in mediation, however, is voluntary.
7. All children with disabilities, even if expelled or placed on long-term suspension, are entitled to educational services that meet the standards of a free and appropriate public education.

## Your Child or Adolescent and IDEA

Each state has developed its own laws, rules, and regulations for carrying out the intentions of this federal law. You will have to speak to your school officials, other parents, or other knowledgeable people to learn about the specifics as they apply in your state and community. Even though ADHD is not listed as a "handicapping condition," knowledge of the requirements of the law is essential to understanding what you can do. Since many children with ADHD also have a learning disability, it is important for many parents to know how to get help for this disability as well.

It is useful to look at the several steps in the process followed to help your son or daughter. Let me be specific.

1. *Search.* Each school system must have a system for seeking out students who might have a disability.
2. *Find.* Once a student with a potential problem is identified, there should be a system for collecting information and designing an evaluation process.
3. *Evaluation.* A comprehensive, multidisciplinary evaluation should be done.
4. *Conference.* Parents or guardians should meet with the school personnel and evaluation professionals to review the evaluation conclusions, any labels or diagnoses established, and any proposed placement and IEP. The details should be presented in writing.
5. *Parents' decision process.* Parents or guardians, with consultation from educational or other professionals and lawyers when needed, decide to accept, request clarification of, request changes in, or reject the proposed placement and IEP.
6. *Appeals process.* If parents reject the label, placement recommendation, or IEP, there should be an appeals process that starts with the local school system and can go to the county or state level.
7. *Follow-up progress reports.* Such reports should be provided to the family. As the end of the school year approaches, a reassessment is done. There should be a *conference* to plan the next school year. Steps 5 and 6 are repeated before implementation of the next year's plans.
8. *Conference.* School professionals meet with parents to discuss findings and recommendations.

Throughout this book, I have urged you as a parent to be informed and assertive. I have suggested what you need for your son or daughter and how to get the services from your school system. Please note that what I have encouraged you to fight for is not based only on what I believe children and adolescents with learning disabilities need. It is based on federal law that mandates this. This federal law requires every state and every school system within the state to meet the requirements of the law. School systems can only get away with not meeting the requirements of the law if you do not know your rights. Since this is so important to you, let me go into more detail on your rights under this law.

### Search

If someone from your school system suggests that your son or daughter might have a problem and needs testing, be positive and agree to the testing. If the tests reveal a problem, you can get help. If the tests find nothing wrong, that should relieve both you and the school. If you are concerned about your child's academic progress and suspect a problem but your school has said nothing about it, speak to the classroom teacher. Share your observations and concerns.

If the teacher agrees with you, he or she can initiate the process through the principal. If you cannot get the classroom teacher to start this process, meet with the principal. (It is best not to go directly to the principal first because this may antagonize the teacher.) When there are two parents, it is always better for both to be present at such meetings. Explain your concerns again, and ask the principal to start the evaluation process. If the principal does not agree and/or refuses to request such an evaluation, follow up on this meeting with a formal request in writing. Under federal guidelines, if a request is made to the principal in writing, the principal must call a meeting of essential people within thirty working days to consider this request. Usually the school psychologist, special education person, and teacher attend this meeting, which is chaired by the principal. This meeting is usually called an education management team meeting, or EMT meeting.

At this EMT meeting, your request will be reviewed. If the team agrees to do the evaluation, you will be asked to sign a release for such testing. If the team does not agree to do an evaluation or suggests observing for several months first, you can accept this decision or you can appeal this decision to a higher level.

If you strongly suspect that your son or daughter has a learning disability, there is another option. If you can afford the cost, get a private evaluation and bring the results back to this team. If the results show evidence of a disability, the team must respond. Such private evaluations are expensive and many families cannot afford them.

Why is it hard for school professionals to see what parents are concerned about? I find that there are several types of students who are struggling but not recognized. One is the quiet, shy, withdrawn student who is not causing trouble. Unfortunately, the school staff might wait until this child is so frustrated and unhappy that he or she refuses to go to school, cries in school, or gets into difficulty before becoming concerned. Another type is the very bright child who manages to do at least average work in spite of his or her problems. This child may have a superior intelligence but because of learning disabilities, may be performing at a C level. School personnel see the student as "just average," yet what is actually happening is a case of significant underachievement.

Another situation is where parents are doing two or more hours of homework with the child each night, essentially teaching the child what was not learned in class or doing the work for or with the child. In addition, parents might be providing a private tutor to help the child. Thus, the child appears to be doing well in school. I always ask the school professionals, must this parent remove all help and supports and let the child fail before he or she is seen as in need of an evaluation?

### Find and Evaluate

Once the school personnel agree to the need for an evaluation, make yourself as informed as possible about what the evaluation is and what is being assessed. Find out what is planned, make sure that the plans cover the areas discussed in the chapters on evaluation. Be sure that someone prepares your son or daughter for each step.

For preschoolers, school systems are required to have a multidisciplinary team available to evaluate children who need assessment. In most school systems, this program is called Child Find.

## Conference

School personnel and special educators will meet with you. If your family has two parents or guardians, be sure both of you are present. You may also bring your own professional consultant to review the results and recommendations and to advise you. You are entitled to receive written copies of each evaluation prior to this meeting so that you can have your consultants review them and advise you. If you feel it necessary, you can bring your lawyer.

Angry, defensive, or demanding behavior won't get you anyplace. Assume that everyone there has the best interest of your son or daughter at heart. In reality, this is true for more than most school conferences. Your school personnel want to do what is best for your child or adolescent. Often, they must weigh this need with the reality of budget and available services. Listen, ask questions, reflect. Even if you completely agree with everything that is advised, ask for time to think and to read the recommendations in detail. On the one hand, anger or defensiveness polarizes the sides. On the other, too quick an agreement may prevent you from asking questions that occur to you after you read the reports and reflect on them.

Do your homework prior to the conference. Reread Chapter 6 on evaluation. Talk with other parents or parent advocates who have been in the same situation and, if possible, learn something about what programs are likely to be suggested.

If someone says that your child has learning disabilities, ask for specifics. You know what learning disabilities are. Let them know of your knowledge and of your need for exact information. Don't let the evaluators overwhelm you with professional words. Ask for definitions and clarification in a calm, concerned way. Let them know that although what they say is important, this is *your* child or adolescent about whom you care very much.

*Remember:* ADHD is not listed in IDEA. I will discuss later ways of getting the child with ADHD included under IDEA. For those parents whose son or daughter also has a learning disability, let me review issues of importance when trying to get services. For the school professionals, the question is not whether your son or daughter has a learning disability—the question is whether he or she is eligible for services. Each school system has a definition of eligibility based on a discrepancy formula. That is, how far behind does the child or adolescent have to be in what areas to qualify for services? (It has been my experience that when the budget is adequate, the amount of discrepancy between ability and performance required to be eligible for services is less than when the budget is tight.)

If you do not agree with the findings, don't challenge them just now. Tell the evaluation team that you would like a copy of the test results and the minutes of the meeting so that you can discuss them with a consultant. You wouldn't consent to your child having open heart surgery or even to being sent to the hospital without a second opinion. Committing your child to at least one year of a special education program or to another year in a regular program without the appropriate help has a different degree but just as great an impact on his or her life.

You will have to agree to the diagnosis or label; that is, to the name your school gives to the problems they say your son or daughter has. You also will have to agree to the level and type of services to be provided and to the placement recommendations. All of these conclusions should be written in the proposed individualized education program (IEP). Ask for clarifications and definitions. Carefully read the documents and be sure you understand. Only if you agree and sign the IEP can actions be taken. No school system can act without a parent's consent.

Keep in mind the difference between an emotional problem that *causes* academic difficulties and an emotional problem that *results* in academic difficulties. If your son's or daughter's behavior problems are due to the frustrations and failures experienced because of ADHD or learning disabilities, don't agree to having him or her labeled only as "emotionally disturbed." If the school personnel insist that your son or daughter has ADHD and/or learning disabilities and an emotional disorder, they may be correct. In making your decision, consider this possibility. If he or she is coded as having a learning disability first, with emotional disturbance as the secondary diagnosis, the placement will be in a program for students with learning disabilities with supportive psychological help. If he or she is coded as emotionally disturbed first, with having a learning disability as the secondary diagnosis, the placement will be in a program for students with emotional disorders with supportive special education help for the learning disabilities. Which do you believe would be best for your child or adolescent? The primary label is critical. Fight for the correct one.

Your school system is responsible for placing your child in an appropriate program within its system. Only if this is not possible will an out-of-system or private placement be considered. You may prefer that your child go into a particular private program that you know about. The public school does not have to concur, however, if an appropriate placement is available within their own system. You might argue that the private placement is better, and this might be true. But even if it were, the law states only that each child must receive an *appropriate* education, not necessarily the *best* education possible.

There are several program levels of service. You want to find the *least restrictive program* that still provides the *most effective educational support* for your child. Remember that this does not always mean being in a regular class program. The least restrictive environment for some children might be the most restrictive environment available. A child may need the security and support of a small, separate, self-contained classroom in order to feel safe enough to relax, take risks again, and become available for learning.

Ask for the details on any placement. Where is it? Will your child have to be transported out of the neighborhood? Ask about the qualifications of the teacher, the size of the class, and the age distribution of the students. Ask for the mix of students—diagnosis, level of intellectual functioning. Ask if you can visit the program. Even if it is spring and you will see a different group of students, you will get a feel for the teacher and program. Try to speak to several parents of the children who are currently in the program. If the teacher has not been selected yet or the class makeup established, ask for a written statement of the qualifications that this teacher must have and the probable makeup of the class.

What about the IEP? This is the written plan identifying the instruction designed especially for your son or daughter and list-

ing reasonable expectations for the child's achievement. There
should be a specific system for monitoring progress.

At a minimum, each IEP must cover the following points:

1. A statement of your child's or adolescent's levels of educational performance.
2. A statement of yearly goals or achievements expected for
   each area of identified weakness by the end of the school
   year.
3. Short-term objectives stated in instructional terms that are
   the steps leading to the mastery of these yearly goals.
4. A statement of the specific special education and support
   services to be provided to the child.
5. A statement of the extent to which a child will be able to
   participate in regular education programs and justification
   for any special placement recommendations.
6. Projected dates for initiation of services and the anticipated
   duration of the services.
7. A statement of the criteria and evaluation procedures to be
   used in determining, on at least an annual basis, whether
   short-term objectives are being achieved.

In addition to an appropriate placement and IEP, your child or
adolescent may need other services. These are called related services. They are to be provided at no expense to the family. The
formal definition of *related services* is "transportation and such
developmental, corrective, and other supportive services (including speech pathology and audiology, psychological services,
physical and occupational therapy, recreation, and medical counseling services, except that such medical services shall be for diagnostic and evaluation purposes only) as may be required to
assist a handicapped child to benefit from special education, and
includes the early identification and assessment of handicapping
conditions in children." These services are usually provided by
the school system or by school professionals.

Related services are expensive. Your school personnel might
make many suggestions about getting the child or adolescent into
psychotherapy but never formally recommend it verbally or in
writing. If they formally recommend a service, thus identifying it

as a needed related service, the school system must pay for the service.

### Parents' Decision Process

After the conference, you are entitled to a full transcript of the meeting. You can also get copies of all tests that were done. The placement and the IEP recommendations must also be provided in writing.

Read all of the documents. If necessary, ask for clarification or for more details. If you see something in writing that was not mentioned at the meeting, ask for an explanation. If you need help, seek consultation and advice from other parents or from professionals.

If you are comfortable with the school's plan for your child or adolescent, you may agree to it and sign the necessary documents. If you do not agree and cannot get the school personnel to modify their proposals, inform them that you wish to appeal. Ask that they review with you their appeal process. Remember that you are entitled by law to due process of appeal.

### Appeals Process

The appeals process differs with each state and local school system. Your school system must provide in writing the step-by-step process of appeal. Many school systems require a mediation process first. You and appropriate school personnel meet with a competent and neutral person who tries to resolve the differences. Only if this mediation process fails may a parent start the formal appeals process.

If you feel that you need legal guidance, try to find an attorney who works in the area of special education law. Ask other parents who is good and who knows your school system. If you go before a hearing officer, you will need an attorney. This is a formal legal process, and the school system will have an attorney to represent it. You need the same.

The final step in this appeals process is a meeting between you and your school system before a hearing officer. He or she is a professional knowledgeable about learning disabilities, school law, and school procedures. The hearing officer is not employed by the school system and acts independently. Both sides present their arguments. Often the decisions are based on the needs of the individual as well as on procedures of law. The hearing officer's decision is binding. If a parent loses at this level, the only other option is to appeal under civil law (Americans with Disabilities Act). This process involves the court system and might take years.

This appeals process may go quickly or may take months. Meanwhile your son or daughter must attend school. In this situation, the usual procedure is for the child to be placed in the program proposed by the school system until the appeals process is complete.

### Implementation

The best designed plans of April and May might fall apart in September. Be observant when school opens. Be sure the placement, the teacher, the related services, the makeup of the class, and the implementation steps for the IEP are correct and in operation. Be concerned, ask questions, but try not to be a nuisance. If you believe that some departure from the agreed-upon plan has been made, ask about it.

Be sure that the regular classroom teachers are aware of your child's special needs or programs and accommodations. Check to find if the regular and special education personnel are interacting with each other.

Programs begun in September may get changed or diluted as the year progresses and the case load for each professional involved increases. Ask your son or daughter to keep you informed or check this for yourself. Does each person see your child or adolescent for the amount of time noted in the IEP? Are more children being added to the program time your youngster receives services? One hour of individual time twice a week might become thirty minutes twice a week in a group of three to five other children. Know your child's IEP, and insist that he or she get what is promised. Remember that no changes can be made without a written notification and your concurrence. If you hear such things as "We just don't have the personnel to do what is on the IEP" or "Our budget is less than expected," inform the principal that you have great empathy for the school's problems. However, these are the school's problems. Your problem is that your son or daughter is not getting what he or she is supposed to get by law.

### Other Thoughts on IDEA

Your son or daughter must be kept informed of the school plan. How much you share, what you explain, and how you explain it will depend on the child's age. If you need help, ask the professionals involved to meet with you and your child or adolescent. If you think it would be helpful, make it a family session.

You may need help in dealing with a son or daughter who resists or refuses special help or being in a special class. Another problem you might have to deal with is stigma. Other children can be cruel, sometimes on purpose, sometimes just by saying all the wrong things. The special programs may be called "retard" or "mental" classes, and the children in them may be called "retards" or "speds" (for *special education*). It all hurts. Speak to the teachers. Ask that they talk to the offending students. Perhaps these teachers could discuss the theme of being different with the whole class. Alert the teacher if his or her insensitivity contributes to the teasing. If necessary, speak to the parents of an offending child in as positive a way as you can. (Here, as elsewhere, hostility won't get you very far.) Support your child, and empathize with his or her feelings. Don't be afraid to show your own emotions, and don't be afraid to have a good cry together. You would do anything in the world to spare the child these problems, but they exist. Make sure the child knows that you care too much to ignore what is going on and that you will do everything possible to support and help. Keep at it until the teasing is minimized or stopped.

Work closely with your school personnel. And make them work closely with you. As a team, both the school people and the family can do the best job of helping your son or daughter reach his or her maximum growth and potential.

## What about Services for the Student with ADHD?

Unfortunately, ADHD is not listed as a handicapping condition under education law, that is under IDEA. I reviewed this issue earlier. Please refer to Chapter 14. The student with ADHD can be classified under IDEA if she or he is found to have a learning disability or to be seriously emotionally disturbed. The third option is to code the individual under the category, "Other Health Impaired." The advantage of getting the student coded under IDEA is that the school system must provide services as well as accommodations.

Another possibility, as discussed earlier, is to use civil law. Recall that Section 504 is used. Most school systems have "504 plans" for students with ADHD. The problem is that civil law only requires that the school system provide accommodations. Services are not required. It is for this reason that parent organizations continue to fight to have ADHD listed under IDEA.

## In Summary

You are standing on the shoulders of many parents who went before you. I have great respect for those parents who fought so hard in the 1950s and 1960s to get what we have today. Without their efforts and the resulting legislation, our children and adolescents would have no rights within school systems. Other parents have taken their place on the "front line" in the years since.

In the spring of 1997, there was a real danger that Congress would change IDEA in ways that would weaken or destroy its effectiveness. I was part of a major effort by parent volunteers who met with their members of Congress and who reminded critical people in the House and Senate day after day of the need for IDEA. I am more than convinced that it was the effort of these parents that saved IDEA in its present form for your son or daughter.

There will be future challenges. Many feel that ADHD should be included as one of the handicapping conditions. Such an addition to IDEA would make receiving services easier. Previous efforts have not been successful. Perhaps you would like to work with parent organizations to try to accomplish this change in the future.

Try to find a way to take your turn as a parent volunteer, fighting for services. Find a way to be active in a parent organization at the local, state, or national level. I list these organizations in the appendix. You will learn much from other parents and from the materials available. You will find informed parent advocates to help you. You will find much to be done. Hopefully, you will join the ever-present need to fight the next battle.

# CONCLUSION

ADHD is a life disability, affecting all aspects of life. For many, ADHD is a lifetime disability as well. Like other chronic developmental disorders, the consequences of not recognizing, diagnosing, and fully treating ADHD can be extensive. Each stage of psychological and social development can be affected as can academic success, self-esteem, and positive peer interactions. The resulting emotional, social, and family problems can become as great a disability for the adult as is the primary disability of ADHD. The secondary academic underachievement can have an impact on choice of career and future success with work. Such an impact influences both work happiness and future income.

Therefore, the early recognition, diagnosis, and start of treatment interventions is essential. Missing the diagnosis or not properly treating ADHD can result in a lifetime of difficulties. It is important for parents to understand ADHD and to be alert to the needs of their son or daughter. It is critical that health and mental health professionals know of ADHD and their critical role. It is equally important to recognize the related emotional and neurologically based disorders so that these problems also can be addressed.

The secondary social and peer problems must be addressed. If having a family member with ADHD has resulted in family problems, these must be handled.

Unless the total individual is understood and helped, progress might be limited. Thus, it is important that a full evaluation be done. Looking only for ADHD might result in missing a learning disability or other related disorder. Seeing the surface emotional problems as the diagnosis will result in minimal success in treating these problems.

Treatment must be multimodal. Parent and individual education and counseling are first. Then, your child might need specific behavioral management or social skills help. The use of appropriate medications, managed correctly, is essential. Further individual, behavioral, group, and/or family therapy might be necessary. Throughout all of these efforts, it is necessary to work closely with your school system.

Since many educational, health, and mental health professionals may not be familiar with ADHD, it is essential that you, as parents, become fully educated. You may have to take the initiative to educate the professionals you seek for help.

Thank you for reading my book. I hope it will be useful to you in understanding your son or daughter. I also hope it will help you help your child and your family. Equally important, I hope it permits you to nurture and help yourself as well.

You must be that special guide to your son or daughter with ADHD, to your partner, and to your family. This task is not easy. But, as you know all too well, you have no choice but to be that person.

May you have success in helping your son or daughter grow into a happy, healthy, successful adult. I wish you the best in your efforts.

# APPENDIX

**Organizations Related to Attention Deficit Hyperactivity Disorder (ADHD)**

*Children and Adults with Attention Deficit Disorder*
Children and Adults with Attention Deficit Disorder (CHADD) is a national alliance of parent organizations that provides information and support to parents of individuals with this disorder.

      499 N.W. 70th Avenue
      Suite 101
      Plantation, FL 33317
      800-223-4050
      (954) 587-3700
      Fax: (954) 587-4599
      Website: http://www.chadd.org

*Attention Deficit Disorder Association*
Attention Deficit Disorder Association (ADDA) is a national alliance of support groups that provides referrals and information to parents and to support groups.

      9930 Johnnycake Ridge Road
      Suite 3E
      Mentor, OH 44060
      (440) 350-9595
      Website: http://www.add.org

## Organizations Related to Learning Disabilities

*Learning Disabilities Association of America, Inc.*
The Learning Disabilities Association (LDA), formerly called the Association for Children with Learning Disabilities (ACLD), is a national parent association with state and local chapters. Membership is open to parents and professionals. Through a network of national, state, and local programs, parents receive educational programs, parent advocacy advice, and support systems for individuals with learning disabilities throughout the life span.

> 4156 Library Road
> Pittsburgh, PA 15234
> (412) 341-1515
> Fax: (412) 344-0224
> Website: http://www.ldanatl.org

*International Dyslexia Association*
The International Dyslexia Society (IDA), formerly called the Orton Dyslexia Society, is for parents and professionals. The primary focus is on individuals with dyslexia, also called a language-based learning disability.

> 8600 LaSalle Road
> Suite 382
> Baltimore, MD 21286
> (410) 296-0232 or (800) 222-3123
> Fax: (410) 321-5069
> e-mail: info@interdys.org
> Website: http://www.interdys.org

*Council for Exceptional Children*
The Council for Exceptional Children is the branch of the National Education Association for educators in special education. The Division on Learning Disabilities is the specific group within the council concerned with learning disabilities.

> 1920 Association Drive
> Reston, VA 22091
> (703) 620-3660 or (800) 845-6232
> Fax: (703) 264-9494
> Website: http://www.cec.sped.org

*National Center for Learning Disabilities*
National Center for Learning Disabilities is a foundation-like organization with extensive fund-raising efforts. This money is used to further

public education on learning disabilities and for specific areas of research. Information is provided to parents and professionals.
381 Park Avenue South
Suite 1401
New York, NY 10016
(212) 545-7510
Fax: (212) 545-9665
Website: http://www.ncld.org

**Professional Organizations**

*American Academy of Child and Adolescent Psychiatry*
3615 Wisconsin Avenue, N.W.
Washington, DC 20016
(202) 966-7300
Website: http://www.aacap.org

*American Academy of Ophthalmology*
1101 Vermont Avenue, N.W.
Washington, DC 20036
(202) 737-6662
Website: http://www.eyenet.org

*American Academy of Optometry*
5530 Wisconsin Avenue
Chevy Chase, MD 20815
(301) 984-1441
Website: http://www.aaopt.org

*American Academy of Pediatrics*
P.O. Box 927
141 Northwest Point Road
Elk Grove Village, IL 60007
(847) 228-5005
Website: http://www.aap.org

*American Medical Association*
535 N. Dearborn
Chicago, IL 60610
(312) 464-5000
Website: http://www.ama-assn.org

*American Occupational Therapy Association*
    4720 Montgomery Ave.
    Bethesda, MD 20814
    (301) 652-2682
    Website: http://www.aota.org

*American Psychiatric Association*
    1400 K Street, N.W.
    Washington, DC 20005
    (202) 682-6000
    Website: http://www.psych.org

*American Psychological Association*
    1200 17th Street, N.W.
    Washington, DC 20036
    (202) 336-5500
    Website: http://www.apa.org

*American Speech, Language, and Hearing Association*
    10801 Rockville Pike
    Rockville, MD 20852
    (301) 897-5700
    (800) 496-2071
    Website: http://www.asha.org

*National Association of School Psychologists*
    4340 East West Highway
    Suite 402
    Silver Spring, MD 20814
    Website: http://www.naspweb.org

*National Association of Social Workers*
    750 First Street, N.E.
    Suite 700
    Washington, DC 20002
    (202) 408-8600
    Website: http://www.naswdc.org

*Sensory Integration International*
    1402 Cravens Avenue
    Torrance, CA 90501

**Legal Organizations**

Many law schools have special units or programs offering reference materials or counsel on children with disabilities. If you or your attorney needs such help, contact your nearest law school and find out what it offers. The following national programs may be of help or may provide a local resource.

*Children's Defense Fund*
> 25 E Street, N.W.
> Washington, DC 20001
> (202) 628-8787
> Website: http://www.childrensdefense.org

*Disability Legal Support Center*
> American Bar Association
> 1800 M. Street, N.W.
> Washington, DC 20036
> (202) 662-1000
> Website: http://www.abanet.org

**Informational Centers**

*The National Information Center for Children and Youth with Disabilities*

The National Information Center for Children and Youth with Disabilities (NICHEY) provides extensive information and literature on all areas of disability.
> P.O. Box 1492
> Washington, DC 20013
> (202) 884-8200 or (800) 695-0285
> Fax: (202) 884-8441
> Website: http://www.nichy.org

## NOTICES

*Adderall*    Richwood Pharmaceuticals
7900 Tanners Gate Drive
Suite 200
Florence, KY 41042

*Benadryl*    Parke-Davis Division of Warner-Lambert Company
201 Tabor Road
Morris Plains, NJ 07950

| | |
|---|---|
| *Catapres* | Boehringer Ingelheim Pharmaceuticals<br>900 Ridgebury Road<br>Ridgefield, CT 06877 |
| *Cylert* | Abbott Laboratories<br>100 Abbott Park Road<br>Abbott Park, IL 60064 |
| *Dexedrine* | Smithkline Beecham Pharmaceuticals<br>One Franklin Place<br>P.O. Box 7929<br>Philadelphia, PA 19101 |
| *Dextro-Stat* | Richwood Pharmaceuticals<br>7900 Tanners Gate Drive<br>Suite 200<br>Florence, KY 41042 |
| *Norpramin* | Hoechst Marion Russel Pharmaceuticals<br>10236 Marion Park Drive<br>P.O. Box 9627<br>Kansas City, MO 64134 |
| *Pamelor* | Novartis Pharmaceuticals<br>59 Route 10<br>East Hanover, NJ 07939 |
| *Ritalin* | Novartis Pharmaceuticals<br>59 Route 10<br>East Hanover, NJ 07939 |
| *Tenex* | A. H. Robins Company<br>1407 Cummings Drive<br>Richmond, VA 23220 |
| *Tofranil* | Novartis Pharmaceuticals<br>59 Route 10<br>East Hanover, NJ 07939 |
| *Wellbutrin* | Glaxo Wellcome Company<br>Five Moore Drive<br>Research Triangle Park, NC 27709 |

# INDEX

audiograms, 242
Audiokinetrons, 242
auditory disabilities:
   controversial therapies for,
      241–43
   distractibility in, 34–35
   education on, 166, 171
   figure-ground in, 54–55, 142
   impact on family of, 142,
      145
   in memory, 64, 145
   in perception, 52, 54–55, 64
   in processing, 55, 241–43
   in sequencing, 60
auditory lags, 55
auditory processing training,
   241–43
autism, 269
autonomy, 90–91
avoidance behaviors, 16, 74
Ayres, Jean, 240–41

**B**
balance, 57–58, 72
Band-Aid stage, 95
basic trust, 88–89, 92
behavioral therapy:
   for modulating disorders,
      75–76, 80
   in treating ADHD, 153–54,
      160–61, 174, 178–79
behavior management programs,
   188–211, 236, 288
   for adults with ADHD, 260
   basic concepts of, 191
   categories of unacceptable
      behaviors in, 194, 196
   chores in, 206–10
   dawdling in, 209–10
   dealing with loopholes in,
      202–3
   dealing with resistance in,
      201–2

developing initial intervention
   strategy for, 192–95
goals of, 190, 203
maid service in, 206–8
noncompliance in, 206–10
property damage in, 208–9
setting up first phase of,
   195–203
setting up second phase of,
   203–5
Sunday boxes in, 208
time-outs in, 197, 199–200,
   203
behaviors and behavioral
   problems, 72–80, 174–79,
   194–96
   ADHD in, vii–ix, xiii–xvi, xviii
   ADHD suggested by, 32–38
   antecedents of, 192, 194–95
   as chronic and pervasive, 44–
      48
   collecting data on, 36
   consequences of, 192, 195
   defining of, 195, 199
   education on, 174
   how professionals observe
      them, 36
   in modulating disorders, 72–77,
      79–80
   in normal psychosocial
      development, 87, 91, 95–96,
      100, 102
   secondary, 105–26, 153–54,
      159, 162–63, 166
   in specific learning disabilities,
      56–57
   in tic disorders, 81
   in treating ADHD, 159,
      175–79, 212, 225–26
   working with schools on,
      181–82, 184–85
Benadryl, 225
Benzedrine, 213

# ABOUT THE AUTHOR

DR. LARRY B. SILVER, a child and adolescent psychiatrist, is in private practice in the Washington, D.C., area. He is clinical professor of psychiatry at Georgetown University School of Medicine. Prior to performing his current activities, he was the acting director and deputy director of the National Institute of Mental Health. Prior to the National Institute of Mental Health, Dr. Silver was professor of psychiatry, professor of pediatrics, and chief of child and adolescent psychiatry at the Robert Wood Johnson School of Medicine. He is the author of *The Misunderstood Child*, now in its third edition.